Your Kingdom Come

"Preparing for basic, prophetic, and strategic level intercession"

Becca Greenwood

Library of Congress Cataloging in Publication Data

Your Kingdom Come
Copyright @ 2012 by Becca Greenwood

Published by Cleansing Stream Ministries
2012, CA

ISBN 978-0-980835-1-9

Unless otherwise noted, Scripture references are from the New American Standard Version of the Bible, A.J. Holman Company.

Scriptures quoted from *The Holy Bible,* copyright © 1973 by The Lockman Foundation, Used by permission.

Message
NIV
KJV
NASB
Amplified Bible

Contents

Book 1: Encouraged to Intercede 9

    Lesson One: Inheriting the Promises of Prayer 9

    Lesson Two: From Prayer to Intercession 29

    Lesson Three: Susie's Story 45

    Lesson Four: My Prayer List 61

    Lesson Five: Having His Heart for Others 77

    Lesson Six: Intimacy with God 93

Book 2: Prophetic Intercession 111

    Lesson One: We "Can" Hear God's Voice 111

    Lesson Two: Learning His Voice 127

    Lesson Three: Prophetic Protocol 143

    Lesson Four: Breakthrough! 159

    Lesson Five: Corporate Intercession 177

    Lesson Six: The Power of Prophetic Intercession 199

    Notes 213

Book 3: Spiritual Warfare 219

    Lesson One: Explanation of Spiritual Warfare Prayer 219

    Lesson Two: Creation is Waiting 233

    Lesson Three: Satan the Unlawful Tenant 249

Contents

Lesson Four: Spiritual Mapping 267

Lesson Five: Rules of Engagement 289

Lesson Six: Engaging in Battle 305

Notes 317

Leader's Guide 321

Introduction.. 321

Your Kingdom Come

Book 1: Encouraged to Intercede

Becca Greenwood

Book 1: Encouraged to Intercede

Praying with Authority

Lesson One: Inheriting the Promises of Prayer

I was driving through the cold and gusty winds of Colorado to the weekly prayer meeting I was leading. It was my favorite time of the week. This group of intercessors and I had been pressing into praying for the nations of the world. We saw dramatic answers to our prayers. Each week brought excitement and expectancy. We wondered how the Lord would lead. What would He speak and when would we see the answers?

As I drew closer to the location of our meeting, I asked the Holy Spirit to speak to me concerning what was on His heart. I felt a deep impression concerning India; so much so, that I knew this was to be the focus of our intercession. When I entered the prayer room several intercessors had already gathered. I quickly asked, "Are any of you feeling impressed to pray for India today?" Three of them responded in unison. They felt the Lord speaking to them concerning India as they were driving to our meeting. We knew at that moment that we had our prayer assignment for the day.

In agreement we began to pray and intercede for India. We invited the Lord to direct us specifically in our prayers. God's presence was tangible in the room. We raised our voices together in unison feeling urgency for this nation. One of the intercessors strongly moved by the Holy Spirit said, "I really feel that there are believers who are being persecuted right now for their faith; and we are to pray for their safe release." Another prayer warrior quickly agreed, "Yes, I am feeling strongly led with the same impression." As the leader of this group, I have learned that when two or three of us hear the same thing, we need to pray in agreement.

Over the next two hours, we cried out for those believers who were held and interrogated for their faith. We prayed that their release would come quickly, swiftly, and miraculously. We asked that God's favor would go before and behind these precious brothers and sisters, and that those holding them captive would release them. We prayed until we felt a release.

Our weekly prayer meeting is held in the offices of an evangelistic ministry focused on spreading the gospel to the nations of the world. At this present time, this ministry is effectively doing this in 92 countries of the world. The morning following, we learned that twenty-four hours earlier workers of this evangelistic ministry in India were captured and interrogated. The region in which they work is highly persecuted. Once a Christian believer is discovered they are almost always imprisoned and tortured for their faith. But miraculously, the police officials released them without torture or imprisonment. It was truly a miracle from the Lord.

Friends, prayer and intercession are truly an exciting adventure and an awesome partnership that we can engage in with our Lord. Let's look at some things we can do to move in that direction.

1. Draw near to God

James 4:8a says, *"Draw near to God and He will draw near to you."* God calls all believers to pray. Not only does He desire that we pray, but He longs to be in a personal relationship with us as well. As we pray we are drawn into close communion and partnership with Him. It is in this place of fellowship that we understand the Father's heart. Here we are further transformed into His image and likeness. And here we continuously receive the mind of Christ.

2. What is this process of transformation?

Just as each of us has friends, Jesus desires to be our friend. All of us have friendships that function on different levels.

A. We all have acquaintances

These are relationships that have just formed and are at the beginning stage of the adventure of growing into a friendship. At this stage we learn to relate to the Lord and to pray to Him in order to have our needs met.

1. We pray because we hunger to know Him more

Matthew 6: 11 says, *"That if we will pray to Him He will give us our daily bread (meet our daily needs)."* As we faithfully seek Him, He becomes the source of all that we need. God's Word says, *"He will meet our needs according to His riches in Glory"* (Eph. 3:16, NASB).

I love the promises that say our God, "will never leave us nor forsake us" (Hebrew 13:5, NIV). Friends, He is always faithful for He cannot deny Himself and He is alive in each of us. We have a heavenly Father who is faithful to meet our needs.

2. We pray because we have sinned

God's Word says, *"That if we confess our sins, He is faithful and just to forgive us our sins"* (1 John 1:9, KJV). We all have things, including sins, which we need to bring before the Lord in an attitude of repentance. Because of the awesome gift of forgiveness and salvation we can enter God's presence and be cleansed from all unrighteousness.

3. We pray because we long for the Lord's presence

"As the deer pants for the water brooks, so my soul pants for you, O God. My soul thirsts for God, for the living God. When shall I come and appear before God?" (Psalm 42:1-2, NASB).

The Hebrew word for "to pant" is *arag*. It means to have a strong wish or yearning for someone or a situation. It suggests the panting of an animal which is overheated or dehydrated. King David descriptively expressed his heart's cry for the presence of the Lord in a similar manner. For each of us there should be such a longing and thirst in our hearts for the Lord that we feel totally dehydrated and depleted without Him. He is the only one who can quench our spiritual thirst.

Imagine a deer roaming through the wilderness—through a new territory. As he wanders further into this new place it soon becomes clear there is no water. It is a dry and barren land. He goes for days without water, but because of his animal instinct he continues to press onward, desperately longing for the sound of a water brook. His desire is to taste that water and quench his thirst. This will save his overheated and dehydrated body. If he does not drink, he will die. He has gone for so many days that the thirst and dryness has grown into an agonizing misery. He must have water! Then, he hears the faint trickle of water. Could that really be the sound that he has been looking for? Is it possible he can now have a deep refreshing drink? His tired lifeless walk quickly grows into a hopeful trot. He cannot only hear the water, but now he smells it. Now he runs. He bounds down the hill to see a fresh running brook of cool water. He plunges his dry cracked mouth into the refreshing stream and begins to joyfully drink. Finally, his intense thirst is quenched. What a powerful picture David has painted for us. Just as the deer longs for this water brook our soul and everything in us should long for the Lord.

Inheriting the Promise of Prayer

In the year 2000, I experienced something new in my life. We moved from Texas to Colorado. Having lived in Texas my entire life, this new relocation became a very difficult transition. I faced a season of feeling misplaced and very lonely. Everything was dry and barren. Thoughts came into my mind, "Lord, why did you bring us here. Surely, we have missed your best for us." During this time, I began to spend a lot of time praying, worshipping, and reaching out to the Lord. I so longed for companionship and I soon realized He was the only one who could fill all the voids in my life. Soon He brought life where there was barrenness. There came a deep satisfaction, and feeling of peace and security that only He can bring. I discovered the more time I spent and rested in His presence the more peace and comfort I received. That empty longing and void in my life was filled by His awesome presence and love. And the joy that I felt was missing in my life soon returned.

Do you long for more of His presence in your life? Are you thirsting for more of Him? Friends, in this journey you will find that place of relationship and fulfillment that only He can bring. This should be our heart's cry.

B. Acquaintances grow into friendships
Growing beyond the acquaintance stage we soon see friendships begin to develop. We find those we like go to dinner with, or shopping with, or golf with, or maybe just talk with on the phone every once and awhile. A similar relationship begins with the Lord as we learn to spend more time with Him. And this is where we begin to build and maintain a special trust relationship.

In this place of trust we learn our position with Him. We start to see ourselves as His children and His friends. Let's investigate further this development process.

1. We are all God's children

"The Spirit Himself testifies with our spirit that we are children of God" (Romans 8:16).

We are not only God's creation, but once we are saved, we become His children. We also become heirs of God and co-heirs with Christ (Romans 8:17, NIV). Our heavenly Father delights in us as His children and desires to relate to us out of a Father's heart of love.

As parents we love to spend time with our children. Actually, being a mom to my three daughters is my favorite thing. I love to spend time with them, love on them, and experience all the stages of their lives. I especially love it when they want to be with me, talk to me, love on me, and be in my presence; simply because they love me. How much more does our heavenly Father want to relate to each of us? He is a loving God who deeply desires fellowship with His children.

2. We are God's friends

There are friends we trust because a relationship has been forged through experiencing life together; both joys and trials. We have learned that no matter what may come there is still a level of commitment and trust that we feel comfortable with. We may even begin to share the deeper things in life together— confidences and aspirations.

As our children grow, we begin to relate to them on a friendship level instead of a parent/child relationship. We talk, we share opinions, we share our hearts, and we share our dreams. This same kind of relationship is possible with God. In fact this is what He desires.

"I've told you these things for a purpose: that my joy might be your joy, and your joy wholly mature. This is my command: Love one another the way I loved you. This is the very best way to love. Put your life on the line for your friends. You are my friends when you do the things I command you. I'm no longer calling you servants because servants don't understand what their master is thinking and

planning. No, I've named you friends because I've let you in on everything I've heard from the Father" (John 15:11-15, The Message).

What a beautiful promise. Because we are His friends, He lets us in on things He has heard from the Father. He entrusts us with His secrets.

C. From friendship to intimacy

As "we" girls would say, this would be our very best friend. This is the one that knows your deepest hearts cry and passions. You share the most cherished part of yourself with this friend. And nothing in life—distance, hardship, or trial will ever separate the relationship—the commitment to one another and the love shared between the two.

After a period of time spouses develop many similar characteristics. In experiencing the covenant of this cherished, intimate relationship we begin to mirror each other in our actions and words. We learn to communicate lovingly and to share and treasure all areas of life together. Without speaking we often know what the other is thinking and our deepest dreams and passions are shared and embraced freely.

In our relationship with the Lord, this is where we enter into that treasured place beyond the veil. We hunger for His presence and to fellowship with Him and to hear His voice.

"This is the passion of God burning inside me! I promised your hand in marriage to Christ, presented you as a pure virgin to her husband" (2 Corinthians 11:2, The Message).

We cannot get to this place without consistently and faithfully cultivating our prayer lives. How is this accomplished? By reading the Word daily, journaling our thoughts to the Lord, worshipping Him, speaking with Him, and silencing ourselves and listening to Him. In these lessons, we will learn how to move into deeper places with Him by engaging in action steps.

D. From bride to ambassador

This is how our Lord has designed for us to relate to Him. Jesus wants us to move beyond acquaintance, friendship, and trust into a cherished and personal partnership. He is looking for a captivated bride where intimacy is developed and forged in a private place with Him. By entering into this level of relationship with our God, we begin to be transformed into His image—we become more like Him. From here our prayer life forms and grows and we begin praying from a heavenly perspective. We actually become what God's Word describes. *"We are therefore Christ's ambassadors as though He is making His appeal through us."* (2 Corinthians 5:20, NIV). When we pray and speak in agreement with Him He makes His plans for His kingdom known. I appreciate the famous quote made by Rees Howells, *History belongs to the intercessors.* Let discuss the way to begin praying to see history made.

Sincere Prayers

The word "sincere" is defined as free of deceit, hypocrisy, or falsehood. It means to become earnest, genuine, real, and pure. When we pray we need to pray from a place of heartfelt genuineness, honesty, and truth. Many times we come before the Lord and pray in a religious or traditional manner. As we have discussed, our prayer life is one built on friendship, relationship, and intimacy. Prayer should never be looked at as a chore, but rather a place of freedom in communing with our Savior, teacher, brother, and friend.

Take some time to reflect on your personal prayer life. Do you have a specific time of prayer?

_____
_____
_____

Inheriting the Promise of Prayer

How often do you pray?
_____
_____
_____

Think of the last time you prayed a sincere and genuine prayer where the Lord responded and the answer came quickly:
_____
_____
_____
_____
_____
_____

Let's take a few minutes to ask the Lord for specific prayer requests. Record what you are believing for and trusting for. Have faith that He will meet you in these requests.
_____
_____
_____
_____
_____
_____

Relevant Prayers

To pray with relevance means to connect what is happening in our personal lives and the world with our heavenly Father. Our prayers are to have some bearing or importance for real world issues and present day events. We should not be praying the same prayer we prayed ten years ago. If you have prayed a long time for an unsaved loved one, or have been praying and believing for a miracle or breakthrough do not stop praying. We must continue praying until the answer comes. Our prayer life should not be done as routine or ritual. We must grow beyond saying the same prayer with the same words every time. If this is the case, we have entered into a kind of "religious" praying that often lacks a spiritual connection with the Lord. God cares about what is occurring in our personal lives, in our church, our cities, our nation, and our world. The motivation for prayer should be both pertinent to those things that are happening in the world around us, as well as a desire to meet and know God personally.

Persistent Prayer

We are to pray persistently while not allowing problems or distractions to hinder our prayer time. It is good to commit to an unrelenting resolve to not to give up or let go. God is not some far off God in heaven that we cannot relate to. He created you and me because of His Father's heart; and His Holy Spirit is here on earth to work in us and through us.

The following story of the widow and the unrighteous judge should inspire us to function in a persistent manner in our prayer life.

"Jesus told them a story showing that it was necessary for them to pray consistently and never quit. He said, 'There was once a judge in some city who never gave God a thought and cared nothing for people. A widow in that city kept after him: 'My rights are being violated. Protect me!'

"He never gave her the time of day. But after this went on and on he said to himself, 'I care nothing what God thinks, even less what people think. But because this widow won't quit badgering me, I'd better do something and see that she gets justice—otherwise I'm going to end up beaten black-and-blue by her pounding.'

"Then the Master said, 'Do you hear what that judge, corrupt as he is, is saying? So what makes you think God won't step in and work justice for his chosen people, who continue to cry out for help? Won't he stick up for them? I assure you, he will. He will not drag his feet. But how much of that kind of persistent faith will the Son of Man find on the earth when he returns?'" (Luke 18:1-8. The Message).

Purpose Focused Prayer

In this season of the Christian world, we are hearing more and more things concerning purpose and destiny. I am a firm believer that this is due to the fact that the Lord has created all individuals with a specific purpose, gifting, calling, and anointing. It might look and be different for each of us, but we all have been given a passion that the Lord desires to see fulfilled. Some are doctors, some teachers, some ministers, musicians, artists, writers, bankers, etc. The point is we are to have a purpose focused life that releases God's kingdom in whatever arena the Lord has placed us.

The same is true in prayer. As we draw close to the Lord we begin to focus our prayers on what is in His heart. We pray with the purpose of joining in agreement with Him to see His kingdom come and His will be done. We pray knowing there will be effective results. The following is a powerful example of what can happen when we hear and respond to God through intercession.

Jeremy lived in a small town in the South, one still steeped in racism and prejudice. As an African-American teenager, he felt he had no hope. He was not good enough. His family had a long history of financial struggles, so he thought he would too. No one ever spoke words of affirmation and encouragement to him. And now he had a new math teacher for the week, and she was another white woman. Jeremy resolved not to do his work because he was sure she would not accept him.

"Jeremy, you need to do your work. Please pick up your pencil and try."

Not willing to look at me as I spoke to him, Jeremy crossed his arms and looked away. You could see the years of hurt, struggles, and the resulting defiance in his eyes as he spoke.

"Mrs. Greenwood, I don't need to do this work. It is not going to help me in life. I do not want to do this work."

"Jeremy, I need you to pick up your pencil and do your work. Please obey what I am asking you to do." I replied calmly and patiently.

"Mrs. Greenwood, I am not going to do this work."

Later, my heart ached as I continued to replay the scene that occurred earlier that day. How could I get through to this young man? That night I went to prayer and asked the Lord for guidance in reaching out to him. The Lord reminded me that Jeremy had to make his own right choices, but there were also issues in his heart that desperately needed healing. I knew the Lord was directing me to be the one to initiate this healing. I spent time in intercession praying before returning the next day as the substitute teacher of this class.

As the bell rang, Jeremy came walking in the door just at the precise moment so that he would not to be late. If he had arrived a moment later he would have been tardy. I could tell this was a well rehearsed routine.

I explained the math assignment. Within a few minutes, Jeremy laid his head on the desk to take a nap while the rest of the class worked. This was my cue to put action to my prayers.

"Jeremy, you need to pick up your pencil and do your work?"

Jeremy responded in the same manner he did the day before.

"Mrs. Greenwood, I told you yesterday, I am not going to do this work. I do not need this math. I am not going to use it in life and I am not going to do it."

I leaned over his desk trying to catch his eyes. In a soft, calm voice I reached out to him. "Jeremy, look at me please. Can you look at me? I would like to talk to you about something."

Curious, he turned his eyes toward mine. "Jeremy, I realize you have lived in an area where you and your family have been shunned and treated poorly because of the color of your skin. Is this true sweetheart?"

Shocked by my words he cautiously and quietly answered, "Yes, ma'am."

"Well, Jeremy I recognize that how you and your family have been treated is not right. As a matter of fact, my ancestors were some of the founding fathers of this small town. I realize that some of my ancestors and relatives might have been some of those who said and did hurtful things to you. I want to say that how you have been treated is wrong. How my race has treated your race is wrong. And I want to ask you to forgive us."

At that moment, he shockingly replied, "This sounds like church."

"Yes, Jeremy it does. I also, as a white woman, want to say that when I look at you, I do not see the color of your skin, but I see a handsome, bright young man who has the potential to break out of the cycle your family has been in and to do something great with your life. Don't let the past and the wrong actions of the white race and the people of this town control your future. Please forgive us."

Fighting back the tears, he emotionally and quietly said, "Yes ma'am."

"Jeremy, do you live with your mother?"

"No, ma'am. I live with my grandmother."

"Does she pray for you?"

"Yes, Ma'am she does. Every night she kneels by her bed and prays for me."

"Jeremy, I know your grandmother wants you to do your work. I know she wants the best for you. I do too. I prayed for you last night. I believe in you. For your grandmother and me, can you please pick up your pencil and do your work? Can you choose to make today a new day in your life."

A tear gently rolled down his cheek as he slowly pulled himself up in his desk, reached for the pencil, and pulled the sheet of paper toward him. As he began to solve the first math problem, he answered in a soft whisper, "Yes, ma'am, I can."

The classroom was so quiet you could have heard a pin drop. I gratefully and lovingly placed my hand on his shoulder and said, "Thank you, Jeremy." As I made my way back to the desk, I was rejoicing on the inside and so moved by the Spirit of the Lord that I could hardly contain my emotions and tears.

During the following four days Jeremy came to class early and would excitedly exclaim, "Mrs. Greenwood are we going to learn something new today? I am going to do my work."

The remainder of the school year, Jeremy would always try to come and find the classroom I was subbing in for the day. One day, he asked to speak with me.

"Mrs. Greenwood, I have friends who want me to hang out with them tonight. They are going to be up to no good."
"Jeremy, are you looking for an adult to help you tell them you can't go?"

"Yes, ma'am."

"Jeremy, you go tell your friends that Mrs. Greenwood said that it is not a good idea for you to hang out tonight and if they have a problem, they can come see me."

I smiled as Jeremy walked out of the classroom confidently exclaiming, "Hey guys, Mrs. Greenwood said it is not a good idea for me to go tonight and if you have a problem with that you can talk with her about it!"

God is awesome. He has positioned us as a people of purpose and action. We are to get in there with God making our prayers full of focus and anointed with God directed purpose.

Faith Filled Prayers

Hebrews 11:1 shares this empowering promise. *"Now faith is sure of what we hope for and certain of what we do not see"* (NIV).

Faith is defined as "confidence or trust in a person or thing, a belief that is not based on direct evidence, a trust in God and His promises." When God speaks we can trust what He says. God is not a man that He would lie. He is truth and His words will not return to Him empty and void. They will fulfill the promises He has spoken! (Isaiah 55:11, NIV)

Let me ask a question. Do we expect God to move on our behalf in response to our prayers? When we pray and ask the Lord for rain, do we have the faith to carry an umbrella? As we pray for lost loved ones do we thank the Lord for how He is answering, even when we cannot see the end result?

Many of us want to put faith in our own works; those things we do that are visible and seen. Our thinking tends to be, "Well, if I work hard enough, I will get the result I'm looking for." This is a performance trap that we must guard against. When we pray, God speaks, we hear, and then we pray in agreement with Him. Soon we see God moving. One of my favorite quotes comes from Andrew Murray: "Beware in your prayers, above everything else, of limiting God, not only by unbelief, but by fancying that you know what He can do. Expect unexpected things 'above all that we ask or think.'"

Your Kingdom Come

Let's pause and reflect
Share a time when you prayed a faith filled prayer.
_____
_____
_____
_____

What was the result of that prayer?
_____
_____
_____
_____

Now that we are finished with this lesson, let's do some personal reflection:

What are some areas in your prayer life where you feel you need to grow?
_____
_____
_____
_____

Where do you feel the Lord is taking you in your prayer life?
_____
_____
_____
_____

Acts 4:31 says: *"And when they had prayed, the place where they had gathered together was shaken, and they were filled with the Holy Spirit and began to speak the word of God with boldness"* (NASB)

Inheriting the Promise of Prayer

What an awesome experience we receive from God's Word. Do you believe the same promises and results are available to you? Not only can we grow in our personal prayer life, but our corporate prayer life can be anointed, powerful, and full of God's presence as well. We can have incredible spiritual experiences with God. God's Word says that if we ask it will be given to us. Now is the time to begin to pray with focused prayers (Matthew 7:7a. NIV).

What happened when the disciples prayed together?
_____
_____
_____
_____
_____

Do you believe the same promises and results are available to us?
_____
_____
_____
_____
_____

Let's pray
Lord, I thank you for the privilege of partnering with you in prayer. What an awesome promise we have to move from acquaintance to intimacy, and from intimacy to a kingdom ambassador. Lord, I invite you to touch my life and also the corporate prayer life of this church, taking us higher and deeper in you. Jesus, we ask that you begin to let us in on everything the Father is doing. Lord, increase our passion and hunger for you. Make our prayer lives sincere, relevant, passionate,

purpose focused, and faith filled. As we begin this journey into prayer and intercession we say, most of all, Lord may our love for you increase and our prayer lives reflect and release what is on Your heart. Lord, we say yes to the partnership of fulfilling anointed kingdom prayers. In Jesus' name we pray, Amen.

In closing, here are some steps to take between now and the next lesson:
1. Set aside a personal time to pray and be consistent in meeting that time. Be aware that once you make this commitment, things will happen to try to stop you. Our enemy does not like it when the church begins to make commitments to pray.
1. Invite God presence into your prayer time.
2. Ask Him to help you grow in your personal and prayer relationship with Him.
3. Begin to pray specific prayers for your family, church, city, and nation.
4. Begin to journal your prayers and also be sure to go back and record the date when the Lord answered your prayer. This is a great faith booster!
5. Do not be anxious in your prayer time.
6. Be expectant that the Lord will meet you in your journey. Do not grow discouraged. There will be times you will feel the Lord's presence and times you won't. This is normal. The important fact to remember is to be faithful in your prayer life.
7. Schedule a weekly time for corporate prayer. Invite God's presence to fill and guide this time.
8. Allow the anointing of the Lord to guide this corporate prayer time. Do not pray through a list, but pray as the Lord leads. While there is nothing wrong with praying through list of things written down, in this time we are learning how to allow the Lord to guide us into new areas of faith and

spiritual experiences. Therefore, let's give Him room to take us to new places in prayer.

From Prayer to Intercession

Lesson Two: From Prayer to Intercession

Isn't it amazing that an all powerful, all knowing, all present God who created the universe would pick you and me, ordinary people to partner with Him in a dynamic prayer life? When we really stop and think about this, it is awe inspiring that our heavenly Father desires us to pray in agreement with Him.

I will never forget the first time I heard the Lord direct me specifically concerning the call to intercession for lost souls. I was kneeling in prayer and asking the Holy Spirit to fill and to guide me. Instantly, I felt a powerful and all-consuming presence flood over me from the top of my head to the soles of my feet. I was embraced in the presence of the Holy Spirit and felt Him filling my spirit to overflowing. I was overcome. I had never felt anything so wonderful. I prayed, "Lord, please don't let this presence ever leave me."

After several minutes, the Lord showed me a vision. Amazed to be receiving such clear revelation from the Lord, I sat quiet and still. He was speaking to me and I knew His voice. My heart raced and tears streamed down my face.

In the vision I was standing on a platform surrounded by thousands and thousands of people. They were extending their hands to touch mine, and I was reaching out to touch each of them. I was reaching for as many hands as I could. I did not understand what this meant. I asked, "What is this You are showing me?"

He answered with a question; *Becca, will you be accountable for the souls I have assigned to you? Will you reach them for Me?* I did not understand the fullness of what He was asking me. I did know at that moment, however, that the Lord had put His hand on Greg and me, and that our lives were going to change quickly. He had a purpose for us, but we needed training. I responded the only way I knew: "Yes, Lord, show me how."

This experience has been the driving force of my prayer life, and also the foundational pillar of partnering with the Lord in intercession. I began to pray regularly for the salvation of lost souls, for family members, our neighbors, the cities in which we lived, and the nations of the world. Since this time, we have travelled into 23 nations and ministered throughout the United States. Many people have come to know Jesus. We see people delivered and set free on a regular basis. But this is not enough. Our hearts are full of passion for the transformation of our nation and the nations of the world. We want out lost world reached with the message of the saving knowledge of Jesus Christ.

Once we are truly captivated by Him and His love, we will always hunger for more. And as I grow in Him, more revelation comes concerning the call to fulfill our responsibilities as Kingdom representatives. There is a lost, struggling, and dying world that needs each of us on our knees in intercession.

1. What Is intercession?

Intercession is carrying a spiritual burden for an individual or situation. This includes cities, states, and nations. It is praying until God's kingdom plan is released and fulfilled. Intercession is also defined as intervention between two parties to reconcile differences. Intercession is standing in the gap between heaven and earth, praying fervently until the God's kingdom plan is fulfilled.

What a tremendous privilege it is to be called to work with God in His kingdom. We are in a divine partnership to see God's plans fulfilled in earth. Let's look at an awe-inspiring scriptural example from the life of Peter in Acts 12:5-16.

"All the time that Peter was under heavy guard in the jailhouse, the church prayed for him most strenuously.

Then the time came for Herod to bring him out for the kill. That night, even though shackled to two soldiers, one on either

From Prayer to Intercession

side, Peter slept like a baby. And there were guards at the door keeping their eyes on the place. Herod was taking no chances!

"⁹Suddenly there was an angel at his side and light flooding the room. The angel shook Peter and got him up: 'Hurry!' The handcuffs fell off his wrists. The angel said, 'Get dressed. Put on your shoes.' Peter did it. Then, 'Grab your coat and let's get out of here.' Peter followed him, but didn't believe it was really an angel—he thought he was dreaming.

"Past the first guard and then the second, they came to the iron gate that led into the city. It swung open before them on its own, and they were out on the street, free as the breeze. At the first intersection the angel left him, going his own way. That's when Peter realized it was no dream. "I can't believe it—this really happened! The Master sent his angel and rescued me from Herod's vicious little production and the spectacle the Jewish mob was looking forward to."

"Still shaking his head, amazed, he went to Mary's house, the Mary who was John Mark's mother. The house was packed with praying friends. When he knocked on the door to the courtyard, a young woman named Rhoda came to see who it was. But when she recognized his voice—Peter's voice!—she was so excited and eager to tell everyone Peter was there that she forgot to open the door and left him standing in the street.

"But they wouldn't believe her, dismissing her, dismissing her report. 'You're crazy,' they said. She stuck by her story, insisting. They still wouldn't believe her and said, 'It must be his angel.' All this time poor Peter was standing out in the street, knocking away.

"Finally they opened up and saw him—and went wild!"
                    The Message

Friends, look at the power of intercession. It was the fervent prayers of believers, partnering with Heaven for Peter's release that caused his supernatural, angelic rescue from the hands of the jailers, the Jews, and Herod. Praying in agreement with the Lord releases the supernatural. It is in these moments where we enter into intercession that our prayers begin to bring forth change. As we persevere in intercession, provision, protection, and breakthrough occur.

The believers prayed with great fervency for Peter and when the miracle came, they almost could not believe it. Doesn't this sound familiar? I can relate. How many times I have witnessed the Lord's miraculous hand as a result of intercession, and in amazement and wonder I have had to pause to truly grasp the miracle. Within moments, just as child opening a present with the surprise; the celebrating, rejoicing, and shouting in gratitude explodes in me!

A. Making it real

Journal an instance where you experienced or witnessed a miracle as the result of prayer.

_____
_____
_____
_____
_____
_____

B. Our miracle

Maybe you were not able to list an occasion. Do not feel bad or have thoughts of frustration and condemnation. Today is the turning point for each of us to go deeper into our prayer lives and to believe God for more. Perhaps, you need the Lord to move in a miraculous way in your life? I remember a time many years ago when Greg and I stepped into working for a ministry full time. We had a four year old daughter and two week-old twins. But we were certain we were right where the Lord had called us, even though walking this journey out at this point in our lives required a lot of faith and prayer.

From Prayer to Intercession

Our pastors had taught and challenged us every week to write on note cards what we wanted God to do. We began to put into action what we had been taught. As a result, the Lord moved faithfully in our lives. It is amazing what I see as I look back at those note cards and the date I recorded when the prayer was answered.

With our growing family, we needed a larger and more dependable car. This soon became the top request on my personal prayer note cards. But, I told no one what we were believing for. After one month of praying, God answered. The Lord directed an elder in the church to give us a minivan He used in his auto repair business. Our pastor still shares the amazement Greg experienced when the exchange of car keys took place. I, too, was speechless and amazed as I watched in great surprise my husband and pastor pulling into the driveway in a minivan! Beyond excitement, Greg ran into the house celebrating the goodness of God. We rejoiced and wept and thanked the Lord! I remember thinking, "God, believing in prayer really does work!"

C. Your miracle list

Now it is your turn to believe the Lord. Write down three things that you want to pray and believe for: *(hernia)*

1. *My Dad would be healed and transferred to Custer before the Holidays*

2. *My mom's pain would be non-existent — Her body/heart/+ Soul would be healed.*

3. *That we would have a permanent position for photo Ids / Parking / Safety.*

Stop and pray and ask the Lord to stir your faith to see the miraculous outcome of prayer. Let's pray together now.

4. I would be able to retire and spend quality time with my mom

Lord, I thank you for your faithfulness to answer prayer. You truly are a magnificent, faithful Father. Lord, I ask that right now you stir my faith to higher heights and deeper depths, so I can truly believe to see supernatural, miraculous answers to prayer. I want my prayer life to be faith-filled and effective. Lord, teach me to intercede as Jesus intercedes. And I thank you, Lord, for the answers to these prayer requests.

Now the answer might come quickly or it might come in time. I had written the request for a car on my prayer notes a month before it was answered. Some of the requests I have believed for took over a year or more for the answer to come. But I never stopped praying until the answer came. Remember to be persistent and faithful.

2. Jesus, our Intercessor

Jesus is an intercessor and amazingly He serves as our intercessor. Luke 6:12 says, *"One of those days Jesus went out to a mountainside to pray, and spent the night praying to God"* (NIV).

God's Word clearly tells us that Jesus only did what He saw and heard the Father doing. It was in these times when Jesus drew aside to pray and to hear the God's voice that He was provided with the insight, instruction, and anointing to fulfill all that His Father desired.

Being a teacher, minister, and intercessor myself, I am sure those times were very necessary for our Lord to remain focused in receiving guidance from the throne room, to pray for all those He was ministering to, and to continually be filled with strength. I appreciate the following quote by Oswald Chambers: *"Prayer does not fit us for the greater work; prayer is the greater work."*

3. Jesus intercedes for us in heavenly places

Romans 8:34, *"Who is he that condemns? Christ Jesus, who died more than that, who was raised to life is at the right hand of God and is also interceding for us"* (NIV).

I feel heartfelt gratitude when I receive prayer from other people. How comforting it is to know that others are walking with us and carrying our burdens. I share repeatedly about my gratitude for praying parents and grandparents, and for the righteous inheritance I have been blessed with in my family line. It was prayer spent on their knees before the Lord that paved a way for me to walk in my purpose and calling. The heart-felt words of my 90 year old grandmother, Memmy, still ring true in my mind and spirit today.

"Becca, your dad shared with me that you feel the Lord is calling you into full time ministry. That you are to travel the nations and pray for these lands, reach the lost and teach the word of God. Well sweetie, I want you to know you are the answer to my prayers. I served the Lord the best I could my whole life in the church. But my heart was always to reach more souls and more people in the world. I prayed many nights for souls to be reached and saved and for further opportunity to teach the word of God. You are and will be the fulfillment of those prayers."

Shedding tears of gratefulness and joy, I thanked her for her faithfulness to the Lord and for her prayers. My grandmother truly did play a key role in what is unfolding in my life today; as have all my grandparents, and especially my parents.

Imagine the Lord Jesus Himself making intercession for you and me in the Heavenly throne room right now. As He intercedes, it strengthens and prepares us to live lives set apart for Him. How comforting this is. These heavenly prayers keep us protected in the ways of the Lord and place us into a life of purpose. As we ascend into His presence, we capture His heart and our prayers and lives become the fulfillment of His prayers.

4. Jesus is our High Priest

"The point of what we are saying is this: We do have such a high priest, who sat down at the right hand of the throne of Majesty in heaven, and who serves in the sanctuary, the true tabernacle setup by the Lord, not by man" (Hebrews 8:1, NIV).

The word "priest" in Latin means "bridge builder." Jesus paid the ultimate price in order to build a bridge of redemption from heaven to earth; and in the process to make a way for each of us to be a partner with Him in His rulership of the universe. Christ's chief purpose as priest is summed up in the Greek word *entunchanein*. This word means that Jesus continually meets with God the Father in order to represent believers, and to act graciously on our behalf. With Jesus as our High Priest we know that if He is for us who can be against us!

5. We are a royal priesthood

I was teaching when a gentleman asked, "If Jesus is making intercession in throne room for all of us, then why do we need to pray?" The answer is that because we are heirs of God, co-heirs with Christ and a royal priesthood, God wants us also to be co-laborers with Him. Just as Jesus serves as our high priest, He has also blessed us with this position in an intercessory priestly calling. Romans 8:17 says, *"Now if we are children, then we are heirs-heirs of God and co-heirs with Christ, If indeed we share in his suffering in order that we may also share in his glory"* (NIV).

The Greek Word for "heir" is *kleronomoi*. It means in order for us to be adopted as joint heirs, we have to accept the responsibility of sharing in both the sufferings and glory of Christ. Webster's dictionary defines "co-heir" as "one who inherits jointly with another or others." What a grand promise from God's Word. All that belongs to Christ as the Firstborn also belongs to us as believers as well! To wear the crown we must also share in and embrace both the cross and His resurrection.

What does it mean to share in the cross? It means we die daily to our fleshly desires and emotions and choose to put God first in all we do. But when we do this we do not stay in this place of death. If we did we can become very religious in our mind-set and actions. Dying to self does not mean we are in this continual place of denying ourselves everything. It means we welcome the Lord into our lives allowing Him to purify our desires, impure motives, sinful thoughts and actions, and to raise us into His resurrection life, purposes, and plans. This is key to an effective prayer life.

When Christ died on the cross, the veil of the temple in front of the Holy of Holies, was rent (torn) in two. As God's sons and daughters we are also His priests, and we have the authority to enter into God's presence of God day or night, and to carry His intercessory burdens.

One of my favorite Scriptures is 1 Peter 2: 9:
"But you are a chosen generation, a royal priesthood, a holy nation, a people belonging to God, that you should show forth the praises of Him who has called you out of darkness into His marvelous light" (NIV).

What does it mean to be a people belonging to God? It means that we are a set apart nation, an acquired, purchased, and consecrated class of people formed for God's own possession. Then we become purpose focused and full of kingdom action.

6. Effectual, fervent prayer!
The effectual fervent pray of a righteous man availeth much! (James 5:16, KJV).

I love this Scripture! One of the purpose focused, action steps we are to take is to engage in effectual, fervent prayer.

Andrew Murray shares: *"God does nothing but by prayer and everything with it."* The Greek word for "effectual" and "fervent" is *ischuo*. It means "to be strong, able, forceful, and to prevail." The Lord has appointed us to be prayer warriors who stand in a place of passionate, fervent, fulfilling intercession. Listen to the many translations of this verse:
- The energetic supplications of a righteous man.
- The fervent supplications.
- The operative petition of the just.
- The unceasing prayer of a just man.
- The earnest prayer of a good man can do much.
- From the heart of a man right with God has much power.
- The inwrought prayer of a righteous man exceedingly prevails.
- Is mighty in its working.
- Has great effect.
- Very powerful effects.

7. Learning to hear God's voice
In order to be focused and passionate we have to learn to hear God's voice. Many believers do not realize that we can hear His voice or even how to recognize it when He is speaking. We each have voices in our lives that influence us in our daily walk—our own voice, the voice of the enemy, the voice of family and friends, and God's voice. In advancing in our call to prayer and intercession we have to learn to distinguish between these voices.

In John 10:27 Jesus says: *"My sheep hear my voice and I know them, and they follow Me"* (KJV). This promise from God's Word emphasizes relationship. The word "know" signifies a "deep" knowing. It is actually the word used to describe a sexual relationship between a man and a woman.

From Prayer to Intercession

The word is not meant to describe any thing similar with God, but rather to emphasis how intense God wants to be in a relationship with us. Therefore, the Lord desires for us to become so familiar with Him and His ways that we "know" when He is speaking, and that we further understand the directives that He is giving. To understanding this better, we must grasp the issue of inheritance and ownership with the Lord. We are the God's sheep. We are not the devil's sheep.

But can the devil and his demons also speak to us? Absolutely, but we are not his children. The enemy's voice will be one of confusion, deception, control, and manipulation. His voice does not bring peace. If we know God's Word, we will know when the enemy is distorting, twisting, and confusing God's promises through deception.

The more time we spend in God's presence and in reading His Word, the more we will recognize His voice, His thoughts, and His ways. They will then become our thoughts and ways.

If a father knows how to give good gifts to his children, how much more will the Lord give good things to those He loves. But there is always the question, "How do I know for sure that I am following God's voice?" One thing I tell people is to bind the voice and lies of the enemy, bring our spirit into submission with the Holy Spirit, and then to welcome the voice and guidance of the Holy Spirit. Not only will we begin to hear God's leading and direction, but His ways will begin to become our ways. Just as Jesus did only what He saw and heard the Father do we, too, will be able to follow Him and walk in His ways. But for this to happen we must pursue God's Word and also the leadings and promptings of His Spirit. As we step out in obedience the more sure we become of the voice we are hearing and following. When our life is aligned with God and we grow, our voice will become like God's voice. What we say is what God wants to say.

8. What are some of the ways God speaks to us?
In the second book of this prayer curriculum we will discuss this topic in depth. But to get started, let's learn some of the ways God speaks to us.

   A. Dreams

Many times God speaks to us in dreams. I often tease and explain that sometimes our dreams can also be the pizza we ate for dinner, especially if they are bizarre and bring confusion. If dreams produce fear, distress, and are evil in nature these dreams are not from God. Sometimes a dream can come from things that are on our minds that we have thought about in excess. Pay attention to your dream life. Write down your dreams in a dream journal and date them. Especially those that you know are from the Lord. If you are not sure they are coming from God, pray for discernment. God does not want us confused about anything.

   B. Visions: Open and closed

We read about many men and women in the Bible who experienced what we call "open" visions. Elisha witnessed Elijah as he was taken to heaven in a horse drawn chariot; angels surrounded the children of Israel as they prepared for battle; and Peter, James, and John witnessed the transfiguration. Open visions are the ability to witness a supernatural event while it unfolds before our natural eyes. I am convinced that the Lord still speaks to us in this manner. Our oldest daughter has experienced open visions from a very early age.

   A "closed" vision is one that unfolds in our spirit. Or, as my dear friend Tommi Femrite so beautifully explains, it unfolds in the theater of our minds. I experience closed visions on a regular basis. This is where my prophetic anointing in hearing God speak directly to me flows the strongest.

C. An impression or knowing in your spirit

This might be compared with what is termed "women's intuition." However, both men and women can operate in this. Most would describe it as something beyond and impression, something that can only be explained as a "knowing" deep within the human spirit when we are walking with God. It involves knowing right from wrong, good from evil; the best decision verses a good decision, and especially what God is saying as opposed to what Satan is saying.

D. A whisper or strong impression in your thoughts

It is not uncommon to hear believers and intercessors make the comment that they hear the Lord speaking. For many this is not God's audible voice, but an impression in their thought life that is very clear as if someone has spoken it to them. It coincides with the "knowing" of part "C."

E. God's audible voice

An experience when a believer hears God's voice audibly speaking to them. This is usually a rare occurrence.

F. Through God's Word

God's Word is like food to our soul and spirit. Just as food nourishes and gives life to our physical bodies, so does God's Word give sustenance to our spiritual lives. Scripture gives spiritual direction and answers to many of our prayers.

G. Through the prayers, voices, and giftings of others

I am sure we can all recall a time when we prayed and then, later, in a church service our pastor would speak and give the answer to our inquiry. There are also the occasions when we receive a word of prophecy from others. I will discuss this in depth in the next book of this curriculum on knowing the type of prophetic words to give and receive. As a preliminary word of caution do not speak words over people concerning marriage, pregnancies, relocations, and job changes. Stay tuned for the next booklet to learn more about these things.

H. Through circumstances

God is always faithful in every circumstance in our lives. He is never early and He is never late. He is always right on time. I sometimes feel like He is late because my answer comes at the latest moment possible. I am sure many of you will agree. But no matter what transpires, God is always faithful. He is also wise to answer our prayers through circumstances. Sometimes He will cause things to happen in order to bring us into new places He has created for us. Then there are the times when we are not certain which direction to go and He will shut one door and then open another. Sometimes our circumstances can speak louder than words.

I. Through angels

Repeatedly we witness in God's word angels delivering messages from heaven. Daniel, Mary, Abraham, Joshua, and many others received divine direction and instruction from an angel. The Lord still speaks to believers today through his angels.

Let's pause and reflect

Share an experience where you know you heard God's voice speaking to you.

_____
_____
_____
_____
_____

Share a time when the enemy attempted to lead you astray?

_____
_____
_____

From Prayer to Intercession

_____
_____

Has there been a time when your emotions or desires took you down a path that you realized later was not God's best for you?

_____
_____
_____
_____
_____

Has there been a time when someone spoke a prophetic word of direction from the Lord to you that provided great clarity?

_____
_____
_____
_____

Has the Lord used you to speak into someone's life? In the following curriculum we will engage in practice exercises empowering you to hear and release God's voice.

The good news is, God still speaks and we can learn to quiet ourselves, pray, seek Him, and know His leading in our lives.

Let's pray
Lord, we come before you and thank you for the awesome price Jesus paid for us on the cross. Jesus, thank you for being our Savior, redeemer, friend, intercessor, and High Priest. Thank you that you continually make intercession for us before the throne room of God. Lord, I invite you into my prayer life. Lord, take me from a place of prayer into the calling of intercession. Let me learn to hear your voice and intercede in agreement

with your purposes and plans. Increase my discernment in order to know your ways and to follow your voice. <u>Lord, where I have lost passion and fervency I invite you to restore it now.</u> <u>Where I have not believed or understood that You still can</u> speak to me, I now recognize that You still speak to people and that you will speak to me. Teach me to know Your voice. I want to carry your intercessory burdens. Let this day be a new beginning of a passionate, intimate, and fervent prayer life.

Things to do before the next lesson:
1. Find a quiet place to pray. Some might even term this "a prayer closet." Many do pray in their closets.
2. In your prayer time continue to invite the presence of the Holy Spirit.
3. Learn to wait on the Lord. Even if it means sitting still in His presence. Silence is still prayer.
4. Do not grow anxious in your quiet place. Allow your heart, mind, and spirit to be quieted before the Lord.
5. One of the difficulties in our culture that hinders prayer is busyness. Have a notebook and pen close by. When thoughts come to your mind of things that need to be done, write them down and go back to focusing on the Lord and waiting in His presence.
6. Do not resort to praying through your prayer list at this time. There is a time and a place for this, but right now you are learning to focus on the Lord, to invite His presence, and to pray His heart.
7. During this time, it is good to pray God's Word out loud. Read Scriptures that talk about the goodness, glory, love, and magnificence of the Lord.
8. Sing songs of worship and exaltation to the Lord.

Susie's Story

Lesson Three: Susie's Story

As a young mother, I taught piano lessons in our home. I understood my students were entrusted and assigned to me by God. I prayed that He would bring me the ones needing a revelation of Jesus' love.

One day I received a phone call from Susie, a sixteen year old girl originally from Thailand. The Lord impressed on me that I was to give her lessons, to intercede for her salvation, and that she had a powerful call on her life.

Before each lesson, I spent time in focused intercession for Susie's salvation. She was placed in my care and it was my responsibility to see her brought into God's Kingdom. Even so, I did not preach or force my beliefs on her. I reached out in love and built a relationship based on trust. One afternoon in the middle of a piece of music, Susie suddenly stopped. "Miss Becca, can I ask you a question?"

"Of course" I replied.

"You are a Christian, right?"

"Yes, I am. Why do you ask?"

She said, "I have Christian friends in my high school who talk to me about Jesus. I am curious to know Him, but my family worships Buddha. I know he is a false and powerless god. I do not want a religion focused on the worship of a false god. I must know that Jesus is real before I commit to follow Him."

"Susie," I said, "Jesus is the Savior of the world. He wants to reveal Himself to you. Do you have a need in your life? We can pray and ask Jesus to help you. He will answer our prayer, and you will know that He is the one true God."

She replied, "I do have a need. I lost my glasses two weeks ago. My parents were mad at me because of the expense to replace them. Yesterday, I lost my new pair of glasses! I am afraid to tell my parents. Can we pray that I find my new pair before my parents realize I lost them?"

"Absolutely," I responded. We prayed asking the Lord to help Susie find her glasses. After she finished her lesson, I earnestly began to seek God in prayer. My faith was ignited simply because she had asked something, which seemed so simple. I knew that when the answer came it would be pure evidence of His love for her. My prayers went deeply into asking God to reveal Himself to this girl from a Buddhist family. What a blow to the kingdom of darkness to convert one still in his camp! I prayed continually during the rest of the week for God to show Himself through her circumstance.

The following week, Susie arrived for her lesson beaming with excitement. She quickly exclaimed, "The day after we prayed I went to school. After English class, my teacher called me to her desk and opened a drawer. She pulled out the first pair of glasses I had lost! That afternoon, the bus driver handed me the new pair my parents had just bought me! Not only did Jesus help me find my new pair of glasses, He also found my first pair. I know He is the one true God. Please lead me to Him." We both wept tears of joy as Susie received Jesus as her Savior.

Susie began to experience a hunger for God's Word. A Bible was purchased. We spent the first portion of the class working on piano lessons and the last portion learning about God. Her Buddhist parents would have forbidden her to read the Bible, so she stayed up late at night reading in bed under her sheets with a flashlight. During this time, the Lord began to give her an intercessory burden for her parents, and other family members in Thailand trapped in worshipping Buddha.

One day Susie explained a difficult situation. Her parents were requiring her to go to the Buddhist temple to pray to Buddha and to receive a blessing from the monk. She didn't want to go, but was given no choice. We asked the Lord to work mightily on her behalf.

The day arrived for her blessing from the monk. After her parents prayed to Buddha, the family was approached by a monk for the blessing. As he reached out to touch Susie's shoulder his hand hesitated. He attempted again to put his hand on her shoulder, but it was as if something hindered his touch. He bowed, as if acknowledging the power within Susie, and left. God performed a miracle. In doing so, He showed her the authority she carried because of His presence in her.

During her last music lesson, Susie said, "Miss Becca, thank you for leading me to Jesus. When I graduate from college, I am going to Thailand as a missionary to lead my people to Him and to reach those gripped in darkness who worship Buddha." We both thanked the Lord for saving Susie, for His faithfulness in her life, and for her calling to reach the Buddhist people of Thailand.

Friends, you never know where your prayers will take you. We do not know what might occur in terms of salvation and transformation until we hear God's voice, recognize it, agree with Him about it, and obey.

1. Who is to intercede?
All believers are called to pray and to intercede. Luke 11:2 says, *"When you pray."* It doesn't say, *"if"* you pray, but *"when"* you pray. Let's look further at what God's word says concerning our prayer lives.

Three Important Ways to Pray:
A. Pray always
"Praying always with all prayer and supplication in the Spirit, being watchful to this end with all perseverance and supplication for all the saints" (Ephesians 6:18, NKJV).

B. Pray earnestly

"And being in agony, He (Jesus) prayed more earnestly. Then His sweat became like great drops of blood falling down to the ground" (Luke 22:44, NKJV).

C. Pray persistently

"Also, [Jesus] told them a parable to the effect that they ought always to pray and not to turn coward (faint, lose heart, and give up). He said, in a certain city there was a judge who neither reverenced and feared God nor respected or considered man. And there was a widow in that city who kept coming to him and saying, Protect and defend and give me justice against my adversary. And for a time he would not; but later he said to himself, Though I have neither reverence or fear for God nor respect or consideration for man, Yet because this widow continues to bother me, I will defend and protect and avenge her, lest she give me intolerable annoyance and wear me out by her continual coming or at the last she come and rail on me or assault me or strangle me" (Luke 18:1-5, NKJV).

Think of a time when you prayed for something for a long while. What was the length of time you prayed and believed for the answer?

_____
_____
_____
_____
_____

When and how did the answer come?

_____
_____
_____
_____
_____

SUSIE'S STORY

Let's pause and reflect
Think back to the emotions you felt at the moment the answer to your prayer came. Remember, share and journal that kingdom moment in your life:
_____
_____
_____
_____
_____

2. Thy Kingdom come
Our ultimate mission is to have a secret place of prayer, a special place and time in order to get away and into God's presence. The word clearly reveals: *"Well done, good and faithful servant! You have been faithful with a few things; I will put you in charge of many things"* (Matt. 25:21, NIV). This is a powerful kingdom principle that applies to all areas of our Christian walk. As we grow in our fellowship with God we move from new beginnings to maturity. Anointing and authority will operate through us. Jesus taught us to pray: *"Our Father who art in Heaven, hallowed be thy name. They kingdom come, they will be done on earth as it is in Heaven"* (Matthew 6:9-10). We become God's agents for furthering His kingdom.

    The "Lord's Prayer" teaches us to pray in a manner that releases God's purposes and plans. This prayer is not to focus on Jesus' return, but to give us the directive we need in order to pray effectively and to see the Kingdom of Heaven released on earth right now. As we pray, we overthrow the schemes of the enemy. We intercede so those trapped in darkness may come to salvation and be set free! We become people of our word, people who walk in integrity, character, obedience, and humility. We reflect the love of Jesus. We are able to hear and see what the Father is doing and then to intercede in unity with Him. As a result, we see miraculous kingdom moments unfold on a personal level, in our families, in the lives of others, in our churches, neighborhoods, government, jobs, states, and nations.

3. Cultivating an atmosphere for revelation
If we are prayerless, then we are also powerless. In order to hear the heart and direction of the Lord we must be faithful in several areas of our daily spiritual walk. We must:
- Spend time in the Lord's presence daily.
- Spend time in His Word.
- Worship the Lord, singing praises of exaltation and adoration.
- Have a spiritual walk of gratitude and thanksgiving.
- Approach God's Throne in awe, respect, reverence, and confidence in His love.
- Talk with the Lord freely sharing your heart with Him.

4. Are there seasons when it is difficult to pray?
Yes. There are times when we pray and nothing happens. Several days or even longer periods of time pass where we do not feel or hear anything significant from the Lord. And there are days where tiredness sets in or our feelings hinder our praying. But, these are the times that we need to continue faithful to our prayer time. This is true for our personal prayer time and for our corporate prayer time as well.

I believe we all experience seasons in which we think or ask, *"God are you there? Do you hear me?"* Beloved, in these times we should walk in the resolve that says, *"Lord, even so, I am here. I will faithfully come before you and pray to you, worship you, read your Word, and even just sit before you. Lord, I choose to be faithful to you."* In these times, if we choose faithfulness, we will experience great spiritual growth.

What about you? Think about the times when you did not feel like praying. Were you faithful in spite of what you felt? If so, what was the resulting spiritual growth that transpired in your walk and life?

_____
_____
_____
_____
_____
_____
_____

5. Hindrances to prayer

Being an intercessor and having been involved with intercessors for many years, it becomes clear that there are certain hindrances that keep us from a dynamic prayer life. I have often heard believers describe it as a wall between themselves and the Lord. They want to draw close to Him, but are unable to fully experience His presence or hear His voice. One thing I share when I am teaching is that we can have and experience as much of the Lord as we want. But we still have to deal with our own personal issues in order to find that place of freedom in relating and connecting with Him. What are some of these hindrances?

A. Pride

A heart of humility is necessary in order to see answers to our prayers. We cannot expect God to answer us if we are walking in pride. James 4:6 tells us that, *"God opposes the proud, but gives grace to the humble."* As we approach the throne in humility, yet in confident faith, God will hear and mighty answers to prayer will result.

B. Preferring others

Learning to have a servant's heart and to prefer others more important than ourselves is vital in intercession. We cannot stand in the gap until we have learned this important principle. This is the heart and essence of intercession.

Before the Lord brought me into intercession and praying for the nations, I had trained nine years to sing. My major in college was vocal performance. Upon graduation I was ready to audition for support and lead roles in opera companies. During that venture in my life, I wanted to go to New York and become a big star on Broadway.

When we moved to Houston, I was quickly asked to join the church worship team, which I readily and gladly accepted. It was a season in our church in which the Lord was moving in releasing new, spontaneous, and prophetic songs. I was thrilled and fully believed that this was what the Lord had created me to do. I believed He wanted me to write and sing new prophetic songs to Him. After all, I had the music training to do it!

One Sunday evening service, the Lord's presence moved strongly as we worshipped and praised His goodness. The worship leader began to play chords on the keyboard waiting for one of the worship team members to begin to receive and sing a new song to the Lord. I was elated. On the outside I was smiling, with hands raised, eyes closed worshipping the Lord. I could feel a song rising up within my spirit. But on the inside I was thinking, "Yes, God this is what I was created to do!" But before I could open my mouth and sing, another lady who never had a music lesson in her life opened her mouth to sing the new song of the Lord!

On the outside, I still appeared spiritual and lost in the presence of the Lord, but on the inside I wanted an immediate and serious discussion with the Lord. "How could she sing before I did, God? Aren't I the one with all the training?"

Upset, I went home and spent time in my prayer closet. God quickly began to speak to me, "You have to learn to prefer others better than yourself. This is not a competition. Learn to prefer others." The words pierced my heart and I realized I was trying to compete for the prophetic song instead of allowing the Lord to use me freely. I genuinely repented and asked the Lord to forgive me and to cleanse me of this performance attitude.

The next weekend in church, the worship leader again allowed time for the release of prophetic song through the worship team. Again, I could feel the anointing to sing that new song. But before I could, I heard the Lord gently speak to me, "Becca, pray that the same lady that sang last week will release the new song." "What? Lord, did I hear you correctly? You want me not to sing, but to pray that that same lady will release the new song?" His response was simple and straight forward, "Yes." Reluctantly, I obeyed. As soon as I prayed that prayer, she began to sing the most beautiful song.

The Lord did this in me until all competition was destroyed. And yes, now the Lord allows me to sing new prophetic songs, and I do as often as He leads me. This principle applies in intercession as well. I have witnessed competition and striving in prayer meetings between well intentioned believers. We cannot always be the one praying out loud, never giving room for others to pray. Preferring others and not competing in our corporate prayer times is vital and necessary to an effective prayer life. God calls us to be an intercessory team and to flow together in unity and agreement.

C. Momma always said not to be lazy!
Watch out for a tendency toward laziness. When it concerns our commitment to prayer, we must set our faces like flint and press into the Lord. Laziness prevents us from growing in our relationship with the Lord, from growing in our prayer lives, and from realizing our kingdom inheritance. Hebrews 6:12

explains, *"We do not want you to become lazy, but to imitate those who through faith and patience inherit what has been promised."* We are to keep our spirits in tune with the Lord. If we become lazy, our hearing becomes dull.

"Concerning him we have much to say, and it is hard to explain, since you have become dull of hearing. For though by this time you ought to be teachers, you have need again from someone to teach you the elementary principles of the oracles of God, and you have come to need milk and not solid food. For everyone who partakes only of milk is not accustomed to the word of righteousness, for he is a babe. But solid food is for the mature, those who because of practice have their senses trained to discern good and evil." (Heb. 5:11–14).

D. Overcome fear

"For God hath not given us the spirit of fear; but of power, and of love, and of a sound mind" (2 Timothy 1:7, NKJ).

"For you did not receive a spirit that makes you slave again to fear, but you received the Spirit of sonship. And by him we cry, 'Abba, Father'" (Romans 8:15).

"Fear of man will prove to be a snare, but whoever trusts in the LORD is kept safe" (Proverbs 29:25).

We all experience fear, that feeling of anxiety in the face of danger, evil, or even pain. Most of us, perhaps, have experienced fear in praying out loud. We sense uneasiness by speaking what we feel the Lord is saying. Fear cripples and disables us in moving forward. It is a snare! Therefore, we have to lay down all fear and intimidation and take a risk in the Lord.

When a two year old child begins to walk and then stumbles and falls, we do not pick them up and scold them. As parents, we rush to them, make sure they are not hurt, and encourage them to keep trying. The Lord also responds in the same manner. We grow in hearing and speaking forth His voice. If we do not get it right, He picks us up, brushes us off, and as a proud Father says, "Good try! Now let's try again!"

Let's pause and reflect
Has there been a time when the Lord encouraged you to step out and into a new place in Him? If so, what happened?
_____
_____
_____
_____
_____
_____

Think of a time when you decided to take a risk in the Lord and the results were great!
_____
_____
_____
_____

Or, maybe you are in a place where this is the first time you have been challenged to move out of fear and into risk taking in the Lord. Make a commitment to allow the Lord to move you out of your comfort zone and into a new place of faith and anointing. Invite Him to release the gifts and anointing He has for you.

E. The necessity of forgiveness
The willingness to forgive is vital to a life of freedom and also to our ability to relate to the Lord freely. We must make the decision to walk in forgiveness even before any breach of trust, hurt, betrayal, or violation has occurred. Jesus said: *"For if you forgive men when they sin against you, your heavenly Father*

will also forgive you. But if you do not forgive men their sins, your Father will not forgive your sins" (Matthew 6:14–15). Christians must be ready and willing to forgive the offenses of others. If we do not forgive, then our heavenly Father will not forgive our sins. This does not mean that we are to wait for an apology from the offender, nor are we to keep a running checklist of wrongs suffered at the hands of others. The choice to forgive is done before any offense has developed and without any expectation of an apology or repayment. Forgiveness is a lifestyle choice.

While Jesus hung on the cross, He cried out, *"Father, forgive them, for they do not know what they are doing"* (Luke 23:34). Jesus did not wait for an apology from those who were taking His life. He cried out for mercy and forgiveness. Jesus' death on the cross establishes redemption for all who will come to Him, even those who have hurt, betrayed, or sinned against us. Christ paid for their sins once and for all just as He did ours. As His followers, we should mirror His example. If we fail to forgive, a wall will be built between us and the Lord and our prayer lives will be greatly hindered.

F. Live a life of holiness

It is essential to deal with open doors that have allowed ungodliness into our lives. When God reveals them or we become conscious of them in some other way we must respond. If we seek Him and ask Him to reveal any open doors leading to sin, He will be faithful to answer.

In 1 Peter 1:15–16 we read, *"But like the Holy One who called you, be holy yourselves in all your behavior; because it is written, 'YOU SHALL BE HOLY, FOR I AM HOLY.'"* Becoming holy means to become consecrated, sacred, and set apart. Christians must no longer live lives characterized or controlled by sin. We can pray and invite the Holy Spirit to fill us daily and to give us the strength to stand against temptation (See Philippians 2:13).

Susie's Story

It is not always the most obvious sins that trap us. Remember: trash in, trash out! What kind of movies and television programs are you watching? What kind of music do you listen to? Is the Lord grieved by your choices of entertainment? If we expose ourselves to things that are polluted with sexual overtones and darkness, then we are polluting our minds, wills, and emotions. Scripture explains that the eyes are the windows to the soul. *"Your eye is a lamp for your body. A pure eye lets sunshine into your soul. But an evil eye shuts out the light and plunges you into darkness."* (Matthew 6:22–23, NLT).

If we are going to walk in holiness then we must obey the standards that the Lord has given to us in Scripture, and we must also follow and honor those in godly authority over our lives. Submissive attitudes and actions are character traits of those walking in obedience. If you do fall into error, remember that immediate repentance is another characteristic of holiness.

As we continue to seek a lifestyle of holiness, hatred toward sin begins to arise within us. We can even ask God to impart revulsion to sin and to the schemes of the enemy in our lives!

In going through this week's lesson, we have learned that we are all called to pray and intercede. We have looked at cultivating an atmosphere of prayer. We have observed hindrances to our prayer lives. Now, let's stop before moving further and recommit our prayer lives to the Lord. If there are issues in which we need to repent, now is the time to do so.

Let's pray
Dear Lord, I thank you for the awesome privilege of partnering with You in prayer and intercession. Lord, I want to take time now to receive a fresh anointing and impartation in my prayer life. I realize in certain areas I have not been as committed as I

need to be, especially in my personal prayer life and also in corporate prayer. Lord, I ask that you help me in these areas (each individual will need to pray as led by the Lord for their personal life). *Lord, I long for more of you. I desire an intimate and free relationship with you. I want and choose to partner with you in prayer and intercession. Breathe fresh life and purpose into my prayer life. Use me to release your kingdom on earth. Lord, may my prayer life be a reflection of You and my life a mirror of Your love. In Jesus' name. Amen.*

This lesson's growth steps:
Between now and the next lesson it is important to invite the Lord to begin to do a cleansing work in your life. This will draw you further into His presence. You will experience a new personal relationship with Him. You will also experience His prayer burdens.

1. This is a time for personal cleansing. It is a time to be obedient and rid ourselves of all that might hinder our prayer and intercession time. Have a piece of paper and pen handy. As the Lord shows you each issue write it down and repent of it.
2. Maybe you struggle with a competitive and performance driven attitude like I did. Invite the Lord to help you prefer others better than yourself. He will be faithful to give you opportunities for this to happen!
3. Continue to seek the Lord concerning areas in your life that you need to bring before Him and make right.
4. Also, ask the Lord to show you any items or forms of entertainment you need to get rid of.
5. Continue to open to the Lord's revelation of anything that would hinder your time with Him.
6. Is there someone you need to forgive? Does the wrong need to be made right?

7. After you have completed this process, mark a big X through your list and write on top of it, confessed, repented, and forgiven on _____.
(Include the date and time). Then take the paper and tear it up and throw it away. This is a prophetic action done to show that these sin patterns and issues have been forgiven and are now officially no longer a part of a new season with the Lord.
8. Invite the Lord to cause you to walk in higher realms of holiness.

My Prayer List

Lesson Four: My Prayer List

1 **Who or what should I pray for?**
As we continue our journey, you might be asking, who or what do I pray for? How do I get started and move forward into an effective intercessory prayer life?

It all begins with spending time alone with God. As I shared briefly in lesson one, your prayer time might last only three minutes, but as you grow it will soon turn into longer periods of time. It is not uncommon for an intercessor to spend several hours in prayer. I recall the first time I prayed for three minutes. it seemed like an eternity. Thoughts of, "How do I pray? And who do I pray for?" raced through my mind. I continued to look at my watch hoping that the three minutes were over only to find that 30 seconds had passed! Eventually, it did not take long for the three minutes to pass. I discovered it was exciting to pray and intercede. I was partnering and communing with my heavenly Father!

Here are some suggestions on how to begin your intercession time. (Note that quietly communing with and worshipping the Lord should precede all other kinds of prayer):

- Pray for your family
- Pray for your co-workers and boss
- Pray for your pastor
- Pray for your church
- Pray the word of God out loud
- Pray for those in authority in your life
- Pray for the widows
- Pray for the orphaned
- Pray for the poor
- Pray for our leaders
- Pray for your city
- Pray for the government

- Pray for your nation
- Pray for the nations

Some of the things we can ask God to do:
- Protect
- Bless
- Sanctify
- Open eyes
- Open hearts
- Open doors
- Convict of sin
- Give wisdom
- Grant health

During your intercession time make sure to put your personal needs aside. They are certainly important, but interceding is meant to go beyond your things relating to you personally. When you intercede, you are standing before the Lord to present to Him the needs of others. You are there to help bring breakthrough into someone else's life. It is time of selfless intervention.

2. The Holy Spirit will reveal the need
"In the same way, the Spirit helps us in our weakness. We do not know what we ought to pray for but the spirit himself intercedes for us with groans that words cannot express. And he who searches our hearts, knows the mind of the Spirit, because the Spirit intercedes for the saints in accordance with God's will" (Romans 8:26-27, NIV).

In reality, Jesus and the Holy Spirit are our intercessors. But we are asked to partner with God in this kind of ministry as His Kingdom people. The Amplified Bible says, *"So too the Holy Spirit comes to our aid and bears us up in our weaknesses."*

(Romans 8:26a) I love this promise from God's Word. The Holy Spirit takes our burdens. He shares the load and makes our part easier. Through the partnering with the Holy Spirit, He is able to express and lead us in prayer for what we cannot put into words by ourselves.

A. He knows God's will

There are many times I need guidance and direction on how to pray. One of the first actions I take is to invite and welcome the Holy Spirit's presence into my prayer time. (We understand the Father, Son, and Holy Spirit to be three in one. This Trinity of being is not something easily understood, but we accept it on the basis of its revelation in the Bible.) Through the Holy Spirit we are able to relate to and grow in relationship with our Heavenly Father and every aspect of Who He is. As shared above in Romans 8:26-27, the Holy Spirit is able to guide our prayer time and direct us to pray in agreement with the Father's heart. Therefore, I welcome His presence to guide the intercession time. I might pray something like this: *Holy Spirit, I thank you for your presence in my life. Thank you for your comfort, conviction, and guidance. I invite you into this prayer time. I welcome your presence to guide and direct me. Show me what is on the Father's heart. What is it that I can pray that is in agreement with the Father's will and heart?*

As I pray and listen, I begin to feel God's presence and His direction. Always remember that one of the most valuable ministries of the Holy Spirit is that of helping us in prayer.

B. He knows Jesus' heart

It is important to understand that intercession is praying in agreement with Jesus. As we grow in our relationship with Him, we will begin to receive understanding and direction concerning how to pray in harmony with His heart. This takes time. The more time we commit to and consistently focus on developing our intercessory prayer lives, the more clearly we will hear His voice and know His heart.

In my personal prayer life I have learned that the Lord longs for souls to be saved. As you enter the Savior's presence it does not take long to realize His heart and passion for the lost. I recently read a powerful quote shared by Reinhard Bonnke on his Facebook page, *"Intercession that is not linked to soul saving is like an arrow shot without a target, an athlete running a race which has no finish line or a football match without a goal net."*

C. Reaching beyond the realm of our words

Powerful intercession reaches beyond the realm of our words and finds expression in the words of the Holy Spirit. Often the Lord will take us into deep places of intercession where we experience *"groaning which cannot be uttered."* This is where the Holy Spirit moves into our spirit alerting us to what is on the Lord's heart. It is so powerful it often feels like a crushing weight.

In this place we might not know the exact situation for which we are praying. But there is the sense that we are standing with the Lord and partnering with Him in an unusually intense way.

In this prayer experience, some intercessors believe or have thoughts that God does not entrust us with knowledge concerning some prayer burdens because we cannot be trusted with the details. However, I believe the contrary to be true. It is a place of higher trust and faith in our obedience to pray in agreement with His heart when we know little or nothing about the situation. It takes more faith to carry a burden without complete understanding. He often places us in positions of needing to trust Him in the direction He is leading us, and also into praying until the burden lifts.

Through the Holy Spirit's guidance, we intercede, *"in accordance to God's will"* or the *"Father's heart."* (Romans 8:27) Since the Holy Spirit knows God's will, we have assurance that the intercession is according to His will and plan. We have the guarantee that the prayer is accurate and will be answered.

D. Standing in the gap for friends

By "gap" I mean that we see ourselves as if protecting a city by standing in a hole in the wall that has been breached by an enemy. In a similar way we actually stand between a person and the enemy of his or her soul.

My husband, Greg, and I were on vacation in Arkansas. I woke up one morning with a sense of crisis and danger. Knowing this was a burden (knowledge of urgency) from the Lord, I quickly moved to another room to begin praying. I asked the Lord who was in danger, but no clear answer came. Sensing the increased urgency of danger, I began to pray in the Spirit.

In sharing this story, I want to clarify the meaning of a prayer burden and praying in the Spirit. A burden is the actual intercessory assignment the Lord is placing on an individual. Praying in the Spirit is when we agree with the prayer burden and engage in praying the Lord's heart and will. It is the place of moving beyond our own understanding and emotions and into lining up with divine inspiration and direction. In some situations, and with certain individuals, it might also include praying in a prayer language. But this is not necessary or required to agree with the Holy Spirit and the Lord's desires. In this instance, I found myself crying and speaking that there would be safety for those who were in this crisis. I prayed for an hour and began to feel the burden lift.

Throughout the day, the Lord kept prompting me to intercede further. I told Greg that someone was in danger. He also agreed with me in prayer. Both of us still did not know who or what this situation involved. Early that evening, I felt a peace settle on me as if this crisis had passed.

When we returned home four days later, the story behind this prayer burden was revealed. Two of our very dear friends had gone deep sea fishing for the day. As they made their way back, large and violent waves overtook their boat causing it to capsize. They had failed to put on their life jackets. When they did not return home, their wives alerted the coast guard who then began the search for the missing men. When the Lord placed the prayer burden on me, our friends had already spent one whole night lost at sea without life jackets, nor anything to hold onto. They literally had to swim, tread, or float in order to stay alive. As I prayed throughout the day, they stayed above water although terribly exhausted. The hour that the sense of danger lifted from me was the exact hour they were rescued.

Why the Lord did not reveal all of this during the time I felt the danger, I do not know. But I am so thankful that I was obedient and prayed even without complete knowledge of the details.

E. What about your prayer experiences?
Has there been a time when you prayed out of obedience to discover later why you were praying?
_____
_____
_____
_____
_____

Maybe you have experienced what I call a "trigger," a unique something that gets our attention in order to bring about intercession. The following are a few ways the Lord will gain our attention.
- Consistent thoughts of a certain loved one or friend.
- An old classmate or friend that you have not seen in a long time whose name or face crosses your mind.
- Physical sensations as intercessory prompts might be new. It is true that not all physical sensations or experiences are triggers to intercede. Be careful with sensations. Make sure they are form the Lord.

- A sudden experience of your heart racing where there is no medical cause for this and no heart condition.
- An overwhelming sense of crisis or danger that comes out of nowhere.
- Going from joy to sadness with no explained reason. This intercessory trigger is quite common, but I know that some people do not understand it. I realize there are times when sudden joy to sadness can be an assignment from the enemy. But if there is no real reason for the sudden depression, heaviness, or sadness, then take the time to ask the Lord if this is from Him. When you begin to intercede and you feel the sadness lifting this gives assurance that it was an intercessory assignment.
- Sudden tears or a feeling of travail.
- A vision from the Lord.
- God's voice in your spirit.
- A dream.
- God's Word with fresh revelation.
- A sudden urgency that is not fear based when watching a news report or reading a news article.
- If you are experiencing these, don't ignore these Holy Spirit prompts. Intercede until you feel the burden lift or the Lord speaks to you that you are done.

3. Peter's lesson becomes our lesson

Peter is a great example of a radical follower of the Lord who did great exploits for God's kingdom, but who also made great blunders out of his intense passion and personality. For our study, let's look at Peter and how he operated before the "tongues of fire" (Acts 2:1-4) fell on him and the 120 in the upper room at Pentecost. I believe the transfiguration is a great example. Let's look at Luke 9:28-33:

*"Now it came to pass, about eight days after these sayings, that He took Peter, John and James and went up on the mountains to pray. As He prayed, the appearance of His face was altered, and His robe became white and glistening. And behold two men talked with Him, who were Moses and Elijah, who appeared in glory and spoke of His decease which He was about to accomplish at Jerusalem. But Peter and those with Him were heavy with sleep; and when they were fully awake, they saw His glory and the two men stood with Him. Then it happened, as they were parting from Him, that Peter said to Jesus, 'Master, it is good for us to be here; and let us make three tabernacles one for You, one for Moses, and one for Elijah'" – not **knowing what he said.*** (Emphasis mine, KJV)

I realize there are many prophetic messages in this Scripture, but for the sake of our study, I want to look at Peter's response to the transfiguration. As usual, Jesus had drawn away to pray. But the disciples who were with Him soon fell asleep. When they awoke they witnessed an amazing supernatural event. But Peter responded in his old way of thinking and in the traditions of men. Even though he had walked with the Lord and witnessed miracle after miracle he and the disciples had not fully grasped that Jesus was releasing the kingdom of God on earth. In the past, where temples, altars, and tabernacles were built to signify and house what God was doing, Jesus came to bring God's Kingdom to each of us in the person of Jesus. Once we are saved the Kingdom of Heaven comes alive in us and we are clothed in Christ. We literally are filled with God's presence. God's word says that we are the temple of God.

Peter wanted to honor the Lord and suggested building three dwellings to house what God was doing. I can see him thinking, "Let's build a place and keep all three of you here in this glorious state." The Scripture says he did not know what he was saying.

But, now let's look at the outcome. The book of Acts records that later when Peter and 120 other people prayed together God answered in a miraculous way! Let's read Acts: 2:1-4:

"When the day of Pentecost came, they were all together in one place. And suddenly there came from heaven a noise like a violent rushing wind, and it filled the whole house where they were sitting. And there appeared to them tongues as of fire distributing themselves, and they rested on each one of them. And they were all filled with the Holy Spirit and began to speak with other tongues, as the Spirit was giving them utterance."

Peter and the others who had gathered to faithfully pray and wait for the manifestation of the Holy Spirit knew that something was going to happen as they waited. They were obedient to pray and seek the Lord as Jesus had instructed them to do before he ascended into heaven. Did they know exactly what would happen? Probably not, but what an incredible answer they experienced. They were baptized in the Holy Spirit. Later, God used Peter to move the church into a season of global evangelization. Where he once wanted to house our Lord, Elijah, and Moses in three dwellings, Peter now became the house in which God would dwell by the Holy Spirit.

I asked this question in lesson 1, but it is important to bring it to light again. Do you believe the same can be true for you and me when we pray and intercede? Friends, our faithfulness to prayer can make and change history. When we are committed to pray and are steadfast in that purpose, awesome things will transpire. You and I are history makers.

Name a time when you prayed and the answer was beyond what you could think or imagine?
_____
_____
_____
_____

4. Travailing in prayer
There are times in intercession when an intercessor is overcome with weeping and emotion. There is a combining of passion with the tears of compassion that result in travail or in other words very hard work. Others observing this might not understand what is happening, but it is very real for the person involved. Let's look at several Scriptures where travail is mentioned.

"Oh that my head were waters, and mine eye a fountain of tears, that I might weep day and night for the slain of the daughter of my people!" (Jeremiah 9:1 Darby Translation).

"And in that day did the Lord Jehovah of hosts call to weeping, and to mourning, and to baldness, and to girding with sackcloth" (Isaiah 22:12 Darby Translation).

"And being in conflict he prayed more intently. And his **sweat** *became as great* **drops** *of* **blood***, falling down upon the earth"* (Luke 22:44 Darby Translation. Emphasis mine).

5. Hannah's travail brings breakthrough
Hannah was deeply grieved because of her barrenness. She had no children. In 1 Samuel 1:9-13, she brings her prayer burden to the Lord. The result of her travail births one of God's greatest prophets. God gave her a beautiful baby boy. His name is Samuel which means "heard by God."

"Then Hannah rose after eating and drinking in Shiloh. Now Eli the priest was sitting on the seat by the doorpost of the temple of the LORD. She, greatly distressed, prayed to the LORD

and wept bitterly. She made a vow and said, 'O LORD of hosts, if You will indeed look on the affliction of Your maidservant and remember me, and not forget Your maidservant, but will give Your maidservant a son, then I will give him to the LORD all the days of his life, and a razor shall never come on his head.' Now it came about, as she continued praying before the LORD, that Eli was watching her mouth. As for Hannah, she was speaking in her heart, only her lips were moving, but her voice was not heard. So Eli thought she was drunk."

As Eli watched Hannah in her anguish of soul and travail before the Lord, he thought she had been drinking wine. He tells her to put it away (vs. 14). Even though he was the priest of the temple, Eli had no comprehension of Hannah's travail. Once Hannah explained her weeping, Eli agreed with her that the Lord would grant her what she had asked. In time, Samuel was born. He began ministering to the Lord in the temple as a young child (1 Sam. 2:18). He eventually grew into one of God's greatest prophets.

When the Lord places travail on us, it can and does release God's supernatural hand. It is important that we do not work up travail with our own emotions and flesh. When true travail comes on us from the Lord, breakthroughs occur.

6. Are we to "wrestle" in prayer?

The answer is yes. Many times in prayer there is an element of what we call "wrestling." It is warfare. The third series of this curriculum will deal with warfare prayer, so for now let's discuss the aspect of wrestling and what it involves.

A. Colossians 4:12:
"Epaphras, who is [one] of you, [the] bondman of Christ Jesus, salutes you, always combating earnestly for you in prayers, to the end that ye may stand perfect and complete in all [the] will of God" (Darby Translation).

In this verse, the word for "combating" means to strive, contend, wrestle, or enter into a contest. Here, Paul shares that Epaphras was contending in prayer for the people of Colossae. It emphasizes that in order for spiritual growth to occur there must be faithfulness in contending and combating for a desired outcome.

This means that we need to understanding that we are in a battle. Sometimes believers will share with me that they do not want to think about contending in prayer or even acknowledge the need for warfare prayer. I usually reply with this question. "Are you saved? Are you truly a believer?" The answer is almost always, "Yes!" Responding to their assurance and confidence, I begin to explain our position. Once we are saved, we have enrolled and enlisted in the most powerful army in the universe. The battle lines have already been drawn and we have chosen the side of ultimate victory. Friends, when we enter God's Kingdom, we have positioned ourselves for war in God's army of Christians throughout the world. The only thing we need is training and understanding of how to wisely use God's authority. By the end of this curriculum, it is my prayer we will be better trained in wisdom and of how to engage in and stand strong in the midst of battle.

Remember intercession does not have to be praying for something big like a nation. It can be praying for a neighbor across the street, or as I shared in the story above, a friend. I believe God requires us to press our faith in small things, in order to see His faith in bigger things.

I remember the first time I was asked to be on a ministry team praying for someone who had a need for God in their lives. The night before, while in intercession, God revealed a list of four items which I believed were on His heart for this person. The following day, during the ministry session, as the pastor led the team, each of these issues was addressed. Often the Lord also will speak to me concerning prophetic direction for cities, states, and nations.

B. Romans 15:30:

"I appeal to you [I entreat you], brethren, for the sake of our Lord Jesus Christ and by the love [given by] the Spirit, to unite with me in earnest wrestling in prayer to God in my behalf" (Amplified Bible).

Here, Paul was imploring the church to pray together, to share in the contest of contending together as a unit. Not only are we to wrestle, but we are to contend in the contest of wrestling together in order to see victory. Beloved, not one of us is meant to battle alone. Not one of us is meant to contend alone. We are called to walk together and to share in the contest in order to see our prayers realized!

C. Ephesians 6:12:

"Because our struggle is not against blood and flesh, but against principalities, against authorities, against the universal lords of this darkness, against spiritual [power] of wickedness in the heavenlies" (Darby Translation).

The word "struggle" in this verse shows us that we are in a very powerful battle—including believers and unbelievers. No one can escape. Another Greek word *pale* refers to a type of wrestling well known in ancient times. It was brought to prominence by the Greek athletic games. The competition required each wrestler to throw his opponent to the ground. The overcomer's hand pinned the defeated one's neck to the ground and victory was declared. This word is used generally to denote a fight or battle, or a Christian's struggle in overcoming evil through heated, intense, and personal battles.

Paul taught the church at Ephesus the position in which believers enter the struggle with darkness. As overcomers, we with intensity, throw our opponent to the ground and declare victory!

D. Out of the mouth of babes

When our oldest daughter was 4 years old, I was cooking dinner and suggested that she clean her room. Being a happy and obedient child, she quickly agreed. Within a short time, she returned to the kitchen and stood with her hands on hips tapping her foot as if she were angry.

"Momma, you want to know what just happened?"

"Sure, baby. What?"

"Momma, you told me to clean my room. Well, there was one of those little bad things. You know momma those bad things in my room"

"Honey, do you mean a demon?"

Let me explain before I go further that we did not talk about demons and darkness in our home, especially around our young children. We did not want to frighten them. But our oldest daughter has always been sensitive to the spirit realm and began seeing into that realm at a very young age.

"Yes, momma, that bad thing. You know what it said to me?"

Not liking the thought that a demon was in my baby's room, I quickly replied, "Yes, baby, I do want to know what that demon said to you."

Tapping her foot quicker and harder, "Well, it told me not to clean my room!"

She had my attention. I asked her what she did. Smiling in pleasure she replied, "Well, I stomped on its head and told it to go in Jesus name! And you know what momma? It disappeared! And you want to know something else momma?"

Totally intrigued and wondering what else she would say, I quickly stated, "Yes, baby. I do want to know something else."

In total confidence in her wisdom and understanding she began to teach me. "Momma, those demons do not like you and daddy. No. not at all! You know what they do when you pray in Jesus name?"

My Prayer List

"No, baby. What do they do?"

"Well, momma they do this." Acting her story, my daughter began to aggressively shake her body as if nervous and in a loud voice exclaimed, "AAAAAGGGGHHHHHH!!!! And then they disdappear! Momma, those demons don't like you and daddy. No, not at all!"

My daughter happily left the kitchen to return to cleaning her room. Amazed and stunned, I called my husband explaining that I just had a spiritual warfare 101 lesson conducted and taught by our four year old daughter!

Look at the authority of a four year old who walked in childlike faith. If a four year old can walk in this level of authority, then friends so can you and I. We all have the same Holy Spirit operating in and through us. There is no junior Holy Spirit!

E. Name a time when you stood in warfare intercession and victories were realized?

My Mom's House
Red Lobster
_____

Maybe some of you are in a battle right now and need a breakthrough. In closing this lesson, let's do what Paul tells us to do. Let's contend together in the contest to see victory. Before moving on, let's pray for our brothers and sisters and believe for victory.

Action steps for growth:
1. As much as is possible, this week do not bring your problems into your time of intercession.
2. Welcome the presence of Holy Spirit.
3. Sing worship songs that glorify the Lord.
4. Continue to practice sitting quietly before the Lord and wait for His direction.

5. Express to the Lord that you want to pray the prayer burdens on His Heart.
6. If someone or something comes to mind after praying this prayer, then pray for that person or situation. Trust what the Lord is speaking to you and the impressions He places in your spirit and mind.
7. If there is not an impression then begin to pray for family, friends, and your church. As you pray you will begin to experience the Holy Spirit's impressions and thoughts. Pray through these as the Lord leads.
8. Pray until you feel the burden has lifted. How do you know the burden has lifted?
   - There will be a peace.
   - There will be a knowing in your spirit that you are done.
   - The Lord will speak that you are done.
   - If you are in travail the tears will stop flowing.
   - If you have engaged in a contending or wrestling place of warfare prayer, you will feel the intensity of the battle lift.
   - The Lord will speak to you that breakthrough has occurred.
   - You will feel the crisis is over.

9. My close friend Alice Smith teaches, "If the horse dies, dismount!" In prayer, if you sense the burden has lifted, then trust what you are experiencing and that the burden has been prayed through effectively. Remember, for some burdens you might be in prayer for weeks, months, and even years. Pray faithfully, but when the burden lifts, have faith that the breakthrough needed for that season has occurred.

Having His Heart for Others

Lesson Five: Having His Heart for Others

1. The Father's heart of mercy

One of my favorite movies is "Brave-Heart." For a woman, that might sound strange to some of you. But at the end of the movie, in the midst of his pain and suffering, William Wallace cries out for freedom for his people. This is the epitome of the heart of an intercessor. Here is one whose heart was so pierced for those held captive that he would give his life and make sure his final cry was for freedom.

The intercessor has the same heart. We cry for mercy. Where people are bound and treated unjustly we cry freedom. Where there is sin and judgment we appeal to heaven's court asking for God to intervene.

Let's look at Exodus 32:30-32 and the heart of Moses concerning the children of Israel: *"The next day Moses said to the people, 'You have sinned a great sin. And now I will go up to the Lord; perhaps I can make atonement for your sin.' So Moses returned to the Lord, and said, 'Oh, these people have sinned a great sin and have made themselves gods of gold! Yet now, if You will forgive their sin--and if not, blot me, I pray You, out of Your book which You have written!'"* (NIV)

What a powerful prayer. Here is a man who said, "Lord, take my name out of the Book of Life instead of those who have sinned against You." The Hebrew word for "blot" is *machah*. It means "to wipe out, wipe away, or to destroy." Moses literally put his life on the line for an undeserving people. This is a resounding cry rising from Moses for mercy for those the Lord had entrusted to him.

2. Jesus cries for mercy

The above example was a foreshadowing, a prophetic picture of what Jesus would do for us. The words of our Savior as He hung on the cross set the stage for our Christian walk, *"Father forgive them for they know not what they do."*

We know that Jesus came to extend grace and mercy to a lost and dying world. He even cried out for those who brutally tortured and eventually crucified Him. Jesus had been in His Father's presence and had received compassion and love for those trapped in darkness in the world He was sent to redeem. Jeremiah 31:34 shares, *"For I will forgive their iniquity, and their sin I will remember no more"* (NASB). Psalm 103:12 is a beautiful promise concerning Jesus' forgiving grace, *"As far as the east is from the west, So far has He removed our transgressions from us."* (NASB). Everything we do in prayer and intercession has to come from the Father's heart of mercy, compassion, and love. This is to be our guide—our example as we intercede.

3. Dangers of witchcraft praying

Witchcraft is the essence of rebellion. It does not only mean the practice of casting spells or of divination or magic. It also refers to someone trying to control or exert their will or agenda on someone else.

As an intercessory leader, many times I have seen and heard the church practicing what is termed witchcraft praying. For instance, praying for our pastor to be the way we desire him to be instead of praying God's heart. Or, praying in a negative way concerning our spouses, family members, friends, or church members.

When Greg and I were newlyweds, I realized that there were things about him that I did not see before we were married. It was nothing sinful. Just little personality issues that I wanted him to change. I began praying for him one evening. My prayer went something like this. "Lord, please change Greg's heart on this issue. Change him, Lord. Make him how I want him to be." I began to pray down my list of what I wanted for Greg. Very soon in the prayer time, the Lord clearly impressed on my spirit, "Becca, worry about the log in your own eye, before you worry about the spec in Greg's eye." Friends, I so plainly heard this, and I quickly repented for praying my own agenda for Greg and not the Father's heart for him.

There are even times where I have heard intercessors pray: *Lord, right now where there have been witches that have cursed us, our church, or the Christian community, we heap the curses back on their heads in Jesus name.*

Please don't pray this way! Jesus died for all who are lost and in darkness. We were also once lost and destined for hell. In this situation the right way to pray is: *Lord, right now in Jesus name, we break the power of every word, curse, hex, and vex placed by witches who have prayed against us. We say their power is cancelled, null, and void. And Lord, we ask for mercy for these people who are trapped in deception so that they will come to the saving knowledge of Jesus.*

4. The mercy of a wise king

I believe one of the best stories of mercy is found in 1 Kings 3:26 when King Solomon was faced with two women each claiming a certain baby as their own. Solomon's decision was to split the baby in two. At that point, we hear the sacrificial cry of the true mother. She pleads with Solomon to give the child to the other woman rather than having it killed. It becomes obvious who is the real mother. Solomon, in his wisdom, learns which woman is the mother.

The same principle applies in intercession. When God asks us to intercede for a particular person or situation, we are standing in the gap (that is, we are standing before God in behalf of someone else) in order for God to change the life of another. God is holy and righteous and we are asking for His judgment to come into the situation. How merciful He is to invite us to pray and beseech Him on behalf of another. We become the one asking for a new direction in someone else's life and we do it without any thought of gain for ourselves. We are seeking a blessing to come to another person who may never realize our prayers brought change into their lives. Intercession is more about other people than it is about us. As we foster this attitude in prayer, we give Christ a chance to make Himself known in other places, lives, and situations.

Making it real and relevant
Let's stop and personally invite the Lord to show us those who need His mercy. It can be a person, business, institution, people group, or crisis in the world, etc. Make a list of those people or situations that the Lord brings to mind. Then, make them your prayer focus for the next week.

A. _____
_____
_____
_____

B. _____
_____
_____
_____

C. _____
_____
_____
_____

D. _____
_____
_____
_____

5. The advantages of fasting

Often in God's Word where there is a need for a supernatural breakthrough, or a cry to the merciful, sovereign hand of God, those praying are also fasting. I appreciate the word of Cindy Jacobs from *Possessing the Gates of the Enemy*. *"Fasting multiplies the effect of prayer at least several times. This is why we ask for fasting chains along with prayer requests for serious issues. Fasting will touch things that prayer alone will not affect."*[1]

Fasting is not a Christian diet. Fasting is not about changing God, but about causing us to change in order to line up in agreement with the Lord and His plans. When you hunger for more, you will receive more. When you hunger for God, He will fill you.

In Matthew chapter 6, Jesus names three things believers should do: *"When you pray..."* *"When you give...."* *"When you fast..."* As stated in Lesson 2, it doesn't say *"if"*, but says *"when."* If we can find the time to pray and give, we as believers can also find the time to fast.

Lou Engle shares a powerful testimony in *The Reformers Pledge,* a book compiled by Che Ahn:

"Five years ago at TheCall School, we received a dream in which I was a referee on a basketball court, and young people were there weeping because of the presence of a demonic barrier on that court. In that dream a 17-year old woman cried out, *'Lou Engle it's your turn now!'* I took the hands of those kids and swept that barrier off the court.

"The definition of referee is judge over the court. We sensed God was calling us to gain a place of spiritual authority

---

[1] Cindy Jacobs, *Possessing the Gates of the Enemy* (Grand Rapids. MI: Chosen Books, 2009), 95.

in prayer over the powers affecting the Supreme Court. Three days before the election in 2004, we needed a pro-life president who would appoint pro-life judges. Seventy kids standing in front of the Supreme Court did and Esther fast-no food or water for three days. At that time, I was invited to take a tour of the Supreme Court. When I asked the young lady taking me on the tour if there was a basketball court in the Supreme Court building, she said, '*As a matter of fact there is, and it is exactly on top of where the Supreme Court holds its hearings. They call it 'the highest court in the land.'*

"I said, 'Take me to that court!' Standing on that basketball court, with the U.S. Supreme Court beneath my feet, I declared, 'From this day forward there will only be pro-life judges.'

"After the elections, we launched a House of Prayer with up to 70 young people praying day and night facing the Supreme Court building. A week before President George W. Bush was to appoint a Justice to replace William Rehnquist, one of our young women, knowing nothing, dreamed that a man named John Roberts would become the next Supreme Court Justice. Those kids prayed. Don't you think they were baptized in confidence before God when the president nominated John Roberts for the position of the Supreme Court Justice?

"We believe through intensive, focused, day-night-prayer and fasting, principalities and powers were shifted, and God got His pro-life man to the top of the Supreme Court Mountain."[2]

---

[2] Compiled by Che Ahn, *The Reformers Pledge* (Shippensburg, PA: Destiny Image, 2010), 117,118

Thank you, Lord for this powerful testimony of fasting and intercession combined as an effective arsenal for believers.

Let's discuss how and what fasting does:

A. It positions us to hear and discern God's heart, voice, and timing more clearly

Our world is full of people with busy schedules. I know I struggle with this on a daily basis! In the midst of full schedules, thinking and clarity of mind can become confused. Coming into a place of fasting lifts the fog from our minds enabling us to connect with God's heart and hear His voice with greater simplicity.

B. It teaches us to deny our flesh in order to receive more of the Lord

One thing that we are not used to, especially in the Western Church, is the concept of denying ourselves in order to receive from God. But in this place of denial and self-control we can better cry out for the Lord to fill our lives more.

C. It is an act of setting ourselves aside solely for the Lord

Listen to the words of Jesus in Matthew 4:1-4:

"Next Jesus was taken into the wild by the Spirit for the Test. The Devil was ready to give it. Jesus prepared for the Test by fasting forty days and forty nights. That left him, of course, in a state of extreme hunger, which the Devil took advantage of in the first test: 'Since you are God's Son, speak the word that will turn these stones into loaves of bread.' Jesus answered by quoting Deuteronomy: 'It takes more than bread to stay alive. It takes a steady stream of words from God's mouth.'" (The Message)

Fasting helps us come to a place of solely depending on the Lord. His Word and Spirit become our daily nourishment in which we say, *Lord, all we want in our lives is you. Jesus, more of you!*

D. Fasting sets our time and priorities in order

Many times a fast may involve separation from worldly entertainment. There are times when we would normally watch television or spend hours on the internet. Instead, we set aside this time for praying, worshipping, and reading God's Word.

Even for those in ministry, a fast can be a sabbatical from busy travel schedules and demands. It allows us to focus on being filled, refreshed, renewed, and revived in intimacy with the Lord.

E. Fasting empowers our praying and our personal lives

We have already mentioned the 40-day fast Jesus experienced in the wilderness. Following the 40 days, He left the wilderness *"full of the power of the Holy Spirit."* It was during this time of total denial of the flesh and an extended time with His Father, that Jesus was set apart, filled, tested, proven true, and empowered for His earthly ministry. If Jesus began His ministry with a 40-day fast, shouldn't this be the model for us as well. I believe there is nothing coincidental with the life and ministry of Jesus on earth. Everything He did, exemplified, taught, and showed us was walked out in order for us to see and understand what is available to us now as His followers. If Jesus could have received the empowerment for His earthly ministry without fasting, he would not have fasted. His heavenly Father required this of Him in order for Him to receive the anointing necessary for His calling.

F. It increases our discernment

I remember the first time I was asked to pray with a deliverance team. For those who are not familiar with this term, it is a ministry time which involves the practice of praying for an individual to see emotional wounds healed and demonic influences broken. It was in 1990. Before this time, I had never seen deliverance take place, nor had I ever witnessed a demonic manifestation. I was thrilled and nervous all at the same time. I fasted the four days leading up to the prayer time. My cry was, *"Lord, give me the authority to pray and to stand against the darkness in this woman's life. And Lord, please help me not run out of the room in fear if a demon should manifest!"* I am happy to report that Jesus' anointing and authority was there, and when a spirit of death made itself known through the woman receiving prayer, I was not afraid. Instead, I was filled with boldness and courage. Fasting really does empower us and increase our discernment.

G. It brings us into greater humility

Fasting is an act of humility when we seek God's mercy and grace. Let's look at Nehemiah 1:4-11:

"When I heard this, I sat down and wept and mourned for days and fasted and prayed [constantly] before the God of heaven,

And I said, O Lord God of heaven, the great and terrible God, Who keeps covenant, loving-kindness, and mercy for those who love Him and keep His commandments,

"Let Your ear now be attentive and Your eyes open to listen to the prayer of Your servant which I pray before You day and night for the Israelites, Your servants, confessing the sins of the Israelites which we have sinned against You. Yes, I and my father's house have sinned.

"We have acted very corruptly against You and have not kept the commandments, statutes, and ordinances which You commanded Your servant Moses,

"Remember [earnestly] what You commanded Your servant Moses: If you transgress and are unfaithful, I will scatter you abroad among the nations;

But if you return to Me and keep My commandments and do them, though your outcasts were in the farthest part of the heavens [the expanse of outer space], yet will I gather them from there and will bring them to the place in which I have chosen to set My Name.

"Now these are Your servants and Your people, whom You have redeemed by Your great power and by Your strong hand.

"O Lord, let Your ear be attentive to the prayer of Your servant and the prayer of Your servants who delight to revere and fear Your name (Your nature and attributes); and prosper, I pray You, Your servant this day and grant him mercy in the sight of this man. For I was cupbearer to the king." (Amplified Bible)

Notice, in the midst of his fasting and praying Nehemiah repented on behalf of the sins of his forefathers and of the nation of Israel. This is known as *identificational repentance*. It is vitally important to know that repentance represents not only a place of humility before the Lord, but that it also breaks the back of the enemy as we pray and intercede.

H. It increases our faith

The prophetess, Anna, is one who fasted and prayed. As a result she spoke from a point of faith concerning Jesus, the Savior of the world and the promise of redemption: *"Now there was one, Anna, a prophetess, the daughter of Phanuel, of the tribe of Asher. She was of a great age, and had lived with a husband for seven years from her virginity; and this woman was a widow of about eighty-four years, who did not depart from the temple, but served God with fastings and prayers night and day. And coming in that instant she gave thanks to the Lord and spoke of Him to all those who looked for redemption in Jerusalem"* (Luke 2:36-38, KJV).

I. It brings breakthrough against darkness

There is a story in Mark 9:14-29 where a father brought his son to the disciples for deliverance. The boy was tormented by a deaf and dumb spirit. But the disciples were not able to deliver him. Afterward, they inquired of Jesus the reason why they were unable to set the boy free. Jesus explained that sometimes demons can only be driven out by prayer and fasting. Often, when you are in warfare, fasting releases a breakthrough!

J. Fasting brings victory in battle

Judges 19 -20 shares a great story showing the difference fasting made in a major battle against a people who were overcome with sexual perversion. A Levite was traveling with his concubine through the land of Gibeah, a land that belonged to the Benjamites. The men of this city were wicked and took great pleasure in homosexual acts. They surrounded the house where the Levite was staying and demanded that he be sent out so they could know him carnally. They ended up brutally raping and murdering the concubine instead, leaving her to die at the doorstep of the house. The Levite found her the next morning and was outraged! He sent pieces of her body with a word to all the tribes of Israel, condemning them for allowing this wickedness to exist in their midst. He demanded that they rise up and do something about it.

The armies of Israel gathered to battle against the Benjamites. On the first day of battle the Israelites lost 22,000 men. They came back, regrouped, and went out to battle again, this time losing 18,000 men. Before the third day of battle, the prophet Phinehas was sent by the Lord to the army of Israel with a message to fast and pray before advancing into battle again. They obeyed the word of the Lord and the men fasted and prayed for 24 hours before going back into battle. When they went back out for the third time against the spirit of perversion and homosexuality it was broken and defeated (vs. 26-28).

K. Fasting brings breakthrough in impossible situations

Esther 4:13-18 shares of the impossible situation in which she had been placed:

"When Hathach told Mordecai what Esther had said, Mordecai sent her this message: 'Don't think that just because you live in the king's house you're the one Jew who will get out

of this alive. If you persist in staying silent at a time like this, help and deliverance will arrive for the Jews from someplace else; but you and your family will be wiped out. Who knows? Maybe you were made queen for just such a time as this.'

"Esther sent back her answer to Mordecai: 'Go and get all the Jews living in Susa together. Fast for me. Don't eat or drink for three days, either day or night. I and my maids will fast with you. If you will do this, I'll go to the king, even though it's forbidden. If I die, I die.' Mordecai left and carried out Esther's instructions" (The Message).

When Esther realized she was in a life or death situation for her people, she responded with a call to corporate prayer and fasting. She understood this would release supernatural power in a time of desperation. There is empowerment and faith released when believers partner and fast together.

Dr. David Yonggi Cho pastors the largest church in the world in Seoul, South Korea. Seven hundred and fifty thousand members go on a twenty-one day fast each year. He has fifteen hundred teenagers camp out on Prayer Mountain in tents to fast and pray for seven days each year. This prayer and fasting has changed the nation of South Korea. Friends, we are called not only to prayer, but also to fasting.

L. Daniel

Daniel, a faithful man of God, was held captive in Babylon almost all of his life. After Nebuchadnezzar, the Babylonian king, surrounded and oppressed Jerusalem and took back captives to Babylon, he took the best and brightest young men. The purpose was to set them apart to be trained in the way of the Chaldeans in order for them to eventually become his assistants. Daniel, along with his three friends, Shadrach, Meshach, and Abed-nego, were among those selected. Daniel and his friends set themselves apart early on by refusing to defile themselves with the foods laid out for them on the king's table. Because Daniel and his friends took this simple stand,

"God granted Daniel favor and compassion in the sight of the commanders and officials" (Daniel 1:9).

Eventually, Daniel rose to positions of great responsibility within the Babylonian kingdom. In Chapter 9 we see Daniel repenting and crying out for mercy for the nation of Israel. In Chapter 10, Daniel, then close to the age of ninety, received a vision that he clearly understood. Troubled by the revelation, he recorded, *"I, Daniel, was mourning three full weeks. I ate no pleasant food, no meat or wine came into my mouth"* (Daniel: 10:2-3, Amplified Bible). It was soon after that fast that Daniel encountered the angel of God along the Tigris River. When the angel spoke to him, he spoke encouragement. Daniel's prayers had been heard in heaven from the very first day he started to fast (Daniel 10:12). The only reason the angel had not appeared sooner was because he was fighting with the "principality" (a territorial demon) of Persia (modern day Iran).

Jentezen Franklin shares a powerful truth from his book *Fasting: Opening the door to a deeper, more intimate, more powerful relationship with God.*

"No matter what is going on in your life right now, you can set yourself to fasting and praying to seek the God who sees you as having great worth. Don't believe the lies of the enemy. Don't sink further under the spirit of heaviness. God has a garment of praise for you. His yoke is easy and His burden is light. As you fast, you will begin to see yourself through His eyes." [3]

---

[3] Jentezen Franklin, *Fasting: Opening the door to a deeper, more intimate, more powerful relationship with God* (Lake Mary, FL: Charisma House), 145.

Friends, fasting empowers and positions us in the midst of impossible situations to see the favor, mercy, and heart of God released.

M. Different kinds of fasting

To help guide you further concerning fasts, the following are different kinds that you can be participated in.

- Personal Fasts—a personal fast is where you feel led of the Lord to fast alone.
- Corporate fasts—in a corporate fast you fast along with others.
- Fasts from solid foods—many call this fast a liquid fast. It involves drinking water, broth, and fruit juices.
- Partial fasts—focuses on refraining from certain foods like meat or sweets.
- Daniel fasts—a fast that only allows the eating of vegetables, fruits, and nuts.
- Total fasts also known as an Esther fast—in a total fast, you fast from all foods.

N. The length of a fast

Fasting can be of any desired length. These are suggestions you might want to consider.

- 1 meal a day
- 1 day a week
- 1 to 3 day fasts
- 1 week
- 21 days
- 40 days

Having His Heart for Others

O. Your personal journey.
Have you ever participated in a fast? Share the outcome of that time.
_____
_____
_____

Does the thought of fasting intimidate you?
_____
_____
_____

In closing, let's pause and pray
Lord, I thank you for Your work in my life, for Your heart of mercy and love. Thank You for the price You paid on the cross for my salvation and the salvation of this lost world. Lord, give me Your heart of mercy for lost souls. Cause me to cry out for mercy for those who do not know You and who are not walking in Your ways. Pierce my heart for the lost. And Lord, I also come to You and ask You to give me strength to make fasting a part of my lifestyle. I need growth in my spiritual walk. I want and desire more of You. I desire to be empowered by You. And Lord, right now, even the sins of my forefathers that have not been repented of, I confess these sins (each person will need to pray what the Lord has been showing them privately) *and bring them under the blood of Jesus to be washed clean and remembered no more. I ask for mercy for my life and my family and for a spiritual awakening to be released in our lives. Lord, where I need to begin walking out Your ways, in simple acts of obedience, in order to draw closer to You and to receive favor and breakthrough, I ask that you show me these ways right now. Help me as I begin to enter into a time of fasting. Teach me how to fast and pray for breakthrough. Lord, give me more*

of You in my life. Increase my hunger and passion for You. Empower me to pray and to intercede with kingdom prayers that will release breakthrough and victory.

Walking it out:
1. After going through this material you may realize that you have prayed witchcraft prayers in the past. Take time to get alone with the Lord and repent for praying harm on others. Do not allow condemnation to set in. Let the Lord release forgiveness, and then rejoice in your new understanding of how to intercede.
2. This week make a commitment to fast for a day or for a meal. Of course, if you have medical issues where this will cause you physical harm, do not enter into a fast.
3. Ask the Lord what you are to believe for in your fast.
4. Make time for the Lord during your fast. We do not fast just for the sake of fasting. When we fast we make time to spend with the Lord.
5. Be aware that everything in you will not want to fast. Things will happen to try to keep you from the fast. I know, trust me, I know! And when you are fasting everything you want to eat will cross your mind. Every commercial, advertising all of your favorite foods will come on the television and radio. Learn to deny your flesh and the thoughts in your mind. Ask for God's help in order to be faithful to your commitment.
6. Do not announce that you are fasting. Do not make a boast about your fasting.
7. Do not forget to journal the things the Lord shows you in your fast. If He does not reveal anything, simply journal your thoughts toward Him.

Intimacy with God

Lesson Six: Intimacy with God

1 **The joy of intercession!**
After my first encounter with the Holy Spirit, which I shared in Lesson One, I began spending long hours in intercession and worship before the Lord. I had a hunger to know Him more. The Lord had me on a journey that would supernaturally teach me that He wants us to experience His presence. He was inviting me into His glorious throne room for fellowship.

Greg and I were preparing to move to Houston. We arrived in town on a house-hunting trip and met with a close family friend who was a highly successful real estate agent. She told us that she had arranged for us to attend a meeting that night in the Summit, a convention center that holds thousands of people. A world-renowned evangelist would be speaking. We were excited because this evangelist was the author of the book containing the prayer that had been the springboard for miraculously changing my life.

Greg and I had never attended a gathering like this, so our friend prepared us as we drove to the event. She spoke of how powerful the service the night before had been. She said it was time to lay down all skepticism and to trust God. By the time we arrived, we were both eager for the service to begin.

As the worship leader and choir led us in songs of adoration, the presence that had become so sweet and real to me some twelve weeks before began to flood the convention center. It was a strong and precious presence. What an anointed time of exalting the Lord! The speaker gave a powerful message and many people came forward for prayer and were healed.

As he was closing the service, this minister said that he felt the Lord leading him to pray an "impartation" to those who wanted more of God's presence. He gave this instruction:

Your Kingdom Come

"Those of you who want this put your hands up and get ready to receive." Without hesitation I threw my hands up to receive from the Lord. As soon as I did, I began to tremble at the touch of the Holy Spirit.

My friend noticed what was happening and quickly came to my side. "Becca," she asked, "do you need a healing?"

I said, "No."

"Well," she said, "this is obviously the Lord so we are going to go with it." There was no argument from me.

The minister extended his hands toward the audience to impart the anointing and exclaimed three times, "Take it, take it, take it!" Every time he spoke those words it felt as if a bolt of lightning shot through my body. We were a great distance from the platform—up in the nosebleed section—but I might as well have been on the stage. By the third command, I fell backward onto the floor and was instantly swept away in the Spirit.

I no longer knew anything of my physical surroundings. I was clueless that I was on the floor, and if I had known I would not have cared. In the Spirit I was taken to the throne room of God and was lying facedown at the feet of Jesus and our Father. The presence was glorious and awesome, but their presence was so holy I stayed on my face and dared not move.

It is difficult to put into words what I felt. It was everything I could ever desire. I wept, sobbed, and rejoiced as I lay at Jesus' feet. I said, *"Lord, this is all I have ever wanted in my life. You are awesome, powerful, wonderful, and holy. Lord, please let me stay here with You. Don't send me back."*

The Lord replied, *Becca, you must go back. You have a husband and daughter and you will have more children. You have a call on your life that I have given you. I brought you here into My throne room to call you to Me and for you to understand the reality and revelation of Who I am. I wanted you to experience the throne room of God. Now go fulfill your call.*

God wants this for each of you reading and participating in this study. In this lesson, it is my heart to write this journey in such a way so that each of you can encounter our Lord, Father, lover of our soul, brother, teacher, the all consuming fire, and friend.

2. God created mankind because He wanted sons and daughters
I would like to pose a question. Why did the Lord create us? I firmly believe it is because He has a Father's heart and wanted children to relate to. When the Lord created Adam and Eve it says in Genesis the Lord would walk in the Garden of Eden in the cool of day with them. I can imagine the joy, intimacy, and friendship experienced between Adam and God. They walked and talked together uninhibited. They shared, and I would like to think they laughed together as well. I am sure it was a glorious time.

I was blessed with a wonderful, loving, encouraging, patient, faith building earthly father. He was my biggest cheerleader and fan. He always encouraged me to be all that I could be. He truly taught me that if I set my mind to it, that nothing was impossible. He used to tell me, *"You can accomplish anything if you set your mind to it. Reach for the stars."* I loved to be with my dad and to spend time with him. I always felt safe, loved, and cherished in his presence. And I knew he loved me unconditionally and I cherished every moment he spent with me. He went to be with the Lord in January 2008, but during one of our last private moments together he lovingly said, *"You are such a beautiful woman. I am so proud of you. I love you. Don't stop studying and teaching the word of God. You keep doing what you are doing."* I will never forget that even in his last couple of days, how selfless and determined he was to tell me how much he loved me. I am very aware that many have not been blessed with this kind of experience in an earthly father. But your blessing will come in knowing your heavenly Father. It will be greater than knowing any earthly person.

I share this because this is how our heavenly Father feels toward us. He loves us. He wants to spend time with us. He is our biggest cheerleader and encourager. He is the kindest, most loving and patient person I know. He is always faithful and completely and perfectly full of goodness, justice, mercy, and love.

Jesus often withdrew Himself from people in order to spend time alone with His Father. He knew there was no way He could accomplish His mission without intimacy with God. I also believe He longed to hear the Father's voice and to receive His love. As I have already mentioned, we see numerous times in God's Word where Jesus went away at night to pray. He not only loved His Father and wanted to relate to Him as His Son, but He was also showing us that we too can enter into God's presence as His sons and daughters. No one is exempt from entering into this secret place or from experiencing His love. How awesome to be so consumed and captivated by Him; so much so that nothing else in life can even compare to His love, presence, and anointing. Once you experience this place, you desire more.

3. The Church is the Bride
Not only are we sons and daughters, but we, the church, are also referred to as His Bride, allowing us to understand just how close He wants us to be to Him. (No sexual intimacy is involved.) The Song of Solomon is a Book of Scripture sharing words of love between a Bridegroom to His Bride. Notice Song of Solomon 2:13-16.

Intimacy with God

A. The Man
"Get up, my dear friend, fair and beautiful lover—come to me! Look around you: Winter is over; the winter rains are over, gone! Spring flowers are in blossom all over.

"The whole world's a choir—and singing! Spring warblers are filling the forest with sweet arpeggios. Lilacs are exuberantly purple and perfumed, and cherry trees fragrant with blossoms.

"Oh, get up, dear friend, my fair and beautiful lover—come to me! Come, my shy and modest dove—leave your seclusion, come out in the open. Let me see your face, let me hear your voice. For your voice is soothing and your face is ravishing" (Amplified Bible).

B. The Woman
"Then you must protect me from the foxes, foxes on the prowl, Foxes who would like nothing better than to get into our flowering garden. My lover is mine, and I am his. Nightly he strolls in our garden, Delighting in the flowers until dawn breathes its light and night slips away. Turn to me, dear lover. Come like a gazelle. Leap like a wild stag on delectable mountains!" (Amplified Bible)

Beloved, these beautiful Scriptures reveal the captivating throne room presence of the Lord. As a bridegroom to a bride, as sons and daughters of the King, we all have an invitation to enter into His secret chamber.

4. So how do we move into the God's presence?

It is imperative to understand that what we are about to discuss applies to our private times of prayer and as well as to our corporate prayer times. But for the most part we will focus on our individual times of prayer. I realize that I have already instructed you to welcome God's presence into your prayer and intercession times. But, this week we are going to go deeper. It is that secret intimate place that He longs for all of

His children to know and recognize; a place of simply experiencing Him.

In order to enter into His presence at the most intimate level, it is vital that you pick a time of the day and a location where you will not be disturbed or interrupted. This is a time dedicated solely to Him. So, if the phone or doorbell rings you will not stop your time allotted to the Lord. Remember not to focus on yourself and do not strive in the flesh to draw close to the Lord. You will find the more you strive the further away from Him you will feel. The key, as we have previously learned, is not to focus on ourselves, but to inwardly think on and outwardly worship Him.

A. Joy in His presence

But let the [uncompromisingly] righteous be glad; let them be in high spirits and glory before God, yes, let them [jubilantly] rejoice!
(Psalm 68:3, Amplified Bible).

In God's presence there is great joy and celebrating. The Hebrew word for "glad" is *simchah*. It means gladness, exceeding joy, extremely festive, happiness, and great pleasure. The idea is to go beyond the limits of one's own understanding.

As we come into God's throne room and experience His love, majesty, holiness, magnificence, and awesome glory, we are brought into a spiritual experience beyond anything we have known or understood up until this time. Friends, every time we experience the Lord we are able to go into places of joy that we have never before embraced. We are able to go higher, deeper, and wider than previous divine encounters. It raises us to a great satisfaction and triumph in Him.

When we pray and celebrate, the angels rejoice with cheers of triumph, and our praise and joy is like the jubilant climax of a heavenly symphony. God's Word says that worship is released around God's throne room continuously. Great praise, exultation, and glory are offered to our King. God's throne room is a place of great celebration and joy!

B. Praise and thanksgiving attract God's presence

"The Lord is my Strength and my [impenetrable] Shield; my heart trusts in, relies on, and confidently leans on Him, and I am helped; therefore my heart greatly rejoices, and with my song will I praise Him" (Psalm 28:7, Amplified Bible).

"Enter into His gates with thanksgiving and a thank offering and into His courts with praise! Be thankful and say so to Him, bless and affectionately praise His name!" (Psalm 100:4 Amplified Bible).

In this lesson, I want to encourage and exhort you to speak out loud in worship and exaltation Him. Brag on Him. Tell Him how awesome and how great He is. Sing praises of His greatness. Read Scriptures from His Word that share of His wonder and attributes. This will draw you into His presence.

C. God's attributes

As we minister to the Lord and speak of His greatness it is important to know the attributes of our Heavenly Father. Why is it necessary to speak of His majestic attributes? We learn from Scripture that there is power in our words. Therefore, as we speak of the greatness of our God it lifts up our spirits and focuses our complete and undivided attention on Him. Being made in the His image, we yearn for and need to receive affirmation and love. And He too wants to hear you and me as His children declaring who He is.

My husband, Greg, and I love our three beautiful daughters. As their parents, we cherish the moments where they are so captivated with love for us that they voice with complete, absolute, and unashamed truth, "I love you." In all honesty, now that our girls are teenagers, these moments are fewer and farther between. If I yearn for more of those precious expressions of love, how much more does our heavenly Father desire for us to voice our love for Him? I often encourage believers to express their love to the Lord without hesitation, expressing this deep love with words. I believe this because:

- Our praise and speaking forth God's greatness attracts the presence of the Holy Spirit.
- It raises us above our earthly surroundings and circumstances.
- It takes our thoughts captive and places our complete focus on Him.
- It causes darkness to flee.

The following Scriptures describe some of God's awesome characteristics. They can be a faithful guide for you in speaking forth His greatness in your prayer times:

1. Exodus 15:6 (Amplified Bible)
"Your right hand, O Lord, is glorious in power; Your right hand, O Lord, shatters the enemy."

2. Exodus 15:11 (Amplified Bible)
"Who is like You, O Lord, among the gods? Who is like You, glorious in holiness, awesome in splendor, doing wonders?"

3. Isaiah 26:4 (NLV)
"Trust in the Lord always, for the Lord God is the eternal Rock."

4. Isaiah 30:18 (NASB)
"Therefore the LORD longs to be gracious to you, And therefore He waits on high to have compassion on you, For the LORD is a God of justice; How blessed are all those who long for Him."

5. Isaiah 40:8 (Amplified Bible)
"The grass withers, the flower fades, but the word of our God will stand forever."

6. Isaiah 43:3a (Amplified Bible)
"For I am the Lord your God, the Holy One of Israel, your Savior."
7. Isaiah 54:5 (Amplified Bible)
"For your Maker is your Husband--the Lord of hosts is His name--and the Holy One of Israel is your Redeemer; the God of the whole earth He is called."
8. Psalm 18:2 (NLT)
"The Lord is my rock, my fortress, and my savior; my God is my rock, in whom I find protection. He is my shield, the power that saves me, and my place of safety."
9. Psalm 18:30 (NLT)
"God's way is perfect. All the Lord's promises prove true. He is a shield for all who look to him for protection."
10. Psalm 29:3 (NLT)
The voice of the Lord echoes above the sea. The God of glory thunders. The Lord thunders over the mighty sea.
11. Psalm 36:6-7 (NLT)
"Your righteousness is like the mighty mountains, your justice like the ocean depths. You care for people and animals alike, O Lord. How precious is your unfailing love, O God! All humanity finds shelter in the shadow of your wings."
12. Psalm 76:4 (NLT)
"You are glorious and more majestic than the everlasting mountains."
13. Revelation 4:8 (NLT)
"Holy, holy, holy is the Lord God, the Almighty— the one who always was, who is, and who is still to come."
14. Revelation 15:3 (NLT)
"And they were singing the song of Moses, the servant of God, and the song of the Lamb: 'Great and marvelous

are your works, O Lord God, the Almighty. Just and true are your ways, O King of the nations.'"

D. Relating to the Father, Son and Holy Spirit

As you read the above Scriptures out loud, begin to talk to your Father, expressing your heart. Here is an example of how to pray:

Father, I come before You today and exalt your awesomeness. You are the Creator of the universe which You hold suspended by Your breath. You truly are a loving heavenly Father whose love is more real and higher than the highest of mountains. You are full of splendor and majesty and holiness. Thank You for loving me. Thank you for Your faithfulness in my life. Father, You are higher and above all darkness and You never let me down. I love You.

Allow expressions of love to bubble up to the Father. Soon you will begin to feel His presence surrounding you. Sing praise songs of love. Sing in the Spirit releasing new songs to the Father.

Once you are immersed in worship, begin to concentrate on the Son. Begin to brag on Jesus and express gratitude for His love and awesomeness. You might want to pray something like this:

Jesus, thank you that You are the Savior of the world. That you came to set the captives free and to heal the sick. Thank You that You loved us so much that you laid down Your life. Jesus, thank You that You are my brother, master, teacher, friend, and the lover of my soul. Jesus, You are beautiful, lovely, and magnificent. I am so captivated by Your love. Jesus, I love You. Thank You for loving me.

After a period of time, include the Holy Spirit:

Holy Spirit, thank You for your presence. Thank You for filling me and guiding me every day. Thank You for Your comfort, joy, and peace. Thank You for the conviction of sin You bring to my life. Thank You for the anointing You impart to my life. Holy Spirit thank You for the times You speak so clearly and sweetly to me. Thank You for the love, peace, and holiness I feel in Your presence. I desire more of You, fill me even more. Fill me to overflowing.

Soon your worship, praise, and exaltation will take you into the throne room where words no longer suffice. It is as if you have reached a place of timelessness, a place filled with the immense glory of our King. There will be times of great joy and laughing. Many times His goodness is so overwhelming, that you will shed tears of delight. As you sit in His presence don't start treating our Lord like a Santa Claus, going down your list of needs. At this point, wait and listen. You will notice that self grows less important as our vision of Him becomes clearer. He is orchestrating this time. Allow Him to take the lead in the spiritual dance; and graciously, yet confidently, follow. My friend Alice Smith shares this powerful truth from her book *Beyond the Veil.*

"*Consistent fellowship with Him produces purity, increases spiritual sensitivity (revelation), and the perception of spiritual realities (discernment). From sacred hours of intimacy spent in His presence, you will experience "transformation by adoration." Burdens lift and frustration dissolve as you nestle under His divine covering.*"[4]

As the Bride to the Bridegroom, as sons and daughters of our Heavenly Father, spiritual intimacy is our destination. This is the beginning of all other adventures and growth in the Lord. It is in this place that we feel and hear the heartbeat of our Savior. It is here that we have the privilege of crawling up onto

---

[4] Alice Smith, *Beyond the Veil*(Houston, TX: Spiritruth Publishing, 1996), 177.

the Father's lap knowing how loved we are as His children. It is here that we learn how truly we belong to Him and to His kingdom.

Scripturally, this can be likened to 2 Chronicles 7, when the Shekinah glory came into the temple. Neither the priests nor the people could stand in the temple when the glory came. When glory comes during intercession, all thoughts of time, space, personal hunger, personal responsibilities, or needs seem to diminish. God wraps you up in Himself. Your will is freed from self-direction, and your one desire is to relate to the Person of Christ. There is no mixture at this point. Your soul is no longer fighting against your spirit. Instead, your soul surrenders as the Holy Spirit draws you into the Holy of Holies.

E. What will unfold here?

Now that we have entered beyond the veil we will experience new things:

1. We are changed from glory to glory. 2 Corinthians 3:18 says, *"And all of us, as with unveiled face, [because we] continued to behold [in the Word of God] as in a mirror the glory of the Lord, are constantly being transfigured into His very own image in ever increasing splendor and from one degree of glory to another; [for this comes] from the Lord [Who is] the Spirit."* (Amplified Bible)

After Moses, was in the Lord's presence, he returned from the mountain top with such glory on his face that he had to wear a veil. As we behold His glory, people will begin to see God's glory on us. We will be transformed.

2. Intimacy becomes a privilege.

We learn how to come to the selfless place where we experience intimacy with the Lord for the sake of intimacy. No set or hidden agendas. Just that place of anticipation and desire to meet with, and to relate to our God.

3. He touches your heart.

During these times, He might flood your thoughts or your spirit with immense revelation and intercessory prayer burdens. Other times, He may be silent. There might be mental images of children, loved ones, friends, cities, or nations. At this point, find and follow the path of the Spirit.

When God places an intercessory burden on you, pray until you feel it lifting. Do not abort what He is imparting to you. Sometimes in my intercession times, I wander off the assignment too soon and begin to feel a lifting of His presence or a numbness in my spirit. If this occurs in your time, go back to the burden and pray it through.

4. You get prophetic revelation.

As will be discussed in depth in the next part of this curriculum, the Lord will begin to reveal His secrets and release prophetic intercessory assignments. Pray through what is being shown and keep a journal nearby to write down what He is speaking.

5. He leads you into warfare praying.

There might be an assignment of the enemy that the Lord shows you concerning an individual. For example, it could be a picture of an automobile wreck or a betrayal from someone close to this individual.

For me personally, I am so grateful for faithful friends who intercede. My husband and I were on our way to a ministry event. We waited and took our turn at a 4-way intersection. As Greg began to accelerate, a car came around the corner right toward my side of the car. The driver was speeding and it was obvious we were going to be hit. I am still not certain how to explain this, but it was as if supernaturally our car was pushed out of the way, avoiding a collision that could have been fatal. No wreck, no injuries, and no dings on the car. We were shaken, but also thankful for His obvious protection.

Upon arriving at the conference, I shared with my dear friend, Alice Smith, what had just occurred less than 15 minutes earlier. She quickly explained that the Lord had shown her earlier that week an assignment of the enemy against Greg and me. It was a fatal car wreck. She engaged in warfare intercession on our behalf. We all knew beyond any shadow of doubt that it was her faithfulness in warfare prayer that saved us that day.

The last portion of this curriculum will focus on warfare intercession. Our authority as believers will be an entire lesson in the Prophetic Intercession book. But to help guide you now, let's briefly discuss how to engage in warfare prayer. With ambassadorial authority, pray against the enemy's plan and fight for God's plan. If you are uncertain of how to pray, then simply agree with the Father and pray, *"Father, preserve and protect your purpose for my loved one's life* (my friend's life or whatever the situation that God is revealing)."

F. He is waiting to commune with you

You can have as much of God as you want. Revelation 3:20 shares, *"Behold, I stand at the door and knock; if anyone hears My voice and opens the door, I will come in to him and will dine with him, and he with Me."* (Amplified Bible).

If you are hungry and thirsty enough and you invest the time, you will experience this sweet and timeless relationship with Him.

Setting our focus on Him
This week is the time to go deeper into your relationship with the Lord:
1. Set at least two extended times aside to focus on entering into His throne room presence. Longer periods of time than in previous lessons.
2. Turn off your phones and determine not to be interrupted in your set aside time.
3. Do not allow negative thoughts of yourself to invade your mind. This will hinder you from entering in.
4. As we have discussed previously, do not forget to have a notepad handy so that if tasks you need to accomplish for the day cross your mind you can write them down and continue to move into the Lord's presence.
5.
6. Be patient as you worship, praise, and speak forth the wonders of our King.
7. Have faith that He will meet with you.
8. Wait for the Holy Spirit to rest on you.
9. Remember to wait and listen.
10. Allow Him to orchestrate this intimate time.

Your Kingdom Come

Book 2: Prophetic Intercession

Becca Greenwood

Book 2: Prophetic Intercession

Lesson One: We "Can" Hear God's Voice

It had been a difficult transition time for our family. I will always remember the sense of relief Greg and I felt as the report came that the church leadership had unanimously agreed upon and issued an invitation for us to come on staff as the associate pastors. I recall feeling relieved that the weight of the burden of pressing into the next season of our lives was coming to an end. As Greg and I talked about this new opportunity we leaned strongly toward accepting the position. Then, from the back seat of the car our nine year old daughter spoke, "But, daddy God told me in my dreams that the next place we are to move to will have mountains and snow. Daddy, I do not see mountains and snow. Where are they?"

During this nine month period, the Lord had given our daughter three dreams and in each one, He visibly showed her mountains and snow. She would excitedly and confidently share with us each time the dream occurred. Now she reminded us again. Unfortunately, in the town where this church was located there were no mountains and definitely no snow. It was completely flat. Not even a rolling hill! We had learned over the years how clearly the Lord spoke to our oldest daughter and how extremely accurate the revelation always seemed to be. When she innocently spoke her concern, Greg and I knew we were to take the matter to prayer. After several days of seeking the Lord for His direction we both came to the same agreement—this was not the new offer and was not the place for us. We graciously turned it down.

I admit that this was a very uncomfortable place for us. We felt we had done the right thing, but there was still no new open door or job opportunity. It was a battle not to be nervous about the decision we made. We struggled in trying not to second guess or question our decision. Within two months, we received a phone call offering Greg a new job. It was located in Colorado Springs, Colorado where there is plenty of mountains and snow.

I share this story to point out how simple it is for children to hear and receive instruction from the Lord. She was confident she had heard and she, in her childlike faith, expected us to have that same confidence.

Communing with God

From the beginning of creation humanity was created to commune with God. Oswald Chambers wrote, "Prayer is not simply getting things from God, that is the most initial form of prayer; prayer is getting into perfect communion with God." [1]

As previously discussed in *Encouraged to Intercede*, God created you and me because He has a Father's heart. He is a relational God, One who wants to connect and converse with His sons and daughters. Just as He showed our daughter the next location of our move, God wants you and me to learn how to commune with Him in order to pray and walk out our lives in agreement with Him. He desires each of us to seek Him in the same confidence and childlike faith of our four year old daughter.

To "seek" is to try to find something by searching and asking. It usually implies a process involving great intensity. Psalm 27:4-8 is a wonderful scriptural promise that David shares concerning his life-long quest to know God:

"One thing I have desired of the Lord, That I will seek: That I may dwell in the house of the Lord All the days of my life, To behold the beauty of the Lord, And to inquire in His Temple. For in the time of trouble He shall hide me in His pavilion; In that secret place of His tabernacle he shall hide me, He shall set me high upon a rock. And now my head shall be lifted up above my enemies all around me; Therefore I will offer sacrifices of joy in His tabernacle; I will sing, yes, I will sing praises to the Lord. Hear. O Lord, when I cry with my voice! Have mercy also upon me, and answer me. When You said, 'seek My face,' My heart said to You 'Your face, Lord, I will seek.'"

David was known as a man after God's own heart. He was willing and obedient to seek God until he received the Lord's mind and strategy. He communed with God concerning the issues he was facing and the struggles he was enduring. He really was a man that set his heart to hearing the Lord.

Seek His Kingdom First

Jesus explained in Matthew 6:33, *"But seek [aim at and strive after] first of all His kingdom and His righteousness [His way of doing and being right], and then all these things taken together will be given you besides."*   Amplified Bible

How do believers today implement Matt. 6:33? We begin by putting God first each day. This means we take time to pray and study God's Word. It means we put God first in order to meet regularly with other believers. And we will also put God first every payday, giving Him our tithe. God becomes first in our choices, arriving at no decision that leaves Him out.

Abraham's nephew, Lot, neglected to include God in his decisions and wound up in the wickedness of a cave, practicing atrocious sin! He did not put God first in his choice of a place to live and raise his family.

There are spiritual parallels for the material things in life. We need to seek to nourish our spiritual lives with spiritual food just as we seek to feed our bodies. We must ensure that our spiritual raiments are in order similar to the way we fuss over our physical garments. We drink natural water, but we need also to drink the water of life that Jesus gives.

I was raised in church my entire life and had a strong foundation in God's Word. Through the Bible I understood right and wrong, and encouraged to stay away from evil. I knew God, based on His Word and what was spoken and taught in church. But, I did not know God in the place of seeking and communing with Him in order to hear His voice. I am thankful that in seeking Him, He allowed me to get to know Him personally.

What are some ways you feel you can strengthen your communication skills in communing with God?

_____
_____
_____
_____
_____
_____
_____
_____

We "Can" Hear God's Voice

Are there areas of seeking Him in your spiritual walk that you need to grow in or practice more faithfully?
_____
_____
_____
_____
_____
_____

During my first experience with the Prophetic, I vividly remember how I received a prophetic word from the Lord. It was in 1990. I was in my early twenties and a new mother. My husband, Greg, and I were the youth pastors of a church in Denton, Texas. We were happily serving the Lord as He touched the lives of the young people He had assigned to us for that season. At the same time, we experienced an increasing desire to know Him more.

Greg's parents had been pastors for many years, and we noticed that God was doing a new and deeper work in their lives. We saw newfound joy and passion in their walks with the Lord. It made us curious. So when they invited us to an upcoming conference about drawing close to God and hearing His voice, we accepted. We were interested, but also a little cautious and skeptical. After all, we had never been to a Christian event where hearing God's voice was discussed.

The conference was intimidating and captivating at the same time. I had always felt the Lord leading me and had an "inner knowing" that He had created me for a purpose, but I did not know what is was. Now, for the first time, I was hearing explanations of what I had experienced even as a young child. I had been hearing God's voice and His direction in my life, but my experience was limited.

When the event came to an end, the conference leaders offered to pray for those who felt God's call and desired a deeper relationship with Him. Greg and I instantly and simultaneously rose to our feet. The leaders then prayed for those standing, asking God to touch each of us in a new way. They prayed that we would have ears to hear His voice and to respond. During the ministry time, I felt God's presence tangibly. It was a presence full of peace, grace, comfort, and love. It was wonderful and left me hungering for more.

As we left the building, a friend of my in-laws whom I had never met, approached us. She asked if I was Rebecca. I said yes. She introduced herself to me and said that earlier that afternoon the Lord had given her a vision of me. She said that He had told her my name and revealed a prophetic word for me. She had to explain what a prophetic word was because I had never heard of such a thing. I thought to myself, *Lord, this is a fast answer to the prayer just prayed over me at the conference. Actually, You answered the prayer before I even prayed it!* I was overcome with gratitude that He had heard my heart's cry.

In the prophetic message the Lord called me by name. As the woman spoke the words He had given her to share with me, I felt and clearly heard that He was calling me closer to Himself and into a season of understanding His love and purpose for my life. It was both tender and powerful, and it sparked an intense desire and hunger to draw close to Him. That night was the beginning of my desire to walk with Him in a new measure of understanding, to hear His voice, and to walk in a new measure of authority.

Demystifying the Prophetic

Since this life changing encounter, my spiritual walk has greatly grown and matured. I am now in a place of intercession and releasing words of encouragement and prophecy to others. The following is a common request I receive on a daily basis. "Please pray for me and give me the word of the Lord for my life. What is God telling you I am to do in this situation?" Seeing how significantly a prophetic word brought such drastic change in my life, I do understand why so many people approach me asking me to pray for them.

I am also aware that many of you reading this curriculum had an experience similar to mine. You new His Word, but did not fully realize that God can and does speak to us today. I believe we all have the ability to hear and respond to God's voice. And I want to de-mystify or take what I call the "woo, woo, way out there" perception out of prophecy.

How do we do this? We start by understanding that everything God does is practical, and that He wants us to learn to live out our lives in practical ways. We learn to fellowship, to tithe, to give beyond the tithe, to pray, and to develop Christ-like character. These are all practical things that eventually lead to other things involving God's giftings and special abilities. The working of God's supernatural power always begins with doing the simple things He asks of us.

The Power of your Testimony

There is great power in our own personal testimony. It causes us to remember all the awesome ways God has spoken and manifested in our lives. This builds faith in us and in others. Based on practical examples and my personal experience mentioned above, think of how God's voice has manifested in your life. Record what God spoke to you and how you responded.

_____
_____
_____

YOUR KINGDOM COME

_____
_____
_____

Record the circumstances regarding your salvation.

_____
_____
_____
_____
_____

How has God supernaturally affected your life and your life events?

_____
_____
_____
_____
_____

Share a time when God's prophetic direction impacted your life?

_____
_____
_____
_____
_____

To continue to demystify the prophetic, let's investigate further the definition of prophecy and intercession.

What Does Prophecy Mean?

The Greek word for prophecy is *prophetia*. It means to proclaim a revelation or message received from God. It indicates the ability to hear God's voice and to respond. At times it can carry additional ideas such as the unfolding of hidden knowledge inaccessible to mere humans as in Matthew 26:68, or the foretelling of future events as in Luke 1:67, or the teaching of God's Word.

What Does Intercession Mean?

1 Timothy 2:1 says, *"I urge, then, first of all, that requests, prayers, intercession and thanksgiving be made for everyone."*

In this verse the Greek word for intercession is *enteuxis*. It means an interview, to meet with or converse, to seek the presence and hearing of God on behalf of others.

Putting Intercession and Prophecy Together

When you put the two words together, prophetic intercession means seeking God's presence in order to converse with Him on behalf of others; and then, to speak forth and to pray in agreement with His mind, counsel, and Word. I appreciate the following quote by Cindy Jacobs in her book *Hearing the Voice of God*, "Prophetic Intercession is the ability to receive an immediate prayer request from God and pray about it in a divinely anointed utterance."[2]

Intercession and Prophecy are Interwoven

Jeremiah 27:18 says, *"But if they are prophets, and if the word of the Lord is with them, let them now make intercession to the*

Lord of hosts, that the vessels which are left in the house of the king of Judah, and at Jerusalem go not to Babylon." (NKJV)

To hear the Lord prophetically we have to intercede (Seek God on behalf of others). Prophetic people spend great amounts of time praying, interceding, worshipping, and listening to God's heart. It is in this place of intimacy that revelation begins to flow. However, not all intercessors and pray-ers are prophets, but all can receive a prophetic anointing.

We Are His Sheep!

"My sheep hear My voice, and I know them, and they follow Me."

John 10:27

We are the sheep of His pasture and have our Redeemers favor. He literally speaks to His people. What an incredible inherited promise from our God! God is not so busy sustaining stars in space, holding galaxies on their course, or causing this earth to spin on its axis that He doesn't have time to speak to you and me. He even gives us the confidence that we will know the difference between His voice and other voices that speak to us.

"And a stranger they simply will not follow, but will flee from him, because the do not know the voice of strangers." John 10:5.

Intercessors should be able to hear God speak. As He speaks, He will reveal areas that need prayer, strategies to overcome the enemy, actions or declarations to break the power of hindrance, and even reveal the sources of warfare. But, victory, when it comes, is always obtained through obedience to God's Word.

We "Can" Hear God's Voice

God's Word reveals many examples of His plan revealed to His servants. Then He gives them the ability to move into His plans in response to His voice. The following are three examples.

An Angel Delivers God's Message

"While I was pouring out my heart, bearing my sins and the sins of my people Israel, praying my life out before my God, interceding for the holy mountain of my God—while I was absorbed in this praying, the humanlike Gabriel, the one I had seen in an earlier vision, approached me, flying in like a bird about the time of evening worship.

"He stood before me and said, 'Daniel, I have come to make things plain to you. You had no sooner started your prayer when the answer was given. And now I'm here to deliver the answer to you. You are much loved! So listen carefully to the answer, the plain meaning of what is revealed.'" Daniel 9:20-23. The Message

God Spoke His Plan to Abraham

"When the men got up to leave, they set off for Sodom. Abraham walked with them to say good-bye.

"Then God said, 'Shall I keep back from Abraham what I'm about to do? Abraham is going to become a large and strong nation; all the nations of the world are going to find themselves blessed through him. Yes, I've settled on him as the one to train his children and future family to observe God's way of life, live kindly and generously and fairly, so that God can complete in Abraham what he promised him.'"

"God continued, 'The cries of the victims in Sodom and Gomorrah are deafening; the sin of those cities is immense. I'm

going down to see for myself, see if what they're doing is as bad as it sounds. Then I'll know.'

"The men set out for Sodom, but Abraham stood in God's path, blocking his way." Genesis 18:16-22, The Message

God Directs Ananias to do What He did Not Want to Do

"There was a disciple in Damascus by the name of Ananias. The Master spoke to him in a vision: 'Ananias.'

'Yes, Master?' he answered.

"'Get up and go over to Straight Avenue. Ask at the house of Judas for a man from Tarsus. His name is Saul. He's there praying. He has just had a dream in which he saw a man named Ananias enter the house and lay hands on him so he could see again.'"

"Ananias protested, 'Master, you can't be serious. Everybody's talking about this man and the terrible things he's been doing, his reign of terror against your people in Jerusalem! And now he's shown up here with papers from the Chief Priest that give him license to do the same to us.'

"'But the Master said, "Don't argue. Go! I have picked him as my personal representative to non-Jews and kings and Jews. And now I'm about to show him what he's in for—the hard suffering that goes with this job."'

"So Ananias went and found the house, placed his hands on blind Saul, and said, 'Brother Saul, the Master sent me, the same Jesus you saw on your way here. He sent me so you could see again and be filled with the Holy Spirit.' No sooner were the words out of his mouth than something like scales fell from Saul's eyes—he could see again! He got to his feet, was baptized, and sat down with them to a hearty meal."

Acts 9: 10-17, The Message

We "Can" Hear God's Voice

God Speaks to Protect Tina

I was attending a corporate prayer meeting in which intercessors from across the city gathered monthly to pray. We were having a powerful time of intercession for the city when the leader of the group asked us to pray for Tina. She did not share why the request was made, but we were all glad to gather around Tina to intercede for her and to minister to her. As we began, the Lord clearly revealed to me a vision in my mind. It was very specific, but it was also extremely difficult to see and to deliver.

Understanding proper protocol, I quietly shared with the leader what the Lord was showing me. Without an explanation, she grabbed my hand and walked me back to the circle and said, "Please share with Tina what you just shared with me."

I was nervous to relay the message and with apprehension turned my concerned gaze to the leader of the group. Seeing the apprehension on my face she sternly stated, "You need to share with Tina, verbatim, what you just shared with me."

Obedient to the leader I had grown to trust, I began to speak. "Tina, the Lord showed me a vision of you and your husband. Your husband was very angry with you and began to yell uncontrollably. Not only did he yell, but he pushed you against the wall and pulled out a weapon and threatened you. I feel strongly that you and your son left knowing you were in danger, but in spite of the severe threat, you are now considering the idea of returning home. I feel strongly the Lord is saying that you are to take your son and go back. Your life and your son's life will be in danger."

Tina, shocked at the accuracy of the word, began to weep. She loudly inquired, "The Lord showed you all of that. No one told you anything?" I, and the prayer leader, in unison quickly replied, "No!" Tina pushed her way through the circle of intercessors grabbed me and hugged me as she wept on my shoulder. "Thank you, thank you for speaking what the Lord was showing you! Thank you for being obedient! I know, now, I am not to return."

I was so grateful that the Lord was able to use me to help her. I remember thinking that night how incredibly important it is to hear God's voice at the right time. The group leader later shared that Tina was going to return immediately following that prayer meeting unless the Lord specifically spoke to her not to return. The good news is, Tina and her son are out of this abusive relationship and are living a peaceful and happy life. Sometimes I shudder to think of what could have happened to my friend and her son if I had not spoken what the Lord was showing me. Because of His intense love for them, I choose to believe that He would have spoken the message through someone else to protect them, but how incredibly crucial it was that night to be obedient in speaking forth His word.

Not as Difficult as Some Might Think

Hearing God's voice might not be as difficult as some of us might think. Once we are instructed on how to comprehend, grasp, and recognize that God is speaking, it empowers us in our personal walk and in our intercession.

Have you surrendered your life to be used of God in any way He may see fit?

_____
_____
_____
_____

We "Can" Hear God's Voice

Have you ever thought about how the gift of prophecy or prophetic intercession might be used to help you draw closer to God?

_____
_____
_____
_____

In closing, let's pray a prayer welcoming this process into our lives:

Jesus, I am so grateful that you commune with us. That as we intently set our heart to seek after You, we will find You. We can commune and fellowship with You. And our prayers can come from a place of agreement with Your written and spoken Word. Show me and teach me to hear Your voice. Lead me on the path of learning to perceive when You are speaking, and then cause me to be sensitive to Your leading in my personal life and also in my prayer life. Jesus, be the guiding voice in my times of intercession. Thank you for the highest privilege on earth, that of communing and partnering with You. Amen.

Steps to Communing with Him:
1. For those who do not keep a prayer journal, now would be a good time to start. Not only do you need to record your prayer requests, but also what you hear the Lord speaking to you in response to your intercession.
2. As we did above, take some time to think through the different times the Lord's supernatural power has moved in your life affecting circumstances. Take the time to write down several of these experiences. You will begin to perceive the patterns and the ways in which God is speaking to you.
3. Pray and invite God to begin to speak to you in new ways. As this occurs, write these in your journal.

4. As you read God's Word this week, ask the Holy Spirit to highlight and illuminate new revelation to you. Be sure to record what God is speaking.

Learning His Voice

Lesson Two: Learning His Voice

I was battling with a spirit of heaviness, also known as depression. I had walked in open rebellion, totally away from the Lord for a three-year period in my life. After a few years I repented, got my life back on course, was married, and became a mother of a treasured toddler. Now, we were in hot pursuit of encountering more of God in our lives. We were in a fast track of spiritual growth.

During this time, the nearer I drew to the Lord, the louder I heard tormenting voices. I needed deliverance from doors I had opened to the enemy. The further I pressed into God, the more intense the harassment became. I heard lies such as, *"God never will forgive you. You are not saved. Your salvation can never be guaranteed!"* I acknowledged these were lies, but the enemy would not halt the onslaught. At times, the badgering was so intense I could barely make myself get out of bed in the mornings. I was so tortured with depression and the horrible thoughts that pressed on my mind that I wanted to pull the covers over my head and remain in bed all day. Some mornings the only reason I got out of bed was the obligation of motherhood.

One day while studying God's Word the Lord directed my attention to the woman with the issue of blood. As I read her story, it was as though I received the same faith that she held. I had the revelation that this woman who was so terribly ill for 12 years was able to press through a crowd, touch the hem of Jesus' garment, and be healed. I recognized that if I stepped out in faith and trusted Him, then He could set me free too!

I knelt on my living room floor and called out, "Jesus, I am setting my face like flint on You. I am grabbing hold of the hem of your garment and I am not letting go until I am set free!" I sensed the presence of the Lord, but nothing really changed.

About this time, my daughter woke up from her nap and began calling for me.

It was lunchtime. I remember working really hard that day on the meal. We had peanut butter and jelly sandwiches. While my daughter ate, I tried to be happy and not be depressed, but I knew I had not been set free yet. In my mind I inquired, *"God where are you? Why did you not bring me freedom in reply to my prayer?"* Almost immediately after I asked the Lord these questions, Kendall started to laugh. Then she said in her two-year-old voice, *"Mommy, it so funny! It so funny! See, mommy, it funny!"* We were aware that our child was gifted prophetically and could see things in the spirit. We had known this for several months. But, I was not seeing what she was seeing, because at his time nothing seemed amusing. I finally asked, *"Sweetie, what is so funny?"*

My daughter climbed out of her booster seat and began to march back in forth in front of me like a warrior. Enthusiastically, she looked at me while marching and asked, *"Don't you see mommy? Don't you see?"* I asked her what I was supposed to see. She stopped in front of me, pointed her little finger toward the back window which overlooked our backyard and excitedly and confidently exclaimed in her little voice *"See mommy. Out there mommy! It Jesus and angel and they do this for you!"* She then continued to march back and forth in front of me like a warrior. I began to cry and exclaimed, *"Lord, if you are here warring for me, then it is time I fight with you!"*

That night at church I asked my home group leader to pray for me. Laying hands on my eyes, she prayed, *"Lord, show her what you want her to see."* At that instant, the Lord showed me a vision. I saw an ancient book with light on the pages. I could see writing, but could not make out what it said. The closer the book was brought to my eyes I could plainly see letters. I could see my name, Rebecca Long Greenwood, penned in the Lamb's Book of Life. I was on the floor weeping when a pastor from across the room made his way over to me. He also laid hands on my eyes and said, *"Lord, show her what you want her to see."* The Lord instantly showed me another vision. This time I could see Jesus. He was approaching me on what looked like the glory and presence of the Hoy Spirit. It was as if Jesus was riding on the power of the Spirit of God. He drew near to me and then beautifully spoke these words, *"Becca, take up your cross and follow me. It is over. It is finished!"* When that declaration came from His mouth, the heaviness and depression instantly left. I rose from the floor completely liberated. The depression has not returned!

Prophecy and prophetic intercession release the life and power of God. What it did for me that day and we have seen it repeatedly do for others during times of intercession.

God's Voice is Creative

In the Genesis creation account, we see repeatedly that God's voice was creative. He spoke and there was light. The power of His voice created the heaven and the earth and all the living creatures on earth and in the seas. Then from the ground He formed human beings. Therefore, you and I and our very existence are a product of His creative voice.

The day I was set free God spoke creatively through His Word. He responded to my prayer and gave a two year old a vision, who then spoke the vision to me. Then I was led into prayer and into a life changing vision and power encounter with Jesus. I was completely set free! I am a firm believer that when God needs to get creative in relaying His purposes He can and He will make the way creative in order to release the revelation and accomplish His plan.

Share a testimony when God moved creatively in your life or a life of a family member.

_____
_____
_____
_____
_____
_____

When Jesus Speaks Things Happen

Jesus was both God and man come to earth to redeem the human race. He was and is the full character of God. Part of that character was the power of His voice. When Jesus spoke, things happened.

His public ministry began in John Chapter 2 when He and His mother attended a wedding. When the wedding feast ran short of wine, Jesus' mother told the servants, *"Whatever He says to you, do it."* (John 2:5, NIV) It was Jesus' creative voice that changed the water into wine.

Whenever Jesus spoke, He carried great authority. He spoke to Lazarus to come forth from the dead and he did. He spoke to the storm, *"Peace be still,"* and it stopped. He commanded the demons to leave and they obeyed. In my personal experience that I shared above, He spoke, "It is finished!" And it was!

Has there been an instance in your life when Jesus clearly spoke? What happened?

_____
_____
_____
_____
_____

The Holy Spirit Speaks to, and Through Us

Jesus had already been crucified, died, and raised from the dead, but had not yet ascended to heaven. In John 20:22 we read that, *"He breathed on them, and said to them, 'Receive the Holy Spirit.'"* At this time the Holy Spirit was released to operate in greater measure through the disciples. He began to speak to them and through them on a regular basis.

We see with Peter that the Holy Spirit spoke to him to go to the home of Cornelius. But we also see that the Holy Spirit was speaking through the men Peter was to go and see as well. Acts 6:10 (NIV) gives an account of Stephen, *"but they could not stand up against his wisdom or the Spirit by whom he spoke."* Here we see the Holy Spirit speaking through Stephen.

In the above shared story it was the Holy Spirit who prompted me to read the encounter between Jesus and the woman with the issue of blood. It was the Holy Spirit who spoke through my two year old daughter, my home group pastor, and my senior pastor.

Discuss a time when the Holy Spirit spoke into your life or through your life with wisdom.

_____
_____
_____
_____
_____

God's Word is Alive and Active

I often tell people that God did not write a best seller and then quit speaking! The beauty of His Word still speaks to us today. There is life and breath from the Holy Spirit speaking God's

Word. He speaks truth and releases His empowering life every time we read it. This is termed the *rhema* Word of God. It guides us in life situations, it brings conviction of sin, it reflects, it makes clear God's path for our lives, and it brings hope, life, and clarity of thought. Hebrews 4: 12 -13, in the "Message," beautifully shares the power of God's Word.

"God means what he says. What he says goes. His powerful Word is sharp as a surgeon's scalpel, cutting through everything, whether doubt or defense, laying us open to listen and obey. Nothing and no one is impervious to God's Word. We can't get away from it—no matter what."
The Message

As we come into prayer and communion, His Word orders our journey. His truths and principles direct us. By knowing God's Word, we know Him and can recognize His voice and how He operates. Chuck Pierce shares an empowering quote in his book, *When God Speaks,* "The Word is the blueprint of heaven and the blueprint of life." [1] I completely agree. It was the power of life and liberty in God's Word that released the faith and trust in Him I so desperately needed in order to receive complete freedom.

What Scriptures carry special meaning for you?
_____
_____
_____

Record Scriptures that God is illumining to you in order to empower your walk and prayer life? If you do not know any, ask Him to begin highlighting them to you?
_____
_____
_____
_____

Some Other Ways He Speaks

Hearing God's voice and the different ways He speaks is not as difficult as some may think. We briefly discussed this in Lesson Two of *Encouraged to Intercede*, but let's investigate these further.

God's Still, Small Voice

When God speaks to us in His still, small voice we simply know that we know that something is either right or wrong. We feel strongly to move ahead in a particular direction or to stop going in the direction we are headed. Sometimes we know that an issue in our heart has been settled. And when it comes to prayer assignments we know what to pray and to speak that is in agreement with the Lord. When we feel these nudges, impressions, or what we also termed "triggers of intercession" in Lesson 4 of *Encouraged to Intercede*, and act on them through intercession, our confidence and faith grows in responding to the Lord's leading. We come to understand that it is God's inaudible voice that guides our spirits in unity with His will.

The Voices of Other People

At times God speaks to us through another person. This is referred to as a "prophetic word." These words are frequently birthed in times of intercession. God spoke to the Apostle Paul through another person:

"After we had been there a number of days, a prophet named Agabus came down from Judea. Coming over to us, he took Paul's belt, tied his own hands and feet with it and said, 'The Holy Spirit says, "In this way the Jews of Jerusalem will bind the

owner of this belt and will hand him over to the Gentiles.""' (Acts 21:10, 11, NIV)

Throughout my Christian walk, I have had those who operate in the gifts of the Holy Spirit speak prophetic words into my life. The revelations have released guidance and have kept me from wrong decisions. They have also brought great clarity at times of major life decisions and given me encouragement and focus on the things the Lord is calling me to do. I have also found that the Lord will speak to me many other ways when I am praying and seeking Him.

I was leading a prayer journey team to Spain in 2003 under Global Harvest Ministries. I originally thought that the Lord said to go in the Fall of the year. But as the team and I met to pray and strategize, we felt uneasy about the timing. Things we were trying to line up were not coming together and everything that needed to be done seemed to be quite difficult to accomplish. I had led enough prayer assignments to know that when this begins to occur it is time to pray and seek the Lord. And this is exactly what the team and I began to do.

It was soon that I heard the Lord redirecting the timing of the trip. But I also asked the Him to bring confirmation. Chuck Pierce flew into town for a few days to be at the Colorado Springs offices with Peter and Doris Wagner and the staff. He came to my office to talk. He asked, *"Are you still taking the team out?"* I told him all that had occurred and that I now felt that I was to take the trip in April or May of 2004. Chuck grew excited and said, *"That is God!* He told me to send out 25 teams in those exact months of next year and yours will be one of them." I, too, was excited and grateful for the confirmation. From that point on, everything fell into place. And we had a powerful time while we were in Spain.

Dreams

In God's Word we read of men and women who experienced life changing revelations and direction in their dreams. One instance occurred when the angel of the Lord appeared to Joseph in a dream telling him to take Mary as his wife because what was conceived in her womb was by the Holy Spirit. (Matt. 1:12) Other instances include Solomon, Pharaoh, numerous kings, and prophets.

A dream is revelation that is released while our physical body and mind are at rest. Sometimes this is the best and most effective way for God to get a message through to us. Jane Hamon shares this insight in her book, *Dream and Visions*.

"It has been amazing to me as a co pastor of a prophetic church when several people in the body, and at times even people who live in another place, have extremely similar troubling dreams. They have, at times, brought them to me because of their disturbing nature only to discover that several others have had similar dreams within a short period of time. Many times these dreams provide revelation concerning our heavenly battle.

"Again, prayer is the key to properly responding to such dreams or visions. God is raising up intercessors around the world who are becoming more and more armed to God's revelations and are ready in an instant to organize and do battle through prayer.

"These prophetic prayer warriors call upon God for His divine angelic assistance as did Daniel when battling the Prince of Persia (see Dan. 10:13). Many times the plans revealed through the dream will enable intercessors to avoid natural disasters such as storms or earthquakes. Some have told of dreaming of destructive storms sweeping through their towns and leveling it flat. As the storm actually began to hit the next day, their prayers prevailed and damage was minimal." [1]

- Dreams can reveal events that will lead the dreamer to make the right decision for his or her future.
- Dreams can reveal situations for intercessory prayer assignments.
- Dreams can reveal battle plans for intercessors.
- Dreams can bring revelation concerning future events.
- Dreams can bring a warning.

Keep a journal of your dreams. Write them down with the date and time. God will teach you how to interpret the dreams and the dream language. Often there will be prayer assignments and strategies birthed in your dreams.

Visions

A vision is like a dream except you are awake when it occurs. The Apostle Peter's commission to eat with and minister to the Gentiles came in a vision (see Acts 10:9-23). Peter Wagner shares in *Acts of the Holy Spirit* the significance of this type of communication.

"God knew that ordinary communication processes would not be adequate to move Peter in the radical direction He wanted him to go. So God did an extraordinary thing and gave Peter the famous vision of the unclean food in the sheet. Peter's background had personally prepared him to receive visions. For one thing, it would fit his worldview. Unlike many today, Peter believed that one of God's normal ways of communicating from time to time was through visions and dreams. He was praying at the time, so his heart was open to God. He may have been fasting, too. Luke doesn't say he was, but we read that Peter became very hungry (Acts 10:10). Prayer along with fasting removes obstacles to hearing God's voice." [2]

There are two types of visions. Open and closed. In an open vision spiritual objects or beings are seen with the physical eyes. Some times objects that are not yet built, but will be in the future, can be seen with the physical eyes as if they already existed.

A closed vision is seeing something play out in the theater of your mind much like happens in a dream. If you experience significant visions, then just as you do with your dreams, journal and date what the Lord is revealing.

We were on a prayer journey to Egypt in 1995. We had been researching and spiritually mapping the regions we were to pray at for over a year. It was awesome to finally be in the land in order to carry out our prayer mission.

Before leaving, one of the intercessors assigned to pray for us received specific instructions from the Lord. She brought each team member a small golden key. She clearly explained that the Lord would instruct each team member to bury the keys as a prophetic act so that breakthrough would occur as a result of our onsite intercession. We were each to be very sensitive to the leading of the Lord concerning the place where we to do this.

One evening, while praying and preparing for the following day, we went into a deep place of intercession. The Spirit of the Lord rested heavily on all of us. Suddenly, I had a vision. I could see an ancient pyramid that I had not seen before. There were columns at the entrance that once made a magnificent entry gate. It was so vivid that I was able to describe this location.

The following morning on the first site of strategic intercession, we found ourselves at one of the oldest pyramids built in ancient Egypt. The entrance was constructed of the columns that I had seen in the vision the night before. I knew this was the assigned place for me to bury the key I had been given.

Experiences and Circumstances

There may be times when God speaks to you through a very specific incident. It might happen in prayer at home or in a corporate gathering. It could be a new spiritual encounter with the Lord. Or, a circumstance that clearly shows that God is changing or redirecting things and asking you to go in another direction.

In 1990, after Greg and I had graduated from college, we had been earnestly praying for the Lord to open His next place of employment for Greg. During this time, we went to Houston, Texas to attend a ministry team training seminar at a church. While there, we went to lunch with a group of church leaders. The Lord spoke to the gentleman sitting across the table from my husband and told him that he was to hire Greg. At first he did not say anything because he had just met us and did not know us. Upon leaving the restaurant that day, he prayed and asked the Lord that if he was truly to hire Greg, it would be confirmed.

Before we left town, Greg gave his resume to two of the pastors on staff at the church. The following night at the evening service both pastors separately approached the gentleman to whom God had spoken and said, *"God, told me to give you a copy of Greg Greenwood's resume."* He called and within two months we relocated from Denton, Texas to Houston, Texas.

Angels

Throughout God's Word, we see repeatedly that the Lord sent angels to deliver messages to His people. We also learn that they fight spiritual battles. The Lord opened the eyes of Elisha's servant so that he could see angels who were dispatched to do battle for His servants.

Learning His Voice

"Now when the attendant of the man of God had risen early and gone out, behold, an army with horses and chariots was circling the city. And his servant said o him, 'Alas, my master! What shall we do?' So he answered, 'Do not fear, for those who are with us are more than those who are with them.'

"Then Elisha prayed and said, 'O Lord, I pray, open his eyes that he may see.' And the Lord opened the servant's eyes, and he saw; and behold, the mountain was full of horses and chariots of fire all around Elisha."   2 Kings 6:15-17, NASB

There is an unseen realm consisting of a host of ministering angels who are active in the lives of God's people. Not only is God for His people, but also are armies of His angels who stand by ready to defend believers. These ministering spirits are not far away, but observe the actions and the faith of believers. I believe that all Christians should pray that God would deliver us from spiritual blindness and open the eyes of our hearts in order to see more clearly the spiritual reality of God's kingdom.

Battles in God's kingdom are not against flesh and blood, but *"against the powers of this dark world ad against the spiritual forces of evil in the heavenly realms"* (Ephesians 6:12, NIV). Actually, there is a cause and effect relationship in spiritual battles. The outcome is determined in part by our faith and prayers. We will discuss in the last curriculum how to engage wisely in spiritual warfare battles.

His Audible Voice

There are times when God chooses to speak in an audible voice. He did so to young Samuel. He spoke audibly when Jesus was baptized. The Bible mentions other times as well. Prayer opens our hearts and minds in order to hear more clearly. Hearing God in an audible voice does not happen frequent, but it does happen.

Thankful for God's Voice Today

I am grateful that God speaks to His people today. In times of intercession we need to discover what the Lord wants us to pray. We need to recognize how to pray in order to acquire powerful outcomes. Love for others and the Lord's purposes are the motivation from which we release prophetic revelation and prophetic intercession. As the Lord opens our spiritual ears, we are able to pray the prayers that change lives. We are also able to pray the kinds of prayers that change cities and nations.

Cultivating New Methods of Communication

1. As we took time last week to begin perceiving how He has previously spoken to us, invite Him to speak in new ways.
2. Prepare to receive dreams from God. How is this done?
    - Keep an open mind. Do not be afraid about receiving divinely inspired dreams.
    - Make sure your home is spiritually cleaned of objects that can be a red carpet invitation for demonic harassment. A great resource for this type of spiritual cleansing is *Spiritual Housecleaning* by Eddie and Alice Smith.
    - Specifically, ask Him to speak to you in your dreams.
    - When new revelation comes, write down the dream. I realize some will dream much more than others. We are all gifted differently. So do not be concerned if you do not have dreams right away or a lot of them. The point is to welcome new forms of revelation.
    - Ask the Lord to help you remember your dreams.
    - Allow time when waking up to record your dreams or otherwise you might forget them.
    - Respond to the revelation in the dream as God leads.

3. Invite Him to birth new prayer assignments through HIs Word and visions.
4. Let Him take you into new places of spiritual growth.
5. Do not be timid concerning new spiritual experiences that are scriptural and which line up with God's Word.
6. List areas in your life in which you need direction from God. Believe that He will speak the answer and that you will hear.

_____
_____
_____
_____
_____
_____

7. Does your church need clear direction from God? If so, ask Him to speak to you, the pastors, and the intercessors.
8. Are there areas of warfare in your life that need to be defeated? Seek Him for the strategy.

Prophetic Protocol

Lesson Three: Prophetic Protocol

My husband, Greg, was not sure how to handle the prophetic revelation he had just received. Janice, a close family friend, had been praying for years to have a baby. But after an extended period of time of believing and then a miscarriage all hope was gone. She was in a place of great sadness and hope deferred. Greg continued to stare at her, blinking his eyes as if trying to cause his vision to recover. Was he really seeing what he was seeing?

After a few minutes he pulled the home group pastor, Bill, out of the meeting to speak with him in private. He explained, *"Bill, I am seeing something in the Spirit concerning Janice. When she and Larry walked in the door tonight, I saw her pregnant. Not just a little bit pregnant, but full term pregnant! Every time I look at her, I see her in this condition. What do I do with this? Do I share this with her?"*

Bill paused for a moment and replied, *"You know Greg, I believe God is showing you something. However, Janice has been told numerous times that she is going to have a baby and it does not happen. Let's not put her in a place of getting her hopes up again. You and I will pray in agreement that what God is causing you to see will come to pass."*

They prayed in agreement with what the Lord had revealed and asked that Janice and Larry would be blessed with a baby. Nine months later this couple adopted a newborn baby girl. And within months of the adoption, Janice became pregnant and later delivered a healthy baby girl. Thank you Lord for answered prayer!

Why was it so important for this revelation to be handled wisely? Because God's Word says that prophecy is to build up and edify the church. If Greg had shared this with Janice and it had not come to pass, she would have been even more discouraged.

Testing Prophecy and Prophetic Revelation

It is important to understand that testing prophecy and prophetic revelation is scriptural. First Thessalonians 5:21 says, *"But examine everything carefully; hold fast to that which is good."* There are ways to learn how to handle revelation wisely and to pray and intercede to see God's plan released. Let's investigate further the checks and balances of this process.

Is the Revelation Scriptural?

All believers must know God's Word if He is going to used them. This is especially true when it comes to hearing and responding to God's voice. There is a voice of deception that will try to come in and steal what the Holy Spirit is doing and birthing. Each of us has a weakness or a hook in which that voice of deception can speak. For some it may be fear or lack of trust. For others it might be a place of unhappiness or wounding that makes it difficult to hear clearly. Here is an example to further explain this concept.

There was a time when I was ministering to Diane, a newcomer to our church. During the prayer time, she shared how unhappy her marriage was. She was sure that the ministry God had placed on her life was being put on hold because of her husband. She felt certain that God had told her that her husband would die soon in order for her to be happy and to step into her calling. Diane then further explained, *"I have been praying in agreement with God's Word for my husband to die, so I can then have happiness. And Becca, his health is now failing."*

I remember the more she spoke the more uneasy I became. You could sense her satisfaction in her husband's present condition. I asked her, *"Is your husband saved. Does he know the Lord?"* She thought for a moment and replied, *"He says he is, but he has no desire to go to church, so I am not sure."* I calmly, in a nonjudgmental, but matter of fact tone asked, *"Diane, don't you think that the Lord wants your husband to know Him? Do you think He would want him to die before coming to salvation?"*

Unfortunately, Diane was unwilling to hear the heart of the Lord for her lost husband and quickly exclaimed, *"God told me that He will sacrifice my husband for the call of God on my life."* Sadly, due to her refusal to respond, Diane did not receive freedom and her own health condition grew worse. She soon left the church and never returned.

Does the Revelation Show the Character of Christ?

Sometimes there are wolves in sheep's clothing who will use Scripture to control and manipulate for their own intentions. Just because somebody is citing chapter and verse does not necessarily establish an accurate prophecy. Even though truths from God's Word are spoken, it is imperative to encounter Christ's character shining through the revelation. Two of the most needed attributes for prophetic utterances are kindness and love.

"The kindness of God leads you to repentance. " (Romans 2:4)

"And if I have the gift of prophecy, and know all mysteries and all knowledge; and if I have all faith, so as to remove mountains, but do not have love, I am nothing." (I Corinthians 13:2)

There is a difference between those whose lives are occupied with religious activities and those whose walk is compelled by their love for Jesus, His Church, and a lost world. Love is indispensable to genuine Christian faith. It must be expressed through a value-system that does not injure others and perseveres in loyalty to Jesus and His Word.

How has kindness and love impacted and delivered you through the intercession of others?
_____
_____
_____
_____
_____

Is Anything Tainting the Word?

If individuals are not whole in certain areas or are not aware of their biases, that can affect how they intercede and release prophetic revelation. They may look at someone's outward appearance and make a wrong judgment and intercede from a misperception. Therefore, it is important to ensure that what we are releasing in prayer is not from a judgmental or critical attitude. If the prophetic intercession is coming in a harsh, frightening, condemning, or critical manner, this is a good indicator that it is not flowing from the direction of the Holy Spirit.

What about a religious bias in prophetic intercession? Be cautious when someone takes the opportunity to promote a favorite doctrine. Usually when this is happens, the praying individual will rant on and on about their ideas and agendas. They often do this in ways to try to preach at or manipulate others to get them to line up with their thinking. This is not intercession. This is religious praying with a self-promoting agenda.

Have you been in an intercession time when the motivation behind the prayers was critical?
_____
_____
_____

A Desire Does Not Necessarily Constitute a Word from God

I have been involved in many situations in which I have to reconcile the relationships between pastors and intercessors. The report from pastors has been one of confusion, disunity, and pain due to intercessors who felt they had the word of the Lord for the church, but would not submit to the counsel of leadership. God is calling pastors and intercessors to work together in a dynamic kingdom partnership. But there are times when intercessors can cross a line and get out of order.

It is not the job of intercessors to become the pastor's or leader's Holy Spirit. Intercessors may see something in a conference or another church and decide that it also needs to happen in their own church. As we increase in prophetic intercession it is essential that we learn the difference between our own voice and desires and those of the Lord. Even if the desire is godly and is what God is doing today, it might not be true for another church and its leaders at the moment.

Is the Holy Spirit Giving an Inner Witness?

Remember we shared in lesson one that we are His sheep and know His voice. Let's visit again what John 10: 2-5 says concerning this faith building promise.

"Let me set this before you as plainly as I can. If a person climbs over or through the fence of a sheep pen instead of going through the gate, you know he's up to no good—a sheep rustler! The shepherd walks right up to the gate. The

gatekeeper opens the gate to him and the sheep recognize his voice. He calls his own sheep by name and leads them out. When he gets them all out, he leads them and they follow because they are familiar with his voice. They won't follow a stranger's voice but will scatter because they aren't used to the sound of it." The Message.

When the Lord is speaking to us or through us in intercession, there will be a resounding cry that rises from our spirit that says, *"Yes, Lord, I agree!"* It is as if every part of our being resonates in agreement with what is being prayed. Even in a corporate time of intercession, this will prove to be the case.

A serial killer was on the loose in the city of Houston. He had murdered four individuals and the police had no leads. You could strongly feel spirits of fear and death beginning to grip the city.

Before we gathered for our mid-week intercession time, the police department made it clear that they had no leads on the case and asked the public for help. They were concerned for the safety of the citizens of Houston and cautioned women to not be out alone until the killer was stopped.

We knew that the direction of our mid-week prayer meeting was to focus on the capture of the killer before he murdered his fifth victim. We prayed that the police would be led supernaturally to the killer. We prayed that fear and death would not have access to the city. We declared that this terrorizing would come to an end and that he would be caught that evening. There was not one person in that intercession time who was not resounding with a yes and amen in their spirit as we stood as watchmen for our region. In unison we confidently proclaimed, *"You will stop this killing in our city and the police will locate you tonight and make their arrest. We will not welcome or allow fear and death to grip this region!"*

When I arrived home, I quickly turned on the television to hear the breaking news. I heard the announcer state that the police had received a phone call leading them to the killer and that he had been arrested. The call to the police came during the exact hour that we had been praying. This is breakthrough!

The Problem of Pride

"Before He [the Savior] can lead a chosen vessel into such a life of intercession, He first has to deal to the bottom with all that is natural." [1] Rees Howells

God's Word says that there are things within our own hearts that are evil. God will bring pressure upon us to change these things, but we must respond and open the door by faith and say, *"Lord, I welcome You to create in me a clean heart."* As we open the door, the Holy Spirit comes in as a gentleman and as Rees Howells so appropriately stated, *"deals to the bottom with all that is natural."*

Rees Howells furthers explains his own struggle in the area of the Holy Spirit dealing with Him. God asked Him to give all of himself in exchange for all of the Holy Spirit.

"[It] was not sin He was dealing with; it was self—that thing which came from the Fall. He put His finger on each part of my self-life, and I had to decide in cold blood [because] he could never take a thing away until I gave my consent. Then the moment I gave it, some purging took place." [2]

In the end Rees Howells experienced a glorious infilling of the Holy Spirit. The Lord dug out bitter roots and gave him a clean heart.

When God fills us with His Spirit, it often seems like our sin issues are magnified. Actually, it is God's anointing in cleansing us and making us clean. For me personally, the Lord also walked me through the process of giving all of myself. But I quickly realized the difference in my response. Within moments of sinning I felt deep conviction from the Holy Spirit, and I desired for my heart to become more pliable and soft before God.

Especially in Western Culture a prevalent issue is that of pride. As discussed in my personal testimony of learning to prefer others in Lesson Three of *Encouraged to Intercede,* when God trusts us to pray, He must first cleanse our hearts to the point that the reports we give are not tainted and biased with pride. Are we releasing prophetic revelation in a prideful manner? Do we rush to tell the one we are interceding for that God has revealed bitterness in their life causing them further offense? Do we share dramatic answers to prayer to make ourselves appear more spiritual than others? Are we territorial and defensive over revelation God has spoken to us?

False humility is also pride. What do I mean by this? When God does use us in an anointed moment, and then people encourage us and us a compliment, it is perfectly fine to say, *"Thank you."* Sometimes we can get "religious" in our responses and say, *"I had nothing to do with it. It was all God."* Granted, we do give God the credit, but we did open our mouths and spoke, and prayed and shared with the person. Do not get into the trap of false humility. Thank the person who is encouraging you and move on.

On the other side of the coin, when God calls you to intercession, it is often a hidden place with little or no credit that will ever be seen on earth. Do not grow frustrated and try to force recognition on yourself. Your heavenly Father knows and sees the labor of love for your pastor, family, church, city, and nation. Be content in His knowing and do not strive or enter into self-promotion.

Prophetic Protocol

The Need for Spiritual Alignment

I often teach that the best leaders are the best followers. What do I mean by this? Those who lead well also understand the necessary value of spiritual relationships and alignments. There is an undeniable significance to other people's spiritual guidance and input in our daily walk. Our hearing is imperfect. We don't even hear others clearly at times. Spiritual leaders are given to the Body of Christ to help us grow, to protect, guide, and to see spiritual gifts released to the fullness in our lives.

"Obey your spiritual leaders and submit to them [continually recognizing their authority over you], for they are constantly keeping watch over your souls and guarding your spiritual welfare, as men who will have to render an account [of their trust]. [Do your part to] let them do this with gladness and not with sighing and groaning, for that would not be profitable to you [either]." Hebrews 13:17, Amplified Bible

Intercessors get in trouble when they develop independent attitudes. There should never be a lone ranger mentality in the Body of Christ. Even leaders are to receive from others and in return welcome their guidance, wisdom, and accountability. Cindy Jacobs in her book *The Voice of God* shares how the Lord clearly spoke to her concerning this truth.

"When I received my call from the Lord, the subject of authority was heavy on my heart. One day in prayer the Holy Spirit cautioned me, "Cindy, if you want to move in great authority, you must be subject to others in authority. Your anointing will grow in proportion to your understanding of spiritual submission. Remember the centurion who came to Jesus and asked Him to heal His servant boy. A great miracle occurred because he understood authority." [3]

Accountability and control are not synonymous. A better term for accountability is alignment or relationship. Those who are called to lead should do so with the heart of seeing others under them soar higher and go further in advancing God's kingdom.

The Lord's Close friend

Psalm 25:14 says, *"God-friendship is for God-worshipers; They are the ones he confides in."*   The Message

Are you one who God can trust with His secrets? Can He confide and entrust His heart and prayer burdens to you? God will only share and reveal prophetic prayer burdens with those He can trust. Just as we have friends we transparently share our hearts with, the Lord is looking for those He can also trust at this level. Prophetic revelation must not become slander or gossip. Sometimes the Lord will speak and it is something that can be shared right away. Other times, He will share something and it will require the ability to hold onto the revelation until the timing is right. Or, He might require you to never share what has been revealed, but to faithfully carry it until the breakthrough occurs.

God's Timing

First Chronicles 12: 32 speaks of understanding God's times and seasons. *"Men of Issachar, who understood the times and knew what Israel was supposed to do."* (NIV). In prophetic intercession, gaining the understanding of the Lord concerning His timing is a key component in interceding with breakthrough results. In order to do so let's investigate the two Greek words for God's timing. *Chronos* is time in general. Meaning the time we live in everyday. *Kairos* is a strategic time when something should be spoken or done. As we grow in our maturity and learn to hear and respond to the Lord, we will release what is shared at that *kairos* time and supernatural things will occur. I have reached a place in my intercessory life where I will hear the Holy Spirit say to me, *"Becca, pray the prayer now. Or, speak the prophetic revelation now."* Then there are those times when I will hear the following direction. *"Becca, do not speak the revelation yet. Hold it. It is not my timing to release this. Carry what I have entrusted to you in intercession."*

Then we have another aspect concerning God's timing. This is the place of tension where God speaks a promise, but it might be years before the fulfillment is realized or the answer comes. Abraham was promised a son. It took 25 years before this prophetic promise was fulfilled.

Then there is the reality that it takes time to grow and mature into hearing God's voice. Samuel grew in his ability to hear from the time he was a young man. With Eli's guidance, he learned to recognize God's voice and to respond.

God's Word says there is a season and time for everything under heaven. (Ecclesiastes 3:1-15). So coming into agreement with how God wants you to pray in His seasons is imperative. There is a time to war, and a time to praise. A time to rest and a time to be active. A time to weep and a time to rejoice. A time to repent and a time to declare. A time to dance and a time to sit still. A time to ask and a time to claim. God is always willing to show us the right path to take at the right moment. He does not leave us to figure it out on our own. We can ask Him how to pray in each season. And, we also have each other and our leaders to serve as confirming voices.

Red and Green Lights for Prophetic Revelation

As is true with all spiritual practices, there are also points of wisdom and guidelines to ensure that we do not get off track or cause another to become sidetracked. When we come into a place of hearing and receiving prophetic revelation, God will begin to speak to us concerning others. Prophetic revelation is meant to build up and edify. 1 Corinthians 14: 3 states, *"But one who prophesies speaks to men for edification and exhortation and consolation."* Let's investigate further the meanings of these words.

1. Edification
The Greek word for edification is *oikodome.* It means the act of building up, strengthening, and making more able. It is the act of one who promotes another's growth in Christian wisdom, piety, happiness, and holiness.

2. Exhortation
The Greek word for exhortation is *paraklesis.* It means an earnest appeal of encouragement, comfort, and refreshment.

3. Consolation and Comfort
The Greek word for consolation is *paranuthia.* Any address, whether made for the purpose of persuading, or of arousing or stimulating, or of calming or consoling.

It is clear that prophetic revelation should not bring confusion, but encouragement and comfort. It is for the purpose of promoting another's Christian walk and growth. Let's look at practices to avoid when considering prophetic revelation:
    A. **Feeling spiritually above leadership.** Never use an intercessory leadership role to speak against the leaders of a church or ministry. Do not become the Holy

Spirit to the leadership and pray from a place of superiority or correction. In stead, pray that God will cause them to want more of His presence, that He will impart further anointing and spiritual wisdom and insight. Ask the Lord to bless the leadership.

B. **If God releases prophetic revelation for the church, submit the word to the pastor and trust him to carry it out.** Once you have shared what God is saying, you have been obedient to your part of the process. The pastor can them take the revelation, pray through it, and respond in the timing and direction God speaks to him.

C. **Using prophetic revelation against a person.** If sin is discerned, do not announce it or use it against the person as a point of manipulation. Intercede so that the Lord will bring freedom from the trap and bondage of sin.

D. **Presumption.** *Presumption* means to undertake or act on unwarrantable boldness. When intercessors begin to hear and respond to God's voice there can be an immature zealousness in operation. Revelation is immediately shared instead of waiting for God's direction and timing. Some begin to address the realm of darkness without proper alignment and wisdom from God.

E. **Praying from a point of fear or woundedness.** When we intercede from this place, it is a for sure guarantee that what we think we might be hearing is not clear guidance from God. God never causes fear. If we are wounded, it is easy to project our own hurtful experiences from the unhealed portion of our emotions.

F. **Witchcraft praying.** This is praying what we want and not what God wants. This is nothing more than control and manipulation.
G. **Becoming a self-proclaimed prophet.** This is where no one else recognizes, confirms, or agrees that the individual is truly operating as a gifted prophet to the Body of Christ. We can all hear and release God's voice. But, this is the person who claims their voice is the only one with all the answers. Usually, this type of individual is lacking in humility and spiritual alignment. They are usually a lone ranger in their spiritual walk.
H. **What about relocation?** I am very cautious and believe we should all be slow to speak concerning giving direction for moving and relocating. I vary rarely have ever spoken to someone that they are to move to another area. This is something an individual needs to hear for themselves from the Lord.
I. **Marriages.** Never speak to someone concerning who they are to marry. I have ministered deliverance to couples who were married because of a prophetic word, and who did not hear the Lord for themselves.
J. **Babies.** If you are praying for someone who is barren or has been trying for years to get pregnant, do not prophesy that they will become pregnant. Even, if you feel this strongly. Simply pray and ask the Lord to open the mother's womb and to bless the couple with a child. Do not prophetically declare a pregnancy.

4. Tuning our Spirits through Wisdom
I was a vocal performance major in school. Before performances, we would practice hours in order to prepare. Prior to the opera, the singers, choir, and orchestra warmed up by tuning their vocal chords and instruments. This ensured that the performance would be in fine tune and in pitch. The same

is true for us spiritually. We have to engage in the necessary practice and perseverance of hearing God's voice. This creates an atmosphere that helps us to respond in wisdom.

This lesson has given us guidelines on how to fine tune our hearing in order to intercede and release His God's wisdom. Only His wisdom brings victory, peace, and spiritual breakthrough.

5. Self-Examination

While I realize we went through a cleansing process in Lesson Three of *Encouraged to Intercede,* this lesson specifically deals with areas of releasing God's prophetic revelation. Therefore, let's get specific about how we operate, and like Rees Howells allow the Lord to deal with our self-nature.

When God reveals something to you about another person, what is your first impulse? What does this reveal about your heart's motives?

_____
_____
_____
_____
_____

- Invite the Holy Spirit to do a cleansing work in your heart.
- As He begins this process, respond to those issues He is calling into order. Your flesh will be uncomfortable, but let Him do His work.
- Ask God to make you soft, pliable, humble, and teachable.

Your Kingdom Come

Do you sometimes feel more awed toward an effective intercessor than toward the God who answers prayer?
_____
_____
_____
_____
_____

Have you ever given yourself a pat on the back when your prayers were answered or God used you in a significant way?
_____
_____
_____
_____

In closing, here are some steps to take between now and the next lesson:
1. Repent for wanting the credit and recognition for what God has done.
2. Make the commitment to give God the glory for how He uses you.
3. Make sure that all places of woundedness are healed in your hearts, thoughts, and emotions. Where necessary release forgiveness to those who have caused pain.
4. Invite God to give you the ability to respond to His leading in a *kairos* time.
5. Thank God for the leaders He has placed in your life. Pray blessings on them.
6. Welcome God's guidance and empowerment for you to receive prophetic prayer burdens for others that will bring edification, exhortation, and comfort.
7. Be expectant that He will answer this request.
8. Respond in faith as He leads.

Breakthrough!

Lesson Four: Breakthrough!

I was teaching a group of intercessors in the town of La Junta, Colorado. They asked if I would be willing to join them in prayer on the property owned by one of the intercessors. On that ranch is a hill. This hill is the meeting point of three counties in Colorado and is the high point of all three counties. Individuals involved in the New Age movement travel to high places such as this to pray and seek spiritual enlightenment.

After the couple purchased the property they began to receive phone calls from people asking if they could climb this hill. They gladly allowed these strangers access with no knowledge of what was occurring when they reached the top. Once they became aware of spiritual warfare, the landowners surmised that demonic and witchcraft practices had occurred there. They knew they needed to climb the hill and pray, but they wanted someone with spiritual warfare experience to pray with them. A group of intercessors from their church, the pastor, his family, and I climbed the hill.

Upon reaching the top we discovered three altars. They were built of rocks and were in the formation of a triangle. One of the rock altars contained the bones of an animal. It was obvious that we needed to pray and destroy these demonic altars. God directed us to perform several prophetic acts which we will discuss in depth in this chapter. First we threw all the rocks down the hill; then we threw down the animal bones. We declared that the demonic powers of these altars were broken off the land. As we continued to pray and read Scripture, God began to impress upon us to perform another prophetic act and to make a prophetic declaration.

Colorado was in a severe drought at this time. It was especially bad in this area of the state; all of the vegetation was dead. From the top of this hill as far as the eye could see was dead grass. Four of the team members were impressed by the Lord to perform a prophetic act to declare the drought broken. We divided the team into three groups. Each group stood on a location where the rock altars had been built. We anointed each site with oil and poured water on the ground at the center of the triangle. After we poured the water, we drove stakes into the ground with Scripture written on them.

We stood in a circle surrounding the altar and worshipped the Lord. Suddenly, while singing with my eyes closed, I felt it raining on me. Actually, the pastor's teenage sons also had the same spiritual experience. Without opening our eyes, all four of us began to dance and celebrate as we truly believed it was raining. When we did open our eyes, the rest of the group looked at us as if we had lost our minds. We all explained the spiritual encounter that had just transpired. We all felt strongly what we were to do next.

The pastor, who has spiritual authority in this region, declared prophetically that the drought would be broken in that region and on the land. Then I declared that the grass would begin to turn green, that life would return to the land, and that the people of the region would see the green grass and life on the land and give God the glory. Within a month, four inches of rain had fallen. As you approached the property line of the ranch, the grass was noticeably greener than that of the surrounding land.

Greater Things than These Shall You Do

Now some of us might feel skeptical about the idea that we can do greater things than our Savior. And for many of us this verse conveys the message that we will reach more souls than He did during His earthly ministry. Jesus said we would do even greater works than He did. This includes all He did while ministering His Kingdom on the earth. *"I assure you, most solemnly I tell you, if anyone steadfastly believes in Me, he will himself be able to do the things that I do; and he will do even greater things than these, because I go to the Father"* (John 14:12, AMPLIFIED BIBLE).

What an incredible promise from the Lord. When Jesus ascended to the right hand of the Father, the Holy Spirit was in turn sent back to us. As believers we are empowered to do the work of God's Kingdom. Upon receiving our orders from our King, we have the right and power of jurisdiction to execute them in our personal lives, the lives of others, in our allotted territories and prayer assignments, in our cities and in the land, and in the spiritual realm against the ranks of darkness.

Paul's Powerful Revelation Concerning Believers

"[For I always pray to] the God of our Lord Jesus Christ, the Father of glory, that He may grant you a spirit of wisdom and revelation [of insight into mysteries and secrets] in the [deep and intimate] knowledge of Him, by having the eyes of your heart flooded with light, so that you can know and understand the hope to which He has called you, and how rich is His glorious inheritance in the saints (His set-apart ones), And [so that you can know and understand] what is the immeasurable and unlimited and surpassing greatness of His power in and for us who believe, as demonstrated in the working of His mighty strength, which He exerted in Christ when He raised Him from the dead and seated Him at His [own] right hand in the heavenly [places], far above all rule and authority and power and dominion and every name that is named [above every title that can be conferred], not only in this age and in this world, but also in the age and the world which are to come. And He has put all things under His feet and has appointed Him the universal and supreme Head of the church [a headship exercised throughout the church], which is His body, the

fullness of Him Who fills all in all [for in that body lives the full measure of Him Who makes everything complete, and Who fills everything everywhere with Himself]." Ephesians 1:17–23, AMPLIFIED BIBLE

We are the Church, His Body, and the fullness of Him who fills all in all. It is difficult to fathom the great and awesome inheritance made available to us. With Paul, may we pray that the Lord gives each of us a Spirit of wisdom and of revelation, and that the eyes of our hearts may be enlightened to the hope to which we have been called, and to the glorious inheritance with which we have been bestowed.

Have you been involved in praying in a manner that is different from your personality? How did you pray?

_____
_____
_____
_____
_____

What is Breakthrough?

Obviously, one of the main roles of prophetic and warfare intercession (which will be the focus of the final portion of this curriculum) is to execute God's plan and to see breakthrough realized. Breakthrough is defined as a strikingly important advance or discovery in any field of knowledge or activity; the act, result, or place of breaking through against resistance, as in warfare.

In *The Breaker Anointing*, Barbara Yoder explains the widespread effects of breakthrough: *"It is an anointing that affects individuals, churches, and cities. When the breaker anointing comes into an area it results in changes not only in individuals but also in churches, the socio-political structure, and the belief systems of the city."*[1]

Micah 2:13 says, *"One who breaks open the way will go up before them; they will break through the gate and go out. Their king will pass through before them, the* LORD *at their head."* (NIV) It is awe-inspiring to watch as the Lord goes forth into a region and lives are transformed.

We Become God's Voice for Breakthrough

One of the most exciting facts concerning prophetic intercession is that we can pray down barriers to holiness and to goodness that result from evil rulers. By standing in the gap or breach, as the voice of the Lord to bring healing to the earth, mighty answers to prayer can be realized. Isaiah 58:12 states, *"And those from among you will rebuild the ancient ruins; You will raise up the age-old foundations; And you will be called the repairer of the breach, The restorer of the streets in which to dwell."* Having sought His guidance, we stand as one who rebuilds, raises up, repairs, and restores.

We can speak words inspired by the Holy Spirit. Psalm 29:3-9 tells us of the many things the voice of the Lord accomplishes: *"The voice of the Lord is upon the waters; The God of glory thunders, The Lord is over many waters. The voice of the Lord is powerful, The voice of the Lord is majestic. The voice of the Lord breaks the cedars; Yes, the Lord breaks in pieces the cedars of Lebanon. And He makes Lebanon skip like a calf, And Sirion like a young wild ox. The voice of the Lord hews out flames of fire. The voice of the Lord shakes the wilderness; The Lord shakes the wilderness of Kadesh. The voice of the Lord makes the deer to calve, And strips the forests bare, And in His temple everything says, 'Glory!'"*

There is great power in God's voice and the authority in what He speaks. As His ambassadors, when our words line up with His words, the Lord's power flows through our words.

To further explain, let's look at John 7: 38-39: *"He who believes in Me, as the Scripture said, 'From his innermost being shall flow rivers of living water.' But this He spoke of the Spirit."* NASB

Each of us has the Holy Spirit flowing through us; that river of God that brings His life, love, healing, breakthrough, the fire of His presence, deliverance, and freedom. According to Psalm 29, His voice is upon the waters. His voice is therefore on the living waters that flow from the mouths of His intercessors. As this river flows in obedience to God's direction it produces God's miraculous intervention and breakthrough.

Psalm 29:5 says that the voice of the Lord "breaks." The Hebrew word for break is *shabar*. As most Hebrew words do, this one encompasses many meanings all at the same time.

- To burst
- To break into pieces; to rend; to tear in pieces
- To destroy, to perish(such as a kingdom)
- To be broken by penitence (to be contrite)
- To cause to break forth, to open (the womb, the infant appears)
- Birthing purposes in the earth[2]

Looking at the definitions of *shabar*, it is easy to see how the voice of the Lord through intercessors can help destroy the works of evil and release brokenness and repentance to those not walking with the Lord. The voice of the Lord through His people also, "opens the womb," so to speak, for the Lord to "birth" His purposes in the earth.[3]

The voice of the Lord also "shakes." The Hebrew word for shakes is *chuwl*. It, too, is a word rich in meaning. It expresses

the complete fullness of what God can accomplish in one spoken proclamation or act.
- To be afraid
- To tremble with pain
- To be terrified
- To be in labor (as in childbirth)
- To bear a child
- To produce
- To cause to bring forth[4]

Barbara Wentroble further explains in *Prophetic Intercession*: "*The voice of the Lord causes the enemy to be afraid. It causes him to be so terrified that he will tremble with pain. God's voice also causes the words spoken to produce and bring forth. His voice births the fruit of our labors. I am convinced that if we could see into the realm of the spirit, we would pray more. Often we pray, but because we don't see an immediate answer, we think nothing has happened. Remember, it took 21 days for the answer to come to Daniel (see Dan. 10:12, 13). Sometimes it will take even more time before we see the results of our intercession.*"[5]

Describe a time when you were involved in prophetic intercession that brought breakthrough?
_____
_____
_____
_____

We are His Ambassadors

We believe that God has incredible, majestic power in His voice. When He speaks things happen. So as sons and daughters of God, how can this apply to us?

We are therefore Christ's ambassadors as though He was making His appeal through us.   2 Cor. 5:20

To be His ambassador means we are His representatives. We have been given His stamp of approval and His legislative authority to act on His behalf as He leads and guides us. We do not have the right or authority to tell or dictate to God what He can do. This would be presumption. But we do have the right to execute His blueprint plans and to carry them out in His timing and wisdom. What are some of the ways we can do this?

Prayerwalking

The term "prayerwalking" is simply an expression used to define a particular function in intercession. I appreciate how Steve Hawthorne and Graham Kendrick describe this prayer activity:

"Many people have begun to use a new word to describe the recent burst of citywide intercession. Yet to walk while praying is probably not a new activity, though it seems different from the well-known formats of prayer. The rising interest is so substantial that it can only help to add a new word to our vocabulary: prayerwalking. We define prayerwalking simply as praying on-site with insight." [6]

There are two goals when prayerwalking:
1. Pray blessings upon the land and the people.
2. Discern and remove the enemy and his influence.

As you walk through the land praying, you will not only be petitioning the Lord on behalf of the people, but you will be praising Him for what He is doing throughout the land. As you praise the Lord and pray blessings for others, the Light of Jesus and His Kingdom shines where you are. Wherever there is light, the darkness cannot remain.

BREAKTHROUGH!

Dutch Sheets in his book *Intercessory Prayer*, tells the story of Sue Doty who prayer walked and gained knowledge so she could pray effectively.

"I sensed the Lord wanted me, along with a team of intercessors, to go on a prayer walk over a specific route, but that some preparation was necessary. First, I talked with my pastor about this and then went to drive along the route I knew we were to prayer walk. As I approached a theater (X-rated movie house, video shop and bookstore) the Holy Spirit started to give me specific instructions. He told me to cast out spirits of pornography and lust, and I did so. He also told me to pray in the Spirit. After a short time I was released from praying, and I continued on the rest of the route before going home.

"On that Friday the Lord revealed to me what had actually happened. I turned on the local news to hear that this particular theater had been ordered by the city to close it s doors. The day after I had been there to pray, the city conducted a surprise inspection. The theater was cited for several violations and its doors were immediately closed and locked."[7]

Prophetic Acts

A prophetic act is something we do. It is having the powers of a prophet to establish an action or decree that foreshadows. A scriptural example comes from the Battle of Jericho recorded in Joshua 6:3–5:

"And you shall march around the city, all the men of war circling the city once. You shall do so for six days. Also, seven priests shall carry seven trumpets of ram's horns before the ark; then on the seventh day you shall march around the city seven times, and the priests shall blow the trumpets. And it shall be that when they make a long blast with the ram's horn, and when you hear the sound of the trumpet's all the people shall *shout with a great shout; and the wall of the city will fall down flat, and the people will go up every man straight ahead."*

I can imagine that as the children of Israel continued to march around Jericho some of them thought what they were doing was crazy. Sometimes in intercession the Lord will direct us to do things that take us out of our comfort zone or that are contrary to our personality. Prophetic acts might be just one of those activities. So what does a prophetic act look like? The following is a list of just a few of the things we have been directed to do in our twenty years of experience.

- Praying in government buildings and anointing all the chairs with oil.
- Anointing every chair in a church building with oil before each church service or conference.
- Pouring anointing oil, water, or salt on land, altars, rivers, and oceans.
- Praying and worshiping outside lewd, dark, rock concerts.
- Doing Jericho drives around a city.
- Flying in helicopters and planes over a city while declaring God's Word.
- Climbing the high point of the city and declaring God's Word.
- Climbing the high point of the city and sounding the shofar.
- Burying Bibles under newly constructed school buildings, government buildings, businesses, and homes.
- Writing Scripture on the framing of a new home before the dry wall goes up.
- Raising and spending thousands of dollars to go to nations to pray on spiritually troubled spots.
- Dancing a prophetic warfare dance on the land.

BREAKTHROUGH!

- Driving stakes into the ground with Scripture promises written on them.
- Singing and worshiping Jesus in temples dedicated to idols.
- Fasting during the Muslim timeframe of Ramadan and praying that those who are fasting Muslims will have an encounter with Jesus.
- Fasting and praying for 40 days for revival in our nation.
- Shouting "freedom" at the ancient gates in Russian cities.

A note of wisdom, we must be discreet when performing prophetic acts. Try not to draw attention to yourself or do something that will put the safety of your team in jeopardy. Do not destroy historic relics or property of a temple. Not only does this put Christians in a bad light, it could get you and your team thrown in jail.

Have you seen a prophetic act done as a part of intercession? How did you feel about it?

_____
_____
_____
_____
_____

Some of this lesson might take some people out of their place of comfort in prayer. Is praying in this manner contrary to your personality?

_____
_____
_____
_____

Prophetic Worship and Intercession

Worship is one of the most formidable weapons in our spiritual arsenal. We see many times throughout God's Word where worship paved the way for supernatural deliverances. Different forms of worship intercession involve spontaneous new songs. This may happen while someone is prophetically dancing. It is also seen in the waving of flags and banners to show glory and honor to God. It could be a song of gratefulness sung or played with the anointing in order to release His presence, healing, love, and liberty. Prophetic worship is not just meant to make us feel good or better, it is a spiritual dynamic that when released carries the ability to see captives set free and spiritual battles won.

In ancient Israel when the Moabites, Ammonites, and their allies began their plan to invade Judah. Jehoshaphat found out about it and called a corporate time of fasting and prayer in order to receive spiritual revelation on how to engage the battle. In their time of corporately seeking the Lord, the Spirit of the Lord fell on Jahaziel and he prophesied the clear Word of God to secure victory in the battle. The following encounter in 2 Chronicles 20:20-25 clearly shares the strategy and outcome:
"They rose early in the morning and went out to the wilderness of Tekoa; and when they went out, Jehoshaphat stood and said, 'Listen to me, O Judah and inhabitants of Jerusalem, put your trust in the LORD your God and you will be established. Put your trust in His prophets and succeed.' When he had consulted with the people, he appointed those who sang to the LORD and those who praised Him in holy attire, as they went out before the army and said, 'Give thanks to the LORD, for His loving kindness is everlasting.'" When they began singing and praising, the LORD set ambushes against the sons of Ammon, Moab and Mount Seir, who had come against Judah; so they were routed. For the sons of Ammon and Moab rose up against

the inhabitants of Mount Seir destroying them completely; and when they had finished with the inhabitants of Seir, they helped to destroy one another.

"When Judah came to the lookout of the wilderness, they looked toward the multitude, and behold, they were corpses lying on the ground, and no one had escaped. When Jehoshaphat and his people came to take their spoil, they found much among them, including goods, garments and valuable things which they took for themselves, more than they could carry. And they were three days taking the spoil because there was so much."

Prophetic Proclamations

A prophetic proclamation is an announcement or decree given with the authority of a prophet. An example found in Scripture is 2 Timothy 4:17: *"But the Lord stood with me, and strengthened me, in order that through me the proclamation might be fully accomplished, and that all the Gentiles might hear; and I was delivered out of the lion's mouth."*

This is not a random outcry, but a partnering with a process released from heaven. God makes known His direction to the Church and the Church makes known God's intentions by speaking in agreement with Him. The outcome is breakthrough! To further explain the significance of prophetic acts and declarations, let me to share the following story.

I was leading a prayer journey team to Russia and Ukraine. We were praying in Ukraine onsite at the Monastery of the Caves. My team and I had researched the history of this location for almost a year before embarking on this prayer assignment. We also spent a long period of time with an ex-priest who had previously served in the monastery before Jesus appeared to him in a dream, and he was radically saved. Due to his encounter with Jesus and his unhindered desire to lead others into the saving grace of our Lord, he was forcibly excommunicated from the priesthood and his service in this monastery.

Jesus is not worshipped in this location, but instead dead bones are revered. This location has an underground cemetery that houses the decayed bodies and dead bones of 120 saints. The bodies are buried in glass coffins and shrouded in expensive ornate robes. People come from all over the world to visit the underground cemetery and worship the bones. It is believed that oil is emitted from the bones which in turn bring salvation and healing to the sick and oppressed. You and I know this is not the way to salvation, but people in this region of Ukraine believe it is the only way to a secure eternity. It was our heart to pray prophetically and strategically to see this deception torn down and Jesus lifted high. It was our hearts cry in intercession to see those trapped in this demonic lie and false worship set free and gloriously saved!

The day we visited the Monastery was actually the Feast of the Bones day. We did not know this until we arrived. This is the day where thousands come from all over the Russian province to sing to, worship, and touch the glass coffins in hopes of obtaining their spiritual security and healing. The Lord gave us clear instructions to go inside the caves for a brief time in order to gain understanding of all that transpires there. Before we entered, we were required to purchase a candle and carry it in our left hand between our two middle fingers. Once inside, we saw a heartbreaking scene.

The tunnel was three feet wide with manmade niches that contained coffins of the dead saints. The people were singing to the dead bodies. They would lean over and kiss the glass cover of the coffins. Yana, our Christian interpreter, quickly escorted us through the tunnels while we observed their worship. They were trying to believe for a healing miracle. It was also explained that numerous priests try to live in the caves with the dead bones. Many only live ten to twelve years, but there was one priest who lived in the caves without ever coming outside for thirty-seven years before dying.

We began to lay hands on the coffins and anoint them with oil and announce their defeat. Yana would slip us into niches that had altars to idols or a dead saint and say, "Pray here, it is very significant."

There was an old woman in front of us with a toddler around the age of eighteen months who was sick. She would take him and lay him over the coffin causing him to kiss the glass. He was perfectly quiet until his lips touched the coffin. He would then let out this terrible shriek. It sent chills down our spines. We wept as we witnessed this scene. We were furious with the enemy at the same time. Everything took place very quickly because the priests who were in the caves were not happy we were there. We prayed for about ten to fifteen minutes before leaving. Then, we went directly above the caves where we interceded.

We wept and began to agree for the salvation of these deceived and trapped worshippers. In unison we asked God to cause supernatural encounters and divine appointments. We asked that those who were lost and bound in this practice would meet believers who would influence them. As we prayed, the Lord showed me a very specific prophetic act to perform and a prophetic declaration to release. I have learned when God shows me something this specific to step out in faith and obedience. He instructed us to do the following. We were to stand in a circle and place the candle in our left hand between our middle fingers. Then we were to sing a worship song to the Lord. After signing we were to take the candle in our hands and in unison break it in two, throw it onto the ground, stomp on it, and shout out loud three times that Jesus Christ is Lord. I then told everyone to run for the bus because at this point the priests of the monastery were not going to be happy. So we did exactly as the Lord had directed and walked quickly to the already running and waiting tour bus. We worshiped God's goodness and glory while we went.

God is absolutely amazing. One month after returning home, I was doing further research on this location. I still had no understanding of the very specific prophetic act and declaration the Lord had directed us in. A book I was reading for my research went into explicit detail of what the priests do when someone leaves the worship of the monastery. Guess what? They stand in a circle, light a candle, and place it in their left hand between their two middle fingers. The they sing one of their worship songs to the idol, blow out the candle, take it in their hands and in unison break it in two, throw it on the ground, stomp on it, and out loud three times shout a curse over the individual who left the monastery and their family members for generations to come. God had us do this same act. But we did it in a united prophetic declaration, *"Jesus Christ is Lord,"* which in turn broke the power of those demonic word curses over the excommunicated members, and over the deception of the worship in the region. Since this time more priests and worshippers of this pagan belief have been saved.

Called to the Ministry of Reconciliation

"Now all these things are from God, who reconciled us to Himself through Christ, and gave us the ministry of reconciliation." 2 Cor. 5:18.

As Christ's ambassadors we have also been given the ministry of reconciliation. The basic meaning of the word "reconcile" is "to change thoroughly." Just as God loved mankind and gave His son to die in our place, the Lord also has bestowed on us the ministry of reconciliation in order to express His unconditional love toward us and others. Ministry, then, is done with the expectancy that causes those who are struggling, walking away from the Lord, and lost to be drawn to Him.

When we engage in prophetic intercession birthed from the heart of the Father we can and will see lives thoroughly touched and changed through His love. By interceding and speaking forth His prophetic utterances we reach the pinnacle of intercession where our Father's heart is to reconcile all men and things to Himself. It might take time and perseverance to see the breakthroughs realized, but as we steadfastly intercede and believe, supernatural answers will transpire.

Putting Intercession Into Action

This week we are going to put feet to our prayers.

1. Schedule a time for a prayerwalk.
2. Ask the Lord to show the assigned area for this prayer venture.
3. Be sure to have at least one prayer partner.
4. If a prayer group is involved be sure to divide into teams and assign each team a location to pray. I prefer teams no larger than 6 people in this type of assignment.
5. Assign a team leader to each team.
6. Discern what God is speaking concerning the land and the people.
7. Make a journal of all that He is revealing.
8. Pray, welcoming His presence.
9. Speak that His light will dispel the darkness.
10. Believe that God will move and touch lost souls.
11. Do prophetic acts as led by God.
12. Speak forth prophetic proclamations as He leads.
13. Speak to those who are out and about.
14. If He directs you to, share the gospel message with those you come in contact with.

15. Be expectant.
16. Have fun.
17. If divided in teams, after prayerwalking, gather together and share all that transpired and the revelation the Lord revealed.
18. Schedule another time to prayerwalk and be sure to pray through all the prophetic revelation the Lord has released.

Corporate Intercession

Lesson Five: Corporate Intercession

The weekly prayer meeting begins. One brother with a strong gift of mercy prays with passion and tears as a restless crisis surges in his heart. His impassioned emotion irritates the woman next to him. She has the primary gift of administration and loves to pray through her prayer list each week. In her thoughts she is saying, *If they would just let me organize this group and assign everyone their prayer focus, we could really accomplish something.*

In the back of the room is an intercessor who is aggressively pacing. She discerns an unfolding crisis. Because of a strong gift of discernment, this prayer warrior reacts with excited intensity, urging everyone in the room to shift their attention and prayers to the impending danger at hand. Others sitting in the room grow uncomfortable and roll their eyes at each other. It is obvious this poor sister has a history of taking them down this prayer path. One gentleman leaves the room as she continues in her attempt to manipulate everyone else to pray just like her. He is thinking, *Can someone please calm this woman down? I am tired of her demands to engage us in her spiritual theatrics! I am going home.*

Following her is the administrator who tries to fix the problem by pulling out her prayer lists. For ten minutes, she methodically rehearses her list out loud urging others to join in. As she prays in her calculating manner, others are grieving God by saying, *"This is a waste of time."*

Next is the seasoned prophet who completely intimidates the rest of the group by praying refined, yet fiery prayers, all the while making others feel they are spiritually out of tune with the Holy Spirit.

Then, there is the one who is totally "off-focus." When the group is directed by the leader to pray for the pastors of the city, this "out of step" individual ignores the instructions and shifts gears and begins to pray for Uncle Joe who is not sleeping well. There is no focus, no flow. The result is a frustrated group of intercessors and an ineffective prayer time with a lot of confusion! Of course this is a scenario involving a lot of different difficulties all at one time, but these kinds of problems are very real. What is the answer to the problems often involved in corporate prayer?

Corporate Prayer Can be Dynamic!

Many people have participated in these types of prayer times. No focus and everyone praying in their own direction without any clear unity of purpose. But corporate prayer times can be dynamic and have great spiritual effects. Not only can they flow in the Spirit, but they can also prove to be a powerful prophetic time of praying in accordance with God's heart. The key is to learn each other's individual giftings and embrace the diversity while still praying in unity. In order to achieve this goal, let's investigate the different giftings and anointings intercessors can operate in. In my earlier years, I learned many of these various anointings through Alice Smith, an intercessory mother to the Body of Christ. Others I have also witnessed in my years of leading prayer groups. The list continues to grow. I am sure five years from now I will add even more to this list.

Warfare Prayer

This prayer warrior will have a strong gift of discernment and function in full confidence in Kingdom authority. They know the schemes of the enemy and how demonic spirits operate. They have no fear and readily address the rulers of darkness with great intensity, fervor, and passion. Faith, prophecy, the word of knowledge, and discernment flow freely through this individual.

Crisis Prayer

This intercessor also has a sharp gift of discernment. It is as if their spiritual antennas are always up ready and able to receive those urgent emergency prayer assignments. Involved will also be gifts of prophecy, words of knowledge, mercy, faith, healing, and pastoral love (This intercessor will sometimes be motivated by a pastoral heart as he or she who carries great compassion and concern for people.) Praise God for these who come to attention and intercede, no matter what time of the day or night they are prompted.

Prophetic Intercession

This intercessor has the gift of prophecy. Prophecy was defined in Lesson One, but to explain further this prayer warrior is one who operates in this gift with accurate and consistent revelation from God which is then spoken out to edify Christ's Body. They are able to hear God clearly and precisely. I recall the commercial that advertised, *"When E.F. Hutton speaks everyone listens."* The same is true for prophetic intercessors. They have a track record of recognizing clear revelation, and therefore people listen to what they speak forth in intercession.

In our prayer group we have an intercessor who is a gifted prophet. When my friend prays everyone listens! There is an anticipation to hear what God is revealing. There will also be gifts of faith, words of knowledge, words of wisdom, discernment, exhortation, mercy, and teaching involved in this gifting.

Prayer for Leaders

The heart and focus of this intercessor is to pray for leaders. It does not matter what type or kind. This prayer warrior has a heart and calling to empower and strengthen those who are in charge. Their top priority is to stand in agreement with God's desire for the anointing and protection of their leaders. Gifts of service, helps, exhortation, mercy, leadership, administration, faith, and discernment might also be present.

Personal Prayers

Mercy is a strong driving force for this kind of intercessor. They are always concerned for the personal needs of others and want to know the specifics of how to pray. Their primary focus is centered on personal needs and concerns for other people. This intercessor also has the gift of faith, service, and hospitality. Their prayers will be driven and molded from a pastor's or shepherd's heart of exhortation, always wanting God's love and best for others.

Worship Intercession

This prayer warrior has the heart of worship. They want to sing the song of the Lord, or that specific song that is anointed for that time. They will often lead in worshipping the Lord. Many are gifted in prophetic song; those God-breathed, spontaneous songs that flow in unison with intercessory prayers. Some of these intercessors love to dance and wave banners and also worship with flags.

Prayer for Pastors/Churches

Every pastor needs this intercessor. Their focus is to pray for the pastor and his family, making sure they are covered, protected, and anointed to fulfill their leadership role. These individuals will also have a heart for the local church and pray for God's presence, anointing, and vision. They will frequently inquire of the pastor's needs concerning his family and church. Pastors, do not allow this to threaten you or make you insecure. If it is coming from a sincere heart of love and concern, rejoice that the Lord has placed one or more in your midst to regularly intercede for you.

Cafeteria Style Praying

This actually is my main gifting in intercession. Yes, I am a warrior and a prophet. I love praying for the nations and also for the government. But I often sense where the Holy Spirit wants to go and have the ability to take an entire group to that place. I am grateful to Alice Smith who showed me early on in my prayer life that this is my gifting in intercession. It empowered me to freely move and mature in the anointing of this call.

A cafeteria style intercessor is a chameleon in the spirit. We feel and discern the direction of the Lord and pray in whatever anointing that is needed for that moment. As we pray we cause the corporate gathering to go in a Spirit led direction. Often, this kind of intercessor will lead a group to go higher and deeper in the Spirit during intercession times. If it is time to warfare, we go to war against demon spirits. If it is time to weep, we weep. If it is a time to prophesy, we prophesy. If it is time to move into throne room intimacy, we go there and bring the rest with us. I like to call it, *"catching the wind of the Holy Spirit and flowing with Him."*

Evangelistic Praying People

"Lord, give us souls!" is the cry of this intercessor. They pray so that a harvest might be reaped, and also that God's people will

go to the streets and evangelize. Putting feet and action to their prayers is highly important. Their motto is, *"Let's not just pray it, let's open our mouths and do it!"* They are intense in their pursuit of lost souls. Mercy, compassion, service, evangelism, discernment, faith, healing, and signs and wonders often flow through these prayer warriors.

Business/Finance Intercession

These believers love to pray and believe for finances and resources for God's Kingdom. They are gifted in administration are called to pray for those in business and the marketplace. If they are not running their own business, they will work for one. They will arrive at work an hour early to intercede through the office, anoint the doors with oil, and believe God for an anointed productive work day. They will agree for resources for the business to increase and often times receive revelation of new creative ways for the business to grow and succeed. This intercessor will have great faith, discernment, prophetic gifting, and often the gift of giving. They are able to lead and teach. They are generally not pastors, although they might feel led to start a lunch time Bible study or prayer group. And when their fellow workers or employees have need they are there to walk them through the situation.

Governmental Intercession

Government is their mission field. This person will be at capitol buildings walking and praying. They will know their government leaders and pray for them by name. They will desire righteousness to reign and will believe for a miraculous move of God to save those in governmental positions who are lost. They will have God's heart's cry for justice to rule in the land. They will know the legislation to be voted on and will carry the ability to mobilize an army to stand with them until God's laws are instituted. Some will pray at a city level, some at a state level, and others at a national level.

Prayer for Schools/Education

This prayer soldier is driven with a heart for the next generation. They have a passion to see the education system and individual schools touched by God's presence. Their focus is to see salvation and empowerment for the next generation and for those who teach and guide. Sometimes they are teachers planted in the schools. Some will even run for school board positions. Others will hold seminars and even go to college campuses to preach, pray, evangelize, and pray for the sick. Some are very radical and are like John the Baptist preparing the way for the Lord.

Prayer for Families

"Lord, touch the hearts of my spouse and my children! Cause them to be on fire for you and to walk in the confidence of Your love." This is often the type of prayer you will hear this intercessor pray. They will have great fervor and a heart to pray the prodigals home. God's Word will be a guiding voice in their prayers. They will spend long hours in intercession within their home. It is not uncommon that they are kneeling in prayer even through the night hours while their loved ones sleep.

Prayer for Arts and Entertainment

There is an army of radical, young prophetic intercessors, warriors, and evangelists whom God has positioned strategically to take back the arts and entertainment industry. Many have moved to and live in Los Angeles, New York, and other strategic locations. They prayer walk places like Hollywood, Times Square, and Broadway believing God for miracles. For many, God has opened incredible doors and made amazing relational connections with those in the industry. They have great faith to see God's Kingdom released where He is not yet glorified.

Prayer for the Media

My daughter has a heart and zeal for the media of our society. She will say, *"I will be the Kingdom influencer of this liberal field. And mom, I am your daughter; I know how to war and pray to see the demonic structure the enemy has established within the media world brought down. Not a problem!"* These warriors have great faith, discernment, and the prophetic and warfare ability to see things set against God changed for His glory. They are sold out to truth and have the fervor to pray until God's truth is released.

Administrative Intercessors

This intercessor will set up prayer and fasting chains, and enjoys transcribing the intercessory prayer times. They will write down the prophetic words, revelations, and the Scriptures that were prayed out loud in a corporate prayer gathering. They will also form prayer team lists and want to communicate regularly with the group. Sometimes if this individual feels that a prayer request has been forgotten or overlooked in an intercessory time they will be sure to let you know and remind the group it needs to be prayed through before everyone leaves. For those like me who do not enjoy administration work, they are a gift from God. They will pick up the slack where I am weak. Solid gifts of administration, service, and leadership will be present.

Corporate Intercession

Those Who use Prayer Lists

This intercessor has a list they faithfully pray through daily. It is their primary focus in prayer. For example, this list could be comprised of lost loved ones, leaders, prayer needs for the church or nations in crisis. They are very methodical in their prayers and are very persistent and focused in praying the list until a tangible answer comes. It is not uncommon for this individual to also demonstrate gifts of administration, mercy, and teaching.

Apostolic Intercessors

This is a prayer leader who carries great authority in their sphere of influence. They mobilize prayer networks to strategically pray for regions, cities, states, and nations. They are recognized by other leaders in the Body of Christ as very influential and many will look to them for guidance, training, and impartation. (Impartation is the giving and bestowing of wisdom, spiritual insight, and giftedness from one to another.) When they intercede and make prophetic and apostolic decrees things happen. Prophecy, leadership, teaching, discernment, faith, healing, signs and wonders, and often mercy are key giftings in this individual.

Prayer for the Nations

This person has an intense zeal and vision for the nations and people groups of the world. They will raise thousands of dollars to travel to these lands to prayer walk, spiritually map the region, and strategically pray for revival and transformation. They believe God for the impossible and have an intense passion for lost souls. Prophecy, mercy, evangelism, teaching, leadership, faith, discernment, and healing will also be evident.

Your Kingdom Come

Corporate Intercession

In corporate intercession all gifts should work together for the common good, and for the focus of the prayer assignment God is birthing. But corporate intercession can be ineffective when we expect everyone to pray like we do as though we all had the same spiritual gifts. When others do not conform to our criteria of prayer or prophetic intercession we then grieve the Holy Spirit by rejecting their way of communicating with God. The individual who judges others is the one that will hinder the effectiveness of the corporate gathering.

Another reason why corporate intercession can be ineffective, causing us to miss the prayer assignment and breakthrough, is because everyone is at different levels of spiritual maturity. This is not a negative thing; it is just a fact. What usually occurs is that someone will step in and try to imitate the anointing of another instead of being who they are truly gifted to be. This in turn grieves the Holy Spirit and hinders the prayer meeting. Alice Smith shares in her book *Beyond the Veil*, "*Corporate intercession can be effective, and as powerful as a nuclear warhead if each member will accept each other's spiritual gifts. Remember that gifts must be governed by love. As we come to understand teamwork and cooperation, our different ways of praying will work like a well-oiled machine.*"[1]

I always instruct those in my classes to make these statements out loud, "*I have a voice! I have a unique voice! And God wants me to use and release my voice!*" In doing this, I instruct and encourage intercessors to see that they each have a unique gifting and ability to hear, respond, and pray in agreement with God's heart. Often times, we as believers do not recognize the value each of us carries in God's Kingdom. Each one of us has something to contribute. When these statements are spoken out loud, it releases a belief and understanding that we are all gifted, valuable, and part of a team. It also releases faith, confidence, and belief to those who might be timid to pray out loud in front of others. As a leader and intercessor, I do not expect everyone to pray like I do. I rejoice in the fact that they don't. If everyone prayed like me then our prayer times would not have flavor and variety. Nor would they carry the same measurable results of breakthrough.

When we accept each others' style of prayer, understanding that we all pray and function from a different motivational gift, then God will be blessed, the enemy crippled, and the group united. Prophetic revelation will flow as each individual, through their own prayers and giftings, adds further revelation to what the Lord is speaking.

Revelation upon revelation builds in each unique gifting. Combined together they release great strength and momentum in order to bring spiritual breakthroughs and miraculous answers. When prayer groups begin to function in this manner, the numbers will grow. Even those within the church who had no previous desire to participate will hear and want to get involved. This type of praying is exciting, thrilling, and fulfilling.

Guidelines for Intercessory Prayer Groups

Here are some practical guidelines for the corporate prayer time that will keep the meetings in order and flowing in the anointing of the Holy Spirit.

1. Follow the leader

Recognize that the person leading the time of intercession is the one who has the spiritual authority to do so. Do not try to become the leader yourself even if you feel you know more than he or she does.

The leader should welcome the presence of the Holy Spirit and ask the Father to reveal His assignment. A note to the leader and to all intercessors: This prayer meeting is not about you. It is time to ascend into the heavenlies as one. This is not a time for the leader to pray the entire time while everyone else watches and listens.

Corporate intercession is not a spectator sport, but a team united for the sole purpose of partnering with our Lord. I use the phrase "going fishing in the Spirit" to describe seeking God's heart for the moment. If there is no clear course, then the leader should encourage everyone to pray in the direction they feel led. When the anointed focus of the hour begins to come together in a tapestry of intercession all those praying will know. There will be that "yes and amen" agreement in the Spirit.

The leader is responsible for giving clear, firm, and loving direction to the group throughout the prayer time. This may include gently interrupting someone who may begin to pray in a misguided way. It is essential that if the group begins to drift from the direction of the Holy Spirit that the leader not be afraid to direct everyone back on track.

Do leaders get it wrong sometimes? Yes. This should be admitted upfront, but there needs to be someone who takes the lead. Leaders and intercessors should always remain teachable and humble. We will all miss it or mess up at times. Give grace and enjoy the process of learning, growing, and journeying together on this prophetic prayer journey. It is important to maintain and keep unity of heart and mind.

2. Pray with the flow of the meeting
The Holy Spirit will begin to flow with certain emphases and moods such as rejoicing, weeping, stillness, and maybe even warfare. It is out of order for anyone to express different emotions—to be weeping and travailing. For example, when

the rest of the group is rejoicing, if you feel that God is genuinely leading you into a different flow, then excuse yourself and quietly find another place to carry this burden.

3. Do not break from prayer in order to have a deliverance session
Keep in mind your purpose is to gather together. It is to pray and stand in the gap. Satan will sometimes try to abort God's purposes by manifesting through someone else in the meeting. If someone does start to disrupt the group have someone assigned to take this individual outside so that the intercession can continue. If further prayer is needed for this person, it is best to make an appointment, other than the appointed time for prayer. People needing deliverance prayer should not be brought to the intercession time.

4. Pray in a positive fashion
This can be accomplished through praying God's Word. Sometimes prayer groups can turn into gossip sessions when everyone's eyes are closed and heads are bowed. In other words, prayers are sometimes used to speak ill of someone or to reveal something that others should not know about a person. This, of course, is never appropriate. Do not air other's dirty laundry. Share only what is necessary.

5. Do not use the prayer time to prophesy over one another
If you feel you are receiving a personal word for someone in the group share it following the meeting. If it would be edifying for the group to hear it then check with the leader before sharing it, and submit to whatever directive they give. Of course, there are times, as the leader, I feel the Lord wants me to speak into and bless the lives of those who have chosen to be faithful in intercession. But this is not to be the main focus of the prayer group and should not occur on a regular basis.

6. Be sensitive to the needs of the group as a whole
There are several ways this can happen. Do not monopolize the group by praying lengthy prayers. Individual prayers should be concise and to the point. Do not pray on a different topic simply because you have a need. Listen to what other intercessors are praying and agree with them. Listen to the volume they are praying in and observe how they position themselves in prayer. If they are praying quietly, do not pray loudly yourself. If they are all sitting in a circle then join them in this circle. Remember it is about the corporate setting and not a setting geared toward individual preferences.

All of the verbal, spiritual, and physical directives should come from the leader. Be sensitive to new people who might be in the group. Will they be offended by what is said? For instance are you being critical or putting down other denominations, churches, ministries, or leaders? This should never be practiced and will cause disunity and hinder the effectiveness of your prayer time.

7. Prefer others more important than yourself
Intercession means "standing in the gap," or standing before the Lord on behalf of others. Be willing to give of yourself for others and prefer them in love. Do not get into spiritual competition. Do not be pushy or aggressive. Guard your heart against jealousy. Pray in agreement.

8. Diligently guard your heart
Check your heart motives in prayer. Do not pray from a critical spirit or a desire for personal vengeance. Are you praying out of a root of bitterness or woundedness? Know and discern why you are praying the prayers you are praying.

9. Do not talk about the leader or the other team members behind their backs

If you have problems with the leader choose an appropriate time and place, separate from the meeting, to talk with him or her. Do not become like Absalom as described in 2 Samuel 15 when he turned the hearts of the men of Israel away from his father David and brought division and strife.

Leaders, listen to the conversations of people who would like to join the group in prayer. If they share too openly about the problems of other ministries, churches, and prayer groups be cautious. Anyone who shares other's problems too freely will more than likely treat your group the same way someday.

10. Do not pray from a place of unbelief or doubt

And He said to them, "Because of the littleness of your faith; for truly I say to you, if you have faith the size of a mustard seed, you will say to this mountain, 'Move from here to there,' and it will move; and nothing will be impossible to you.'" Matthew 17:20

Oligopistos is the Greek word for littleness. It suggests the possessing of little faith or trust. When we pray from a place of little faith or of unbelief and doubt it hinders the effectiveness of our prayers. When we walk in unbelief we are exhibiting the mind-set of unbelievers.

The above reference to a mustard seed points not only to size but also to quality. Just as a tiny seed is planted in the ground grows into a serviceable tree, so faith in God can be cultivated to grow in usefulness. As we have already discussed, time spent in worship, in the Word, and in the presence of the Lord will result in increased faith. When we partner with God, we will see the release of Kingdom power. Expect Him to move when you pray in agreement with Him.

11. Be expectant, full of faith, have fun, and catch the flow of the Holy Spirit
Come expectant that God will meet with you and guide you. Encourage each other to pray out loud voicing your agreement as others intercede. This means that as prayers are voiced we agree with them by saying, "Yes, Lord we agree." Or, "Yes and amen." Trust and release what the Holy Spirit is revealing and expect that God will do more than you can think and imagine. Expect the unexpected.

We are History Makers

The following historic portrayal from *Rees Howells Intercessor* written by Norman Grubb is a powerful example of what united, focused, corporate, faith-filled prayer can achieve.

In one of the battles of World War II the Nazis were attempting to destroy Britain. They had already failed in the battle of Dunkirk, which some attribute to the constant corporate prayer and fasting that occurred at the Bible College Rees Howells had founded, the Bible College of Wales. Obeying specific direction from the Holy Spirit, Rees Howells and others prayed for days believing that they could hold back the invasion through intercession. Their prayers were successful. Later, the Nazis would attempt, yet again, to bomb Britain into submission.

In this next battle involving intercession over the "Battle of Britain," Hermann Goering, Commander-in-Chief of Germany's famed air force, the Luftwaffe, made his great attempt to gain mastery of the air in preparation for the invasion of England.

In each of these vital matters, nothing was left to chance or a "shot-in-the-dark" type of praying. Everything was examined in God's presence. Motives were sifted until the Holy Spirit could show His servants intelligently that there was an undeniable claim for answered prayer. Then faith would stand

CORPORATE INTERCESSION

to the claim and lay hold of the victory; and there would be no rest until they had God's assurance that faith had prevailed and victory was certain. It was not just praying and the hoping for the answer.[2]

The faithful group prayed through the entire battle that surged from September 2, 1940 through September 15, 1940. On September 8, a National Day of Prayer was called. All the while Rees Howells led corporate prayer at his college. The following is the account of the results.

"Mr. Churchill, in his War Memoirs, gives September 15 as 'the culminating date' in that battle of the Air. He tells how he visited the Operations Room of the R.A.F. that day and watched as the enemy squadrons poured over and his own countrymen went up to meet them. The moment came when he finally asked the Air Marshal, 'What other reserves have we?'

"'There are none,' he answered, and reported afterwards how grave Mr. Churchill had looked. 'And well I might,' added the Prime Minister. Then another five minutes passed, and "it appeared that the enemy were going home. The shifting of the discs on the table showed a continuous eastward movement of German bombers and fighters. No new attack appeared. In another ten minutes the action ended." There seemed no reason why the Luftwaffe should have turned for home just at the moment when victory was in their grasp. But we know why.

"After the war, Air Chief Marshal Lord Dowding, Commander-in-Chief of Fighter Command in the Battle of Britain, made his revealing observation: "Even during the battle one realized from day to day how much external support was coming in. At the end of the battle one had the sort of feeling that there had been some special Divide intervention to alter some sequence of events which would otherwise have occurred."[3]

When we engage in effective corporate intercession we, too, become history makers. We can see individuals, churches, cites, governments, nations, businesses, schools, laws, and much more moved into God's glory and kingdom plans.

Identifying Who You Are

Let's discover your intercessory anointing and identity:
Read through the different intercessory anointings and make a list of the ones you operate in the most. It can be more than one.

_____
_____
_____
_____
_____

Think through the corporate prayer times you have been involved in. Have there been some that did not go well?

_____
_____
_____
_____

Share about those corporate times that have been powerful?

_____
_____
_____
_____

Have you released your voice and anointing? Begin to ask the Lord to give you boldness to do so in preparation for the next corporate gathering.

_____
_____
_____

Corporate Intercession

Here are some steps to take between now and the next lesson:
1. Plan a corporate prayer time with those you are studying with.
2. Resolve in your heart not to judge others in their anointing and gifting, but to embrace the diversity that God has given each of us.
3. Come expectant that God will meet you there and supernaturally move.
4. With the direction of the leader, share your intercessory giftings with others in the group.
5. Do not cross over into judgmental thinking of the giftings of others, but rather receive and welcome a diversity of gifts.
6. Pray toward one focus, not several random directions which will prove to be ineffective.
7. Keep your attention on God, the unity of Spirit, and the divinely birthed assignment for that hour.

In order to aid in understanding the spiritual gifts that also function with intercessory anointings, I have included the Spiritual Gifts Glossary: adapted from *Discover Your Spiritual Gifts* by C. Peter Wagner (Regal Books: Ventura, CA. 2002) pp. 91-95.

Administration: The ability to understand clearly the immediate long-rang goals of a particular component of the Body and to formulate and execute effective long range plans for the accomplishments of those goals.

Apostle: The ability to assume and exercise general leadership within God-assigned spheres accompanied by an extraordinary authority in spiritual matters that is spontaneously recognized and appreciated by those within the sphere of influence.

Discerning of Spirits: The ability to know with assurance whether certain behaviors professed to be of God are in reality divine, human or satanic.

Evangelist: The ability to share the gospel with unbelievers in such a way that men and women become disciples of Jesus and members of the Body of Christ.

Exhortation: The ability to minister words of comfort, consolation, encouragement and counsel to others in a way that they feel helped and healed.

Faith: The ability to discern with extraordinary assurance the will and purposes of God for the future of His work.

Giving: The ability to contribute material resources to the work of the Lord with freedom and cheerfulness.

Healing: The ability to serve as human intermediaries through whom it pleases God to cure illness and restore health apart from the use of natural means.

Helps: The ability to invest talents in the life and ministry of other members of the Body, most frequently leaders, enabling the leader to increase the effectiveness of his or her spiritual gifts.

Word of Knowledge: A supernatural word God gives directly that is understood as prophetic knowledge that brings revelation that the person ministering could not have known, that greatly edifies the listeners.

Leadership: The ability to set goals in accordance with God's purpose for the future and to communicate these goals to others in a way that they voluntarily and harmoniously work together to accomplish these goals for the glory of God.

Mercy: The ability to feel genuine empathy and compassion for individuals, who suffer distressing physical, mental or emotional problems and to translate that compassion into cheerfully done deeds that exhibit Christ's love and ease the suffering.
Miracles or Signs and Wonders: The ability to serve as intermediaries through whom it pleases God to perform powerful acts that are perceived by observers to have altered the ordinary course of nature.

Pastor: The ability to assume long-term personal responsibility for the spiritual wellbeing of a group of believers.
Prophecy: The ability to receive and communicate an immediate message of God to His people through a divinely anointed utterance.

Service: The ability to identify the unmet needs involved in a task associated to God's work and to make use of available resources to meet those needs and help accomplish the desired goals.

Teaching: The ability to communicate information significant to the health and ministry of the Body and its members in such a way that others will learn.

Word of Wisdom: The ability to know the mind of the Holy Spirit in such a way to receive insight into how given knowledge may best be applied to specific needs arising in the life of an individual or the Body of Christ.

Worship Leading: The ability to usher a group of believers into the presence of God through music, prayer, dance, waving of flags and other visual forms.

The Power of Prophetic Intercession

Lesson Six: The Power of Prophetic Intercession

In his book, *Praying with Power,* Peter Wagner shares a commanding story of how intercession and hearing God's voice can greatly benefit and supernaturally sway the outcome of events.

Just three weeks before Ed Silvoso arrived for his prayer evangelism seminar, a riot broke out in the Goiania prison. The rebellious inmates took two judges, a chaplain, many guards and others hostage. They set entire cell blocks on fire. After several days of violent confrontation, they threatened to kill the hostages. The situation had reached a crisis. The governor of the state sent in his best troops, but they could not penetrate the prison.

As Silvoso tells it:

"The governor chose better and more powerful weapons. Having heard about the praying ladies, he called them. When the ladies, together with several pastors, showed up at the governor's palace, with tears streaming down his cheeks, he told them, 'My weapons are useless for the emergency I am facing. I need a better weapon and you have it – prayer. Can you take over and bring resolution to this major crisis?'"

The intercessors were not surprised. They had been praying, along with 100,000 others, for the city in the midst of crisis. They practiced two-way prayer and received a clear enough word from the Lord to say to the governor, "Do not worry anymore. Within 24 hours everything will be resolved with no bloodshed!" The governor then turned over his cellular phone, which had a hot line to the army colonel in charge of the government troops, instructing the colonel to take whatever action the ladies indicated, because they were hearing what the Holy Spirit had to say.

The result? Ed Silvoso reports, "Before the 24 hours were over the inmates surrendered, all the hostages were released, the two judges as well as many guards received the Lord, and the ladies were publicly honored by the governor for having resolved an impossible situation. Now the governor's palace is wide open for prayer meetings, and a city of over one million people knows that God cares!"[1]

Dr. Wagner visited Goiania a few months later, and witnessed firsthand how the harmony between pastors and intercessors has opened the spiritual atmosphere over the city for the rapid advance of the Kingdom of God.

Benefits of Intercession

It is hard to read stories like this without thinking, "I want to be involved in this kind of effective prayer. Lord, let this happen in our church and city!" There are many churches and intercessory prayer groups around the world that are functioning and operating in this manner. Many are seeing miraculous answers to prayer as a result of what Peter Wagner terms two-way prayer, the ability to send up the prayer request and hear God's response. In this last lesson, let's investigate further those benefits of prophetic intercession released through individual and corporate prayer.

Standing as Watchman on the Wall

In biblical days a watchman was one who stood on the walls of a city or in the watchtowers to observe whatever approached the city. The Hebrew word for watchman is *sopeh*. It is interpreted "lookout, guard, sentinel, sentry, armor, protection, security, shield, keeper, or turnkey of one's territory." Anything that this individual saw coming near, either honorable or risky, would be announced. Of course it was critical that he warn of arriving peril. He had to remain on the alert for any unfriendly advances against the city, particularly at night. The night watches were most vulnerable to attack.

We are also watchmen in our territories. We must be on alert and recognize what is drawing near in our personal lives, churches, and our territories before it reaches us. I speak of "standing on the wall" as a spiritual metaphor, yet one that is very real. It is a spiritual posture that allows the Holy Spirit to unveil spiritual activity around us.

I was recently leading a prayer meeting. As we were interceding, the Lord revealed to me a vision of the Church. I saw an army filling in rows of perfectly formed lines. The soldiers were dressed in armor and standing at ease. They were simply standing there. They were in line formation, but they were not active and they were not on the alert. It was as though the soldiers in the army were in formation because they recognized they were supposed to be there, but they were passive in their posture and not executing their responsibility.

Suddenly I heard a heavenly command: *Attention!* As the command was issued every soldier in the formation came sharply to attention. The command awoke and energized the army. It appeared to awaken their spirits to become alive and prepared for their orders and assignments. I heard the Lord pronounce, *"It is time to be alert, to come alive from your post of just standing in place and come to attention before the King. It is time to stand in authority, hear and receive your assignments and to advance."*

The Lord has given to each of us the duty to watch, an edict to stand on the wall to see what is approaching, to pronounce it, and then to blow the trumpet. As we stand in a place of prayer, watching on the wall and hearing the voice of the Lord, we can announce and release His directions and commands. We can reveal the presence of the enemy and welcome the presence of the Lord. When we are rightly positioned in our territory or sphere of influence, we can establish a place of habitation for the Lord, and then begin to reach the lost with the Good News of the Gospel.

Gatekeepers for the City

As the watchman stands on the wall and sees who is approaching, he reports to the gatekeeper: *"Then the watchman saw another man running, and he called down to the gatekeeper, 'Look another man is running alone!'"* (2 Samuel 18:26). The gatekeeper is the one who tends and guards the gate. He has the authority to control access through the city walls. If he does not open the gate, then entrance to the city is not allowed. If he opens the gate, entrance is permitted. In Bible days, gatekeepers were Levites, temple officers. They were guardians both of the city and of private homes.

Spiritual leaders in our cities are identifying intercessors, seeking to understand the unique and empowering ministry of intercession, and establishing ministry partnerships with them. The partnership between watchman (intercessors and prophets) and gatekeepers (pastors and leaders) is one of God's strategic moves against the forces of darkness. It is also the key to revival.

In one of Jesus' parables, He described the porter, or gatekeeper, as someone who was also responsible to watch: *"The Son of man is as a man taking a far journey, who left his house, and gave authority to his servants, and to every man his work, and commanded the porter to watch"* (Mark 13:34, KJV). The opening story of Goiania is an example of the watchman and the gatekeeper working together in a city for God's glory to be revealed.

The Power of Prophetic Intercession

Ready to Rumble

Globally, God is bringing the ministries of watchmen and gatekeepers together in a mutually dependent and unified calling. This has resulted in awareness among believers that doing church is a spiritual business that requires spiritual tools. It is no more church or business as usual. We are in a new day and season and it will take spiritual armor and the empowerment of intercession in order to stand.

Eddie Smith shares this truth in his book, *Intercessors: How to Understand and Unleash Them for God's Glory*:

"The army of Christ's spiritual Kingdom is battling against real, spiritual enemies. We can no longer risk flying blind. The stakes are too high!

During the Persian Gulf War, we saw on television the effectiveness of "night vision" infrared technology. Just as the infrared technology allowed soldiers to see in the dark, so will spiritual insight, when developed and properly applied, allow prophetic intercessors to see in the spirit that which lies ahead of us.

Just as God gave prophets to the Old Testament kings, so God has given intercessors to present-day pastors to serve as their ministry partners. Pastors need to employ these prayer warriors effectively in the days ahead to wage war against Satan.

Intercessors can sense dangers on the horizon, but when leadership ignores them, intercessors can become very frustrated. Frustration can produce negativity, which leads them to become part of the problem, not part of the solution."[2]

Pastors and leaders need to realize that intercessors will either war alongside you or without you. Intercessors are prayer warriors born for battle! When there is a battle raging with the enemy's bullets whizzing by, prophetic intercession will be a necessary tool for the victory.

Churches Benefit from Intercession

Many intercessors and praying believers have pastoral gifts and are mercifully moved by the needs of others in the congregation. They are not only passionate about prayer, but also compassionate for the needs of others. Having a culture of prayer and an atmosphere of prophetic intercession within the church will release spiritual support and empowerment for the church and the congregation. This partnership will bring increase, church growth, healing, miracles, salvations, jobs, deliverance, security, and an increased presence of God and His anointing.

Families Benefit from Intercession

The families of those who intercede will benefit greatly from their commitment to pray. Direction is often revealed and provided for each member of the family. And most important God protects us in the process.

Many of us are familiar with the name Corrie Ten Boom because of her exemplary life of faith while in a Nazi prison camp in Holland during World War II. The following is a simple, yet profound, illustration of benefiting from a family member who intercedes.

When she was incarcerated in the prison camp, she caught a severe cold and was distraught because she did not have a handkerchief. She told her sister, Betsie, who was a prisoner with her, that she desperately needed a handkerchief, and said "What can I do?"

Betsie said, *"You can pray!"* When she saw that Corrie's only response was a patronizing smile, Betsie took matters into her own hands and prayed, *"Father, Corrie has a cold and has*

The Power of Prophetic Intercession

not a handkerchief. Will you please give her one? In Jesus' name. Amen."

Soon after this, Corrie heard her name called. At the window was a friend who worked in the prison hospital. She handed Corrie a little package, which Corrie opened and was astounded to find a handkerchief! *"Why did you bring me this?"* Corrie asked her friend.

"How did you know I had a cold?"

"I had no idea," her friend said. *"But while I was folding handkerchiefs in the hospital, a voice in my heart said, 'Take one to Corrie Ten Boom.'"*

Corrie Ten Boom's comment was *"What a miracle! Can you understand what the handkerchief told me at that moment? It told me in heaven there is a loving Father who hears when one of His children on this very small planet asks for an impossible little thing—a handkerchief. And that heavenly Father tells one of His other children to take a handkerchief to Corrie Ten Boom."*[3]

Neighborhoods Benefit from Intercession

Some years ago the Lord blessed our family with a brand new home in a newly established neighborhood. It was a peaceful location with many Christian families; it was also a new field ripe for harvest. Several churches were planting congregations in the vicinity.

One day as we were driving through the neighborhood, Greg and I noticed a sign on the corner lot across from the elementary school. We both assumed it was announcing the building of a new church. Curious to find out, we went closer and read: *"Future Home for the Mormon Church."* This was not the spiritual influence that we desired to see established in our neighborhood.

Your Kingdom Come

Several days later as we passed the corner lot again, I told Greg that someone needed to do something about that Mormon Church before they began to build on the land. With a smile he said, *"You're right! So when are you going to deal with it?"* His challenge surprised me. Even though I did not want a false religion established in our territory, I had not thought about dealing with it myself.

Greg was right. The Lord was calling us to stand on the land and refuse access to that false religion. The following Sunday as our family returned from church, we made a stop at the corner lot. Greg and I stood in front of the sign. I asked him if he wanted to pray. He replied, *"No, you do it. I am here to agree with you as the Lord leads."* What a privilege to be married to a man who blesses and releases the anointing in my life!

So I began to pray. It was not a lengthy prayer as I knew what we were sent there to do.

"Father," I began, *"we thank you for this beautiful neighborhood and all the families you have brought to live here. Father, we thank You for the work You are going to do in their lives. And right now we stand as legal land owners and homeowners in this territory. We stand as ones who have legal spiritual authority in this region. So right now in the name of Jesus we say that no Mormon Church will be built in this neighborhood. We say no to the spirit of lying and error and all antichrist and witchcraft spirits attached to the Mormon Church. You do not have access and you will not gain access into this territory. You are not welcome. We say no in Jesus' name. We speak to the finances that are funding the building of this church to dry up. We say that the required paperwork for this building will not go through and that the bank will not approve the loan. The door is shut to you right now. And, Father, we pray for all those who are involved in this Mormon Church. We agree together that deception will be broken off of*

their minds and hearts, and that salvation will spring forth into their lives. We thank You ahead of time for their salvation. In Jesus' name we pray. Amen!" Before leaving we poured anointing oil around the sign and claimed the land for God's Kingdom. We made this prophetic declaration ten years ago. To this day that Mormon Church has not been built on the property; in fact, the sign was removed within six months of that prayer time.

The Harvest is Cultivated Through Intercession

Ed Silvoso shares the following insight in his book, *That None Should Perish,* "Prayer is the most tangible trace of eternity in the human heart. Intercessory prayer on behalf of the felt needs of the lost is the best way to open their eyes to the light of the gospel." [4]

Anyone acquainted with world evangelism knows that we are seeing record numbers of people coming to Christ. With technology advancing many will benefit from the resulting explosion of knowledge. And there will be even more creative ways of reaching and preaching to the lost world through different modes of communication.

The heartbeat of Jesus is lost souls. As we draw near to Him we are quickly aware that His eyes are filled with compassion for the one who is lost, hungry, poor, and in great need of His touch. Prophetic intercession will carry us on the journey to believe in faith for the great harvest ahead.

Society Benefits from Intercession

In Branson, Missouri, a group of pastors from different denominations began meeting for prayer early in 1996. Initially this was part of a pastors' prayer summit in conjunction with International Renewal Ministries. They proceeded to meet one

Wednesday each month. They began to develop relationships of love, trust, and mutual purpose.

Several years passed. One morning as the pastors gathered, they heard the news that the tragic Columbine High School shooting had just occurred. They agreed that they should go at once to their own local high schools to pray. One of the pastors contacted the principal to explain that the group was coming to pray in the parking lot. The principal's reaction was to invite the clergy to come inside the high school. *"We need your prayers,"* he said. Upon arriving they were welcomed and escorted to the conference room.

Since that day the pastors have been assembling in the conference room of the high school the first Wednesday of every month. Often school administrators join them. This has granted the pastors entrance and favor into other schools in Branson as well. Youth ministers, for example, are received onto school campuses to meet with students and to have lunch with the students.

At one point the school district's superintendent resigned. When the job placement agency explained that it would begin by talking with different focus groups in the community to see what qualities were worthy in a replacement, the school board asked them to meet first with that group of praying pastors. As a result, the ministers' input was instrumental in the search for a new superintendent.

A solid Christian was employed. He assured the students that he expected them to bring their Bibles to school and to study them. He set a righteous standard.

In addition, a Christian businessman has been invited into the city to offer training for all businesses in the area of management and management labor relationships. The training is entitled "Servant Leadership" and is founded on Christian precepts with the Bible as the guide. More than fifty of the Fortune 500 companies apply his counsel. In Branson, at last count, 23 businesses accepted a Servant Leadership model, including the school system and the local hospital. Monthly, a character trait from Scripture such as love, honesty, peace, or integrity becomes the focus for all of these businesses. Employees and students citywide are schooled in the importance of operating in these character traits. In essence the Bible is being taught in 23 businesses. The city is setting a foundation for following Christ.

You Have a Voice

Friends, God has called and empowered each of us to partner with Him. Each of us has an intercessory voice, a role to play in speaking forth His purposes and plans. I would like to end with a story that Dutch Sheets shares about George Mueller and the persevering faith he carried in intercession.

[Mueller said] *"The great point is to never give up until the answer comes. I have been praying for sixty-three years and eight months for one man's conversion. He is not saved yet, but he will be. How can it be otherwise....I am praying?"*

The day came when Mueller's friend received Christ. It did not come until Mueller's casket was lowered into the ground. There, near an open grave, this friend gave his heart to God. Prayers of perseverance had won another battle. Mueller's success may be summarized in four powerful words: He did not quit.[5]

God wants us to hear His voice. And as we stand in the gap through persevering, faith-filled, heaven-inspired, prophetic intercession we liberate people from the powers of darkness through the power of Jesus' name. We can be a part of the powerful prayer army making history in our world today and who will usher in the great awakening and revival we all have longed for. Accept the call, enter in and embark on the incredible spiritual prayer adventure He has ordained.

Your Kingdom Come

Let's pray:
Father, thank You for the journey you have placed us on. What an amazing privilege it is to partner with the Creator of the Universe. Cause us to be anointed in our prayer lives. Take us deeper into Your Spirit and help us to be sensitive to hear Your voice and then to respond. Make us captivated obedient sons and daughters who will walk in agreement with, and proclaim, Your Kingdom blueprints. Father, give us souls, a harvest rich and plenty in souls. Birth strategies to see our families, churches, cities, and nations impacted with revival and transformation. May we not shrink back in this historic time in history, but advance in Your army that is called to attention and in step with You our Leader. We each accept individually that we have a voice. A voice that needs to flow freely and boldly as you lead. We embrace our own anointing and also the gifting of our brothers and sisters in Christ. Father, we accept the call, the call to intercession, the call to prophetic intercession. May we become the house of prayer that we are destined to be. We give You all the glory, all the honor, and all the praise. In Jesus' marvelous name we pray. Amen.

Making an Impact

Now is the time for your intercessory group to seek God in order to find how He would have you make an impact. It is time to discover. Here are some things to think about:

1. What is our corporate prayer assignment that will effect change?
2. Pray as a group and invite Him to reveal new prayer assignments and strategies.
    A. It might be prayerwalking.
    B. Maybe it will be a certain region in your city.

    C. Maybe praying for the neighborhoods that surround the church.
    D. It might be an area downtown where there are the homeless, poor, drug addicted, runaways, and prostitutes.
    E. It might be forming different intercessory groups within the church with prayer focuses such as:
        1. The Church
        2. The Pastor
        3. Families
        4. Government
        5. Nations

3. How your church intercessory group can affect society through your prayers? Ask Him. He will show you.

4. Maybe He will direct your church to coordinate and pray corporately with our churches in your region in order to affect your city.

5. Be obedient to the direction He speaks and be expectant that it will succeed and grow. Do not be discouraged if growth takes time. Once a church or prayer group engages in corporate prayer, the enemy will oppose it. Be committed and persistent in what the Lord is birthing. In time the growth and multiplication will come. When I began my most recent prayer group five years ago, initially only one other person participated. Now, we have grown to a regional prophetic prayer gathering involving pastors, ministry leaders, and intercessors from across our city and beyond. Our prayer time averages 50 to 100 prayer warriors.

Notes

Notes

Lesson One
We "Can" Hear His Voice

1. Terry Tekyl, *Citywide School of Prayer* (College Station, TX: Renewal Ministries, n.d.), 21.
2. Cindy Jacobs, *Hearing the Voice of God: How God Speaks Personally and Corporately to His Children Today* (Ventura, CA: Regal Books, 1995), 39.

Lesson Two
Learning His Voice

1. Chuck Pierce and Rebecca Wagner Sytsema, *When God Speaks: Receiving and Walking in Supernatural Revelation* (Colorado Springs, CO: Wagner Publications, 2003), 15.
2. Jane Hamon, *Dreams and Visions* (Santa Rosa, FL: Christian International Ministries Network, 1997), 104,105.
3. C. Peter Wagner, *Acts of the Holy Spirit: A Modern Commentary on the Book of Acts* (Ventura, CA: Regal Books, 2000), 228,229.

Lesson Three
Prophetic Protocol

1. Norman Grubb, *Rees Howells, Intercessor* (Fort Washington, PA: Christian Literature Crusade), 88.
2. Ibid.
3. Cindy Jacobs, *Hearing the Voice of God: How God Speaks Personally and Corporately to His Children Today* (Ventura, CA: Regal Books, 1995), 145.

Lesson Four
Breakthrough!

1. Barbara Yoder, *Breaker Anointing* (Colorado Springs, CO: Wagner Publications, 2001), 12, 13.
2. Zodhiates, "Lexical Aids to the Old Testament," *Hebrew-Greek Key Study Bible, New American Standard,* p. 1780.
3. Barbara Webtroble, *Prophetic Intercession: Unlock Miracles and Release the Blessing of God* (Ventura, CA: Renew Books, 1999), 78, 79.
4. Zodhiates, "Lexical Aids to the Old Testament,"pp.1723, 1724.
5. Wentroble, *Prophetic Intercession,* 79.
6. Steve Hawthorne and Graham Kendrick, *Prayerwalking* (Orlando, FL: Creation House, 1993), 12.
7. Dutch Sheets, *Intercessory Prayer* (Ventura, CA: Regal Books, 1996), 82, 83.

Lesson Five
Corporate Intercession

1. Alice Smith, *Beyond the Veil: God's Call to Intimate Intercession* (Houston, TX: Spiritruth Publishing Company, 1996), 47.
2. Norman Grubb, *Rees Howells Intercessor* (Fort Washington, PA: Christian Literature Crusade, 1952), 241.
3. Ibid, 245.

Lesson Six
The Power of Prophetic Intercession

1. C. Peter Wagner, *Praying with Power: How to Pray Effectively and Hear Clearly from God* (Shippensburg, PA: Destiny Image Publishers, Inc., 1997), 201,202.

Notes

2. Eddie Smith, *Intercessors: How to Understand and Unleash Them and for God's Glory* (Houston, TX: Spiritruth Publishing Company, 2001), 136,137.
3. The story of Corrie Ten Boom is paraphrased from Quin Sherrer's *Miracles Happen When You Pray* (Grand Rapids, MI: Zondervan, 1997), 23-24.
4. Ed Silvoso, *That None Should Perish* (Ventura, CA: Regal Books, 1994), 57.
5. Dutch Sheets, *Intercessory Prayer* (Ventura, CA: Regal Books, 1997), 197.

Your Kingdom Come

Book 3: Spiritual Warfare

Becca Greenwood

Book 3: Spiritual Warfare

Lesson One: Explanation of Spiritual Warfare Prayer

Marilyn Manson, the popular heavy metal rock star, travels about the globe with his band singing to and exalting the Devil. Each band member is expected to make name changes. The new name has to be one of a renowned actress and the surname one of a noted serial killer. The name *Marilyn Manson*, for example, was prompted by actress Marilyn Monroe and murderer/cult leader Charles Manson.

When this satanic band chose to come to Houston, Texas, the reaction of the church in the city was extraordinary. Numerous churches declared 24-hour prayer watches preceding the concert. They paid for commercial messages on Christian radio stations calling for people to pray. Prayer groups across the city assembled and united. The ungodly effects of the music became the intercessory prayer focus. It is well-known that many youths who have attended concerts by this group returned home to commit suicide. It was astounding how a collective burden for the youth of the city came into focus.

Your Kingdom Come

I sought the Lord and inquired of my intercessory appointment and marching orders concerning the concert. He told me to organize a team and to pray on-the-scene at the theater that was hosting the band's concert. On the day of the concert we departed early in the morning to pray. As we prayed, the Lord began to impart to us a burden to pray for the salvation of Marilyn Manson, all of the members of his band, and the youth in attendance at the concert.

Then the Lord shifted us into warfare prayer. We started to pray that the audio equipment would not work and that the concert would not succeed; that it would fail. We proclaimed that this music devoted to Satan would not be sung over the young of the city. We announced confusion in the enemy's camp and broke every lie that Satan is to be worshiped. I want to clearly state that when we are engaged in warfare prayer we never pray against an individual, but we ask the Lord to reach the hearts of those trapped in darkness and to bring them to redemption. *"For we wrestle not against flesh and blood, but against principalities, against powers, against the rulers of the darkness of this world, against spiritual wickedness in high places"* (Ephesians 6:12, KJV). It was an amazing time of prayer.

The night of the concert was an incredible scene. Many Christians were handing Gospel tracts to the youth and several got saved. An outdoor Christian concert was held across the street with worship to Jesus sung in the direction of the auditorium. The Lord delegated several pastors and intercessors to pray inside the theater.

The concert commenced and during the second song something miraculous took place. One of the fans accidentally spilled his beer on the soundboard. The entire sound system was ruined. The microphones no longer worked, the instruments could not be heard; nor could Mr. Manson. It became impossible for him to proceed. He became so troubled

Explanation of Spiritual Warfare...

he hurled his microphone to the floor, stormed off the stage, and never completed the concert. This was a powerful response to prayer. Within a short time the mayor and city council convened and ordered a city ordinance banning that type of concert in the future.

Those Faithful to Persevere in Prayer

The Lord is looking for faithful people who are willing to persevere in prayer, to faithfully seek Him, to hear His plan for breakthrough, and to execute His plans on the earth. Prayer is behind all great moves of God. It is through prayer that we influence history. Here are a few quotes by great spiritual leaders concerning the value of prayer.

"*Beware in your prayers, above everything else, of limiting God, not only by unbelief, but by fancying that you know what He can do. Expect unexpected things 'above all that we ask or think.*" (Andrew Murray)

"*God does nothing but by prayer, and everything with it.*" (John Wesley)

"*Prayer does not fit us for the greater work; prayer is the greater work.*" (Oswald Chambers)

"*Every great movement of God can be traced to a kneeling figure.*" (D. L. Moody)

And Jesus gave us these transforming words, "*Pray, then, in this way: 'Our Father who is in heaven, hallowed be Your name. Your kingdom come, Your will be done, on earth as it is in heaven. Give us this day our daily bread. And forgive us our debts, as we also have forgiven our debtors. And do not lead us into temptation, but deliver us from evil. For Yours is the kingdom and the power and the glory forever. Amen.'*" (Matthew 6:9-13, NASB) Jesus taught us to pray that God's Kingdom, and the King's agendas and standards were to be established on earth just as they are in heaven. This is not reserved for some future event. It expresses a desire for God to rule in every heart right now so that His will may always be done on earth as it is in heaven. Praying for the presence and manifestation of God's Kingdom includes: walking in God's authority against the works and schemes of Satan, setting the captives free, praying for the sick, reaching the lost, promoting righteousness, walking in the love of the Lord, standing and praying in our regions and territories, and playing a role in transformation. We are to seek the Lord diligently and to pray that His Kingdom will be made known in the earth today. This is where spiritual warfare comes into play.

My journey into spiritual warfare began twenty-one years ago. I was experiencing a hunger and passion to know the Lord more, and a heart to see the lost come to salvation. I received a challenge from our pastor, *"What are God's feelings regarding Satan and how do I feel about Satan?"* He then began to read Scriptures explaining his point. *"The God of peace will soon crush Satan under your feet."* (Romans 16:20) *"God will crush the heads of his enemies."* (Psalm 68:21) *"He will crush the oppressor."* (Psalm 72:4) Responding to this challenge, I prayed that the Lord would cause me to hate Satan and all of his schemes. My intercessory prayer life radically changed from that point on. And since this encounter, I am aware and convinced that God is calling forth a warrior bride to plunder the structures of darkness and to bring forth His kingdom.

Spiritual Warfare Defined

Many of you might be familiar with the term spiritual warfare while others are just now in the process of learning about this

Explanation of Spiritual Warfare...

level of intercession. In order to get us all on the same page, let's begin with a definition. Spiritual warfare is defined as an invisible battle in the spiritual realm involving a power confrontation between God's kingdom and the kingdom of darkness. My experience concurs with the teaching of Peter Wagner in his book *What the Bible Says about Spiritual Warfare,* that spiritual warfare occurs on three levels.

1. Ground-level Spiritual Warfare

This is the practice of a kind of deliverance ministry that involves the breaking of demonic influence in an individual. It occurs on a personal level. Being one who functions as a deliverance minister, I have witnessed incredible breakthroughs in individual's lives through this kind ministry. God is about the business of setting captives set free and His church empowered to walk in victory.

A few years ago I prayed for Frank, a wonderful man of God who has served faithfully in ministry for many years. He had gone through an MRI that showed two blocked arteries to his kidney. One had an 80 percent blockage and the other showed a 40 to 60 percent blockage. He was scheduled for additional tests to confirm the doctor's findings and to determine the steps to take for treatment. Prior to the scheduled day of testing, we prayed over the phone. It was a long-distance deliverance session.

As Frank elaborated on the details of his family history, it became evident that he was wrestling with a generational influence of infirmity with roots established in his ancestors' past involvement in occult and ungodly activities. He confessed and repented on behalf of his ancestors' sinful choices. Then in the name of Jesus we broke the spirit of infirmity and all ties linked to a spirit of witchcraft and to an antichrist spirit. I welcomed the Holy Spirit to fill every empty place with His presence—any and all areas where the house now had been swept clean. Where there had been death, we spoke life. Where there had been illness, we spoke health. We released a submissive spirit to the Lord and called forth all the blessings He has designed for Frank.

The next day, Frank went for the scheduled test. What a faithful God we serve! Frank called, leaving a message of praise concerning the miracle God had performed. I also received the following report by E-mail:

"I just got home from the hospital. I went in to the Cath. lab and they looked for the blockages that the MRI showed my kidney to have an 80 percent blockage on one artery and a 40 to 60 percent blockage on the other. When he injected the dye into my arteries, he checked each side three times and said, 'Well there are no blockages here at all, and you don't have any build up in them either.' Praise the Lord! The curse is gone. These truly are days of freedom. Thank you for your prayers!!"

Discuss a time when you were involved in ground-level spiritual warfare. What was the result of your prayers?

_____
_____
_____
_____
_____

2. Occult-level Spiritual Warfare

This level of warfare involves a more structured level of demonic authority. Warfare prayer at this level focuses on witchcraft, Satanism, Freemasonry, New Age, Eastern religions, and many other forms of spiritual practices. The opening story about Marilyn Manson is a great example of occult-level warfare prayer in action.

Explanation of Spiritual Warfare...

Do you know an individual trapped in occult beliefs and practices?
_____
_____

If so, what was the open door for this lie of darkness to grip this person? _____
_____
_____
_____
_____

Let's stop and pray and ask God to expose the fabrication of deception that has trapped this individual and then enter into warfare intercession for this person's freedom.

Getting the Bigger Picture: Reflect on the city in which you live.
Describe an area or location that is gripped by occult beliefs and activities.
_____
_____
_____
_____

What scheme or lie do you think the enemy used to trap this area in darkness?
_____
_____
_____

Begin to pray and ask God to loose those trapped in darkness, and also seek Him for a prayer strategy to see this area of your city transformed.

3. Strategic-Level Spiritual Warfare

This level of warfare involves focused prayer dealing with high ranking principalities and powers assigned to geographical territories and social networks. These demonic forces are usually referred to as territorial spirits. Let's look at a scriptural example of this type of warfare in action.

Paul and Silas in Philippi

Reported in a Greek legend, the Greek god Apollo killed Python, the wicked earth serpent who resided in the caves of Parnassus in Delphi. He killed Python in revenge for its torment of his mother while she was searching for a location to deliver her twins. Because of his act, Apollo is often referred to as Pythian, predictor or soothsayer of future events.

During Paul's day the inhabitants of Philippi believed that Apollo or Pythian was the influencer of events. The term *python* was used to refer to those through whom the python spirit spoke. In the book of Acts Paul entered into spiritual warfare by casting out this python or fortune telling spirit from a slave girl (see Acts 16:18). The outcome was great turmoil in the city of Philippi. The response and actions that took place as a result of Paul's confrontational deliverance prayer show that the spirit working through this young woman was indeed a territorial spirit. **Let's investigate further.**

Acts 16:19 says that when the owners of the slave girl understood what had occurred they became greatly troubled. It devastated their future opportunity to make money from those seeking information about the future. They captured

Explanation of Spiritual Warfare...

Paul and Silas and brought them before the authorities in the marketplace. In verse 20 the slave owners stated, *"These men are Jews, and are throwing our city into an uproar"*. This accusation is extremely fascinating. Paul addressed a demonic spirit operating through a young slave girl. Next he was charged with throwing a whole city into an uproar. I have prayed deliverance prayers over many individuals, but never has it resulted in a city uproar.

Then we read in verse 22: *"The crowd joined in the attack against Paul and Silas."* Not only was the entire city in tumult, but now a crowd united in an attack against Paul and Silas. Why would casting out a demon from one girl cause a city uproar and a crowd, who knew nothing of the deliverance, to turn against Paul and Silas? The python spirit in operation through this slave girl was a territorial spirit that gripped the city of Philippi. His influence was not just over the slave girl, but over the entire city.

The magistrates ordered Paul and Silas to be beaten, flogged, and thrown into prison. Locked away an inner cell with their feet secured in stocks, Paul and Silas began to pray and worship God. *"Suddenly there was such a violent earthquake that the foundations of the prison were shaken. At once all the prison doors flew open, and everybody's chains came loose."* (Acts 16:26). As a result of casting out this demonic spirit in a slave girl and this unabandoned worship by two of God's men, a fierce earthquake shook the region. Not only were Paul's and Silas's chains loosed, but *everybody's* prison chains were released.

When effective spiritual warfare prayer has been engaged in, signs of what has transpired in the spiritual realm will also manifest in the physical realm; thus, the earthquake. God was shaking the foundational worship of Apollo in Philippi. The outcome of this earthquake was the loosing of *everybody's* chains.

Further indication of effective spiritual warfare prayer is the freeing of the people of a region from the darkness. They are then liberated to experience and to understand the truth and love of God. Note the breakthrough that took place in this spiritual warfare skirmish: The jailer called for lights, rushed in and fell trembling before Paul and Silas. He then brought them out and asked, *"Sirs, what must I do to be saved?"* They replied, *"Believe in the Lord Jesus, and you will be saved—you and your household."* Then they spoke the word of the Lord to him and to all the others in his house. At that hour of the night the jailer took them and washed their wounds; then immediately he and all his family were baptized. The jailer brought Paul and Silas into his house and set a meal before them; he was filled with joy because he had come to believe in God—he and his whole family (Verses 29–34.) The most remarkable demonstration that spiritual breakthrough has been initiated over a region is the salvation of those who have been ensnared in spiritual darkness by a territorial spirit.

Let's recap this spiritual warfare confrontation. Paul cast out a python spirit, also known as a spirit of divination, from a slave girl. The consequential events caused uproar in the city, an enraged crowd, the captivity of Paul and Silas, a violent earthquake that freed everybody's chains, and the salvation of the prison guard and his family. It is evident that the spirit in this slave girl was indeed a territorial spirit that bound this region in darkness.

Gentlemen's Clubs in Houston

Isn't it exciting to learn about spiritual breakthroughs across a region? Now let's bring it to current day issues. The following is a real life example of a breakthrough the Lord brought in the city of Houston.

I was serving as prayer coordinator of the Houston House of Prayer. The church was experiencing tremendous times of corporate prayer and intercession. The Lord began to speak to the pastors and to me about a new prayer assignment for the church. He was leading us to pray over the "Gentlemen's Clubs" in the city. There was a particularly concentrated population of these clubs in the Richmond area of Houston. The Lord then disclosed a prayer strategy. We were to pray onsite at these establishments and break the assignment over this territory that the enemy had established through perversion and whoredom.

Wednesday evening was the regular time for corporate prayer and intercession. For two months this prayer time engaged in a specific direction. I assigned the adults into groups of four to five with a delegated prayer leader. Each individual group was appointed a particular Gentlemen's Club as their prayer focus for that evening. They then drove to those individual establishments. I gave precise direction that we should pray in the parking lots and not go inside the clubs. Praying from inside the car was preferable because this was not the securest neighborhood of Houston.

One Wednesday I was leading a team of women at our assigned location. As we prayed, our faith level rose and we began to ask God to cause conviction to settle on the men who were frequenting that particular club. We prayed and declared that the men would not be able to remain in the club, that they would experience a strong desire to get out. I discovered never to underestimate the power of prayer! While we engaged in intercession, a man drove into the parking lot, got out of his car and entered the club building. We were disappointed but not for long. Within seconds this same individual suddenly exited the club, raced to his car, and speedily drove off.

Soon another man approached the club. Our faith level was definitely higher as we felt assured that our prayers were working. In agreement we prayed that the Lord's conviction would cause this man to be turned toward his family and that he would not be able to enter the club. It was one of those moments that I wish I had taped. As our prayers were voiced we watched this man enter into a visible struggle. He walked to the door and placed his hand on the door handle, but he appeared to be in an intense battle. He visibly trembled as the turmoil of his decision overwhelmed him. Within a short amount of time, he abruptly jerked his hand away from the door, raced to his car, quickly started it, and in an aggressive and speedy manner raced out of the parking lot. Needless to say we rejoiced in this outcome.

Over this two month period, we saw exciting and undeniable answers to prayer unfold in this region of Houston. The Gentlemen Clubs became a hot topic on the evening news. Associations and corrupt practices were uncovered between the Gentlemen's Clubs and city officials. This forced the closing of numerous establishments. New laws were introduced. It became illegal for a man to touch or get within three feet of a dancer. To physically place money in a dancer's costume was prohibited and could lead to tough legal consequences. The clubs were zoned and not permitted to be built near neighborhoods, schools, or churches. This caused business to decrease and the closure of additional clubs.

The most exciting news, though, was the breakthrough for evangelism in Houston. Before we prayed onsite for these establishments, few of the women dancers had been reached with the Gospel and brought to salvation. Following this season of concentrated warfare intercession, they began to respond to the Lord and many received the gift of salvation. This was a powerful response to our prayers.

While some of the Gentlemen's Clubs are still in operation in this city, the evil structure over this area was weakened as a result of warfare prayer. We were obedient to our assignment, and when it is the Lord's timing He will raise up yet another

Explanation of Spiritual Warfare...

group of warriors to break further the darkness in this territory.

Our God is amazingly faithful! Luke 10:19 states, *"I have given you authority to trample on snakes and scorpions and to overcome all the power of the enemy; nothing will harm you."* It is an awe-inspiring thing to see the schemes of the enemy dismantled and God exalted. Likewise, you too can pray and see territories experience transformation. As we move forward, I will share warfare prayer maneuvers that will facilitate and help achieve the goal of spiritual transformation and breakthrough.

What About Your City?

You can be sure that territorial spirits have gripped your city in some way. Who and what do you think these principalities are?
_____
_____
_____
_____
_____

As we move forward in this portion of the curriculum, ask the Lord to speak to you regarding the spiritual dynamics in your neighborhood, city, region, and state. Journal what He shows you.
_____
_____
_____
_____
_____

Your Kingdom Come

Invite the Lord to reveal the prayer assignments that He wants to release to your prayer group. Throughout the next week, journal what He reveals individually and come prepared next week to share the impressions the Lord revealed. He will be faithful to speak and to bring confirmation to the team, and it will be inspiring and exciting to watch as this unfolds within the group!

Revealed Spiritual Warfare Prayer Assignments for the Region.

1. _____
   _____
   _____
   _____

2. _____
   _____
   _____
   _____

3. _____
   _____
   _____
   _____

4. _____
   _____
   _____
   _____

CREATION IS WAITING

LESSON TWO: CREATION IS WAITING

Envision a town where the crime rate is almost zero and all the jails are closed. Think of a farming industry where the produce grown is big and delicious more so than most places on Earth.

This really is happening in a small, humble town by the name of Almolonga, situated in the western mountains of Guatemala. In this remote place, a spiritual awakening led to supernatural breakthrough and transformation. This miraculous transformation has resulted in large blessings for the economy of the region.

Almolonga is a farming community. Most of its 20,000 residents are farmers. What separates Almolonga from the other agricultural villages in Guatemala is the astounding volume of its agricultural yield. Not only is the amount of the crops considerably higher than the norm, it is some of the top quality produce farmed in the western hemisphere. It is now referred to as Americas Vegetable Garden.

On a normal market day, during the eight yearly harvests, large amounts of fresh vegetables are gathered in the town center in order to be exported. There they are loaded onto large tractor-trailers pulled by 40 trucks a day leaving the town.

There is something else that causes this village to be set apart from others. It is something villagers testify about on signs leading into town. It is the declaration that Jesus is Lord of Almolonga. Even some businesses have been named after Scriptures. Friends, this is what has caused the remarkable transformation.

One Almolongan farmer states, *"Definitely it is a blessing directly from God. Before it used to take us 60 days to harvest the radishes, when God moved into town it took 40 days and quite often now takes 25 days. And He also is the one who provides us with the seed. So the only thing we do is follow His instructions, and you can see the results we have."*[1]

Mariano Riscajche, is the pastor of one of the largest churches in town called Calvary Church. He clearly recalls the day that God first captured his attention in 1974. *"I was a real drunk, walking the streets,"* he remembers. *"Then I heard a voice, 'Mariano!' the first time, 'Mariano!' the second time, and the third time, 'Mariano, I've chosen you to come with Me!'"*[2]

Mariano was among the first in a move of powerful salvations that swept through Almolonga. After Mariano was supernaturally delivered from death by town drunks, he and his church began to pray. Churches held prayer vigils on Fridays nights. As a result, the village entered into a season of repentance and holiness which was also accompanied by a period of intense spiritual warfare. Supernatural signs and wonders and healings began to be witnessed by the villagers. Idolatry was dealt with and ancestral worship repented of and renounced. Mariano shares a specific incident, when he felt led to cast a demon out of an alcoholic man.

"And suddenly from that man's throat came a hoarse voice saying 'No! No! This is mine and you cannot take it away from me. I am powerful and all this town is my domain and nobody can come and intrude in here!'" Mariano said.[3]

The demon told the pastor that his name was Maximon. Idols of Maximon have been worshipped for a long time in Guatemala. Candles are burned and hard liquor and cigarettes are sacrificed to his graven image. Historically, Maximon is said to be a combination of Judas Iscariot, Conquistador Pedros Alvarado, and the Mayan demonic deity Ry Laj Man. While on the outside this image appears as a wooden idol, on the spiritual side it once demonically gripped Almolonga as a stronghold and principality of death, violence, drunkenness, poverty and ancestral worship.

Mariano recognized precisely who he was addressing and how to respond. He demanded, *"'Be quiet! The time has come to take authority over you and this town. At this moment, the Spirit of God is over me! "Loose him!"' And instantly the man was free!"* [4]

As a result the town became free! It has been calculated that over 90 percent of the Almolongan population are now born-again Christians. A generation ago, there were only four churches in the town. Now there are 24. The last jail shut its doors in 1988.

Where there was at one time uncontrolled drunkenness, four overflowing jails, and rampant domestic violence, bars have been closed down, or leveled and reconstructed into church buildings. The lot where Calvary Church was constructed was at one time the location of Almolonga's largest saloon.

Reports say that everyplace you look, blessing and prosperity are apparent. Inhabitants who used to pinch centavos to purchase a donkey are at present driving Toyota pickups. And Mercedes Benz trucks marked by God's Word pull the trailers that cart vegetables.

Pastor Harold Cabelleros of El Shaddai Church in Guatemala City says repentance, the gospel, and revival have completely transformed Almolonga.

"The mentality and the way of thinking and the patterns of thinking of the people has changed so drastically, changed from a culture of death, a culture of alcoholism, idolatry, and witchcraft, to a culture today where they think only about expanding the kingdom of God—prosperity, blessing, healing—and everything related to revival." [5]

Mariano says that the miracle of Almolonga should not be unusual at all. *"Just as God did it here, it can happen everywhere in the world,"* Mariano says. *"What the Lord wants* to do, in any place, is to show that, through His power, He can lead people to a better life." [6]

God Created the Earth with a Plan in Mind

"The earth is the LORD'S, and all it contains, the world, and those who dwell in it. For He has founded it upon the seas and established it upon the rivers." Psalm 24:1-2

"In the beginning you laid the foundations of the earth, and the heavens are the work of your hands." Psalm 102:25 (NIV)

"When it goes well with the righteous, the city rejoices, and when the wicked perish, there is joyful shouting. By the blessing of the upright a city is exalted, but by the mouth of the wicked it is torn down."
Proverbs 11:10-11

"Build houses and live in them; plant gardens and eat their produce. Take wives and have sons and daughters; take wives for your sons, and give your daughters in marriage, that they may bear sons and daughters; multiply there, and do not decrease. But seek the welfare of the city where I have sent you into exile, and pray to the LORD on its behalf, for in its welfare you will find your welfare."
    Jeremiah 29:5-7 (ESV)

Isn't the story of Almolonga faith building? Every time I read this historic transformation, a cry rises from my heart, *"Lord, do this in my city!"* This gives us a clear and present account of God the Creator forming the earth with precise intentions in mind. Scripture explains: *"The heavens declare the glory of*

God; the skies proclaim the work of his hands" (Psalm 19:1). The earth and the heavens are a reflection of God's glory, power, and majesty. As the immense expanse and beauty of universe are celebrated, we cannot help but stand in reverence of the Lord our Creator. The earth and heavens were also created in order that God might receive the glory and honor that are due His name. *"Let the sea resound, and everything in it, the world, and all who live in it. Let the rivers clap their hands, let the mountains sing together for joy"* (Psalm 98:7-8). All things birthed through God's Word at Creation, including nature, worship and extol the Lord.

As we have discussed, our God is relational. He is not only our Creator but also our Father. He created the earth so that His designs for humankind can be fulfilled. All men and women are special creations of God made in His image and likeness. No other part of Creation can make this claim.

"Then God said, 'Let Us make man in Our image, according to Our likeness; and let them rule over the fish of the sea and over the birds of the sky and over the cattle and over all the earth, and over every creeping thing that creeps on the earth.' God created man in His own image, in the image of God He created him; male and female He created them."
Genesis 1:26-27

The Hebrew word for *image* is *selem,* meaning that we are the pattern, model, and example of God on earth. The Hebrew word for *likeness* is *demut,* which means something that looks like or resembles something else. This is the only passage in God's Word in which both words are coupled together. The Lord was communicating an important message. He was stating that we are the likeness image of God. Not only are we representatives, but we are also representational. We as humankind are the spokesperson, couriers, diplomats, agents, commissioners, managers, stewards, and ambassadors of God's Kingdom on earth. In the book of Revelation, John identifies the promise for all believers at the closing of history: *"He will dwell among them, and they shall be His people, and God Himself will be among them."* (Revelation 21:3).

God founded the earth and put the nations in place. He instituted an inheritance and boundary for all humankind. He is, consequently, attentive to the cities in which we live, as was so beautifully shared and evidenced in the transformation of Almolonga. The Bible assures us that all of this is true, but throughout the earth it seems that Satan has all-out authority and rule over people and the land (See 1 John 5:19). If God is indeed invested in the land, then why are so many people and lands living in darkness?

Adam Relinquished His Birth Right

When Adam and Eve surrendered their territory to Satan, Creation became enslaved to corruption. They led Creation into the bondage of sin, corruption, and decay when through their sinful act evil was invited to be at home in the world. Likewise, when we adopt sinful actions and rebellion we affect the region to which we have been called. Among the results of our ungodly and wicked choices is a further curse and defilement of land: *"The earth dries up and withers, the world languishes and withers. . . . The earth is defiled by its people; they have disobeyed the laws, violated the statutes and broken the everlasting covenant. Therefore a curse consumes the earth"* (Isaiah 24:4-6).

Let's look at the directive that God afforded man concerning his relationship to Creation: God spoke: *"'Let us make human beings in our image, make them reflecting our nature so they can be responsible for the fish in the sea, the birds in the air, the cattle, and, yes, Earth itself, and every animal that moves on the face of Earth.' God created human beings; he created them godlike, reflecting God's nature. He created them male and female. God blessed them: 'Prosper! Reproduce! Fill Earth! Take charge! Be responsible for fish in the sea and birds in the air, for every living thing that moves on the face of Earth.'"* (Genesis 1:26-28, The MESSAGE)

It is evident that this authorization has been, for the most part, unsuccessful. Rather than taking dependable care of the earth as trustworthy stewards, ruling the earth with wisdom from God, we remain in sin that results in defilement of the land. In reality, much of mankind worships the Creation rather than managing it. The concept of "Mother Earth" as an entity to be revered or called upon for counsel is one more in a lengthy list of trespasses against our Lord.

The reality is that at this point in history we have seen that two cataclysmic occurrences have affected the rule that was humankind's birthright in the beginning: 1) Adam sinned and the earth became the target of corruption. But, 2) then Jesus conquered sin and death at the Cross. As we begin to spiritually discern our cities and regions, where does this leave us now in relation to the created world and our role in spiritual warfare intercession?

Jesus Set Creation Free

Jesus was the first man to walk the earth since Adam in total rule over Creation. The Bible says that the seas became calm at His word and that the fig tree withered at His rebuke. Not only did He rule, reign, and display stewardship during His ministry, but even in His death Creation bowed to the true King. The book of Matthew explains the scene of the power encounter that occurred at Jesus' triumphant sacrifice.

"And Jesus cried again with a loud voice and gave up His spirit. And at once the curtain of the sanctuary of the temple

was torn in two from top to bottom; the earth shook and the rocks were split. The tombs were opened and many bodies of the saints who had fallen asleep in death were raised [to life]; and coming out of the tombs after His resurrection, they went into the holy city and appeared to many people. When the centurion and those who were with him keeping watch over Jesus observed the earthquake and all that was happening, they were terribly frightened and filled with awe, and said, 'Truly this was God's Son!'"
(Matthew 27:50-54, AMPLIFIED)

Creation reacted to the establishment of the government of God and the beginning of the overthrow of Satan's evil rule.

When Jesus voluntarily and obediently gave up His Spirit, He cried out in a loud voice. This was a sign of One who was still functioning in strength. Typically those who are close to dying seem to find it challenging to speak, especially as they release their final breaths. Jesus, however, did not relinquish His Spirit in a feeble manner. He exclaimed with a loud voice—perhaps as a declaration not just to those who were seeing His death, but also to the spiritual realm of Satan and his demonic army. He proclaimed that He had successfully accomplished the mission of redeeming mankind and Creation through His Cross.

Salvation for All

The specific time of day and year that Jesus yielded up His Spirit occurred at the same time of the yearly sacrifice of the Passover lamb, as the priests made atonement for the sins of the Jews. At that instant, Jesus became the supreme sacrifice making atonement for the sins of all mankind. The veil in the Temple was torn in two from top to bottom, establishing a new path for all people, Jew and Gentile, male or female, free man and slave in order to enter into the Lord's presence through a personal relationship with Jesus. Animal sacrifices were no longer required because Jesus' was the everlasting sacrifice given once for all.

The Earth Shook and the Rocks Split

Scripture also explains that the earth shook and the rocks split. This term for *earth* means "the entire earth, all of the land." This was not confined to Golgotha or even Jerusalem. The whole Creation shook. Obviously, this was an intense reaction in response to the blood of our Savior when spilled on the land.

Genesis 4:10 tells us that when Cain killed Abel, the blood of Abel cried out to the Lord from the ground. When the innocent are killed the blood shed on the land calls out for justice. Able's blood was the first case of blood corrupting the land. Throughout the Bible we read that death, violence, idolatry, adultery, sexual immorality, and broken covenants, among other sins, also defile the land and Creation. In Lesson Three, I will explain in depth, the open doors that contribute to pollution of the land, and throughout the rest of this study how to strategically cleanse the land and break the dark powers at these entry points.

On a personal level, we realize that the blood of Jesus cleanses, heals, protects, liberates, forgives, releases, and breaks the power of death and Satan. It is through the shedding of His blood, His death on the Cross, and His resurrection that we are redeemed. But the Lord came not only to deliver us and overcome the schemes of Satan in our lives, He also came to reclaim, restore, and reestablish His reign in earth. As His blood dripped upon the earth and He gave up His Spirit, His blood not only redeemed, healed, delivered, and transformed us; it also did the same for the physical Creation. It is now our Lord's blood that cries out from the land for the souls of man and all of Creation. We are now

His representatives, those who appropriate Jesus' blood in order to partner with Him in seeing regions restored.

The Greek word for shook is *seio*. It is translated "to shake, tremble, quake, move in the earth, or cause a cosmic disturbance." This word is ordinarily used in the context of God's wrath and judgment. In the scene of the crucifixion we might think of the earthquake as a demonstration of God's judgment against those who killed Jesus—and that would be accurate. But there is an additional meaning. *Seio* also refers to "an emotional disturbance through fear, the stirring up or agitation of a crowd, and the upsetting of governmental affairs." The whole earth shook as our Savior died. In this quaking was the tearing down, stripping, disarming of satanic government over Creation, and the reestablishment of the government of God's Kingdom.

The Greek word used for split is *schizo*. It is translated "to break, chop, cleave, divide, open, rend, separate, split, and tear." The rocks split in response to the earthquake, but they also split in response to the tearing down of the authority Satan had established in the Garden. The Old Covenant was fulfilled and the New Covenant in Jesus, as the Rock of revelation upon which the Church stands, was established. When a power confrontation in the spiritual realm takes place and defilement is broken off the land, Satan and his army lose their hold and the land and the rest of Creation responds.

Creation Plays the Music of What We have Composed on Earth

Creation was meant to exalt God and for mankind to steward it. As a consequence of Adam's sin and also humankind's sin throughout history, our world has been subjected to captivity. The very environment in which we were created to rule has entered deterioration because of our disobedience. Creation cannot freely glorify God in its current condition of oppression. It is, therefore, ready and waiting with eager expectation for the sons of God to assume their rightful places. In other words, the land is looking to be liberated from bondage and to be restored unto fruitful and peaceful conditions.

Paul explains our relationship with Creation and our role in seeing it freed in Romans 8:18-25: *"[But what of that?] For I consider that the sufferings of this present time (this present life) are not worth being compared with the glory that is about to be revealed to us and in us and for us and conferred on us! For [even the whole] creation (all nature) waits expectantly and longs earnestly for God's sons to be made known [waits for the revealing, the disclosing of their sonship]. For the creation (nature) was subjected to frailty (to futility, condemned to frustration), not because of some intentional fault on its part, but by the will of Him Who so subjected it-[yet] with the hope that nature (creation) itself will be set free from its bondage to decay and corruption [and gain an entrance] into the glorious freedom of God's children. We know that the whole creation [of irrational creatures] has been moaning together in the pains of labor until now. And not only the creation, but we ourselves too, who have and enjoy the first fruits of the [Holy] Spirit [a foretaste of the blissful things to come] groan inwardly as we wait for the redemption of our bodies [from sensuality and the grave, which will reveal] our adoption (our manifestation as God's sons)."* AMPLIFIED BIBLE

The verses given above follow Paul's declaration, given in Romans 8:17, that we are heirs of God and co-heirs of Christ. Paul states that, as heirs, the sufferings experienced in this present time are not worthy to be compared to the glory that will be made known in us, through us, and given to us. We are recipients of a promising and glorious inheritance. We will rule and reign with Jesus throughout our lives and into eternity.

It is difficult to grasp the thought that an awesome, powerful, and sovereign God has chosen us imperfect beings to partner with Him in this extraordinary responsibility. But He has decided to do just that. We were created for a purpose with areas of responsibility. This is why it essential for us to comprehend the idea that all good things come from our Father, and that all good things He has given us are gifts. We have done nothing ourselves or from our own strength.

Also in the above verses Paul mentions the redemption as the means of "uncovering" in the sense of informing through revelation or disclosing what was not known. In Hebrew this uncovering denotes nakedness or uncovering of all that can be disclosed or revealed. We are not to view salvation as a promise solely for the future, but one that is playing a role right now in the timing of the establishment of the new heaven and the new earth. Peter said: *"You ought to live holy and godly lives as you look forward to the day of God and speed its coming"* (2 Peter 3:11-12).

God wants to raise our bodies and our spiritual position right now and not just in the future. Through the direction of the Holy Spirit we can be, and should be, a surefooted, humble, victorious, and expectant Body of Believers who stand on earth for the Lord. We are to spread the news that God's Kingdom has come, reach the lost for Christ, discipline the nations of the world, and engage in effective intercession in order to bring breakthrough and transformation. We should not see these verses as an escape clause from responsibility now simply because of the future redemption.

Creation is eagerly waiting in earnest expectation and moaning in pains of labor concerning its release from bondage. The phrase *earnest expectation* is derived from the Greek word *apokaradokia*. This word actually incorporates three Greek words: *apo* is interpreted as "away"; *kara* means "the head"; and *dokiem* means "to watch." Combined together the words depict watching with the head erect and outstretched. They suggest waiting in suspense, like a watchman awaiting a beacon or signal to announce a victory in battle.

The Greek word for moaning is *sustenazo*. The word for pains of labor is *sunodino*. The two words joined together signify that the whole Creation is united in travail for deliverance from its burden and oppression. The whole world of nature sighs for relief from the suffering of the ages, convulsing in birth pangs and expecting deliverance. It is not the cry of torment as in the throes of death, but rather that of birth. Just as a woman in labor has the promise of birthing her child, so Creation also waits in hope and expectancy.

The word *creation* here refers to all of God's creation including that which is below human level that also has been enslaved in corruption. It, too, is called to experience the blessing of freedom and redemption. The good news is humankind, you and me, are the first fruits of the changes and blessings that the Spirit has produced in the lives of those saved through Jesus. As first fruits, therefore, we can influence this earth. Kenneth S. Wuest in his *Word Studies from the Greek New Testament* (Eerdmans, 1997) notes that: *"Creation is not inert, utterly unspiritual, alien to our life and its hope. What rises from it is the music of humanity."*

What an insightful statement! Creation plays the music we have composed in this earth realm. What we direct, Creation plays as a well-rehearsed orchestra under the guidance of a famed Conductor. If Creation can resound with melody in the midst of slavery and corruption ascribed by man's sinful stewardship, then it can also play a newly composed song of freedom and fruitfulness when we take our rightful posts as intercessors.

Strategic Spiritual Warfare

This leads us to the role that strategic warfare intercession plays in regions that need to be impacted and transformed. While engaging in intercession at this level is not the only answer to see regions completely restored, it is a key component that we must not and cannot ignore.

In the story of Almolonga, there was a period where the believers of the town engaged in intense spiritual warfare in order to see a complete supernatural breakthrough. They knew who their enemy was and how they must pray to defeat him. As we advance into the next lesson, we will explore how Satan takes what is not his.

In discerning the territory you have been assigned, let's begin to reflect further on your city and identify areas that are under defilement. In other words, evident areas void of the Lord's blessing.

Make of list of those regions where it is evident there is defilement on the land.

_____
_____
_____
_____
_____
_____
_____

Creation is Waiting

Are there regions steeped in poverty? If so, list them.
1. _____
_____
_____

2. _____
_____
_____

3. _____
_____
_____

Are there regions steeped in witchcraft?
1. _____
_____
_____

2. _____
_____
_____

3. _____
_____
_____

Are there regions steeped in perversion, prostitution, and/or homosexuality?
1. _____
_____
_____

2. _____
_____
_____

3. _____
_____
_____

Your Kingdom Come

What about areas of death or high crime rates?

1. _____
_____

2. _____
_____

3. _____
_____

Discover and list the locations of abortion clinics or Planned Parenthood clinics in your city.

1. _____
_____

2. _____
_____

3. _____
_____

Satan the Unlawful Tenant

Lesson Three: Satan the Unlawful Tenant

When we began researching for the Russia prayer assignment the Lord directed us to pray in Novgorod, Russia and Kiev, Ukraine; the two oldest cities in Russian history. The earliest peoples of Russia were steeped in pagan and occult practices. They worshipped Volos, Perun, Mokosha, Svarog, Divanna, Kupala, Sophia, Zeus, and other gods and goddesses. Tribal groups regularly performed human blood sacrifices. Children were kidnapped from other tribes and brutally sacrificed to the gods.

The oldest tribal group the Lord brought to our attention was the Trypillian culture. Their whole existence was intertwined with the worship of the "Great Moist Mother Earth," also worshipped under the name Divanna, better known as Diana. The Dnieper, the Don, and the Danube are all Rivers in the Ukraine and in Russia and are named after this goddess. In the Ukraine, she was worshipped on the Devich Mount. During September, a priestess and nine maidens would climb the mount and perform rituals and blood sacrifices to Divanna. It is interesting that our team consisted of nine members which God used as a prophetic sign.

Through research, we discovered a new age occult group under a man named, Oles Berdnyk of the Ukrainian Spiritual Republic. They were worshipping on this mount and attempting to reinstate the worship of this goddess. They were petitioning individuals of Slavic decent to come and find the spiritual enlightenment of their ancestors under the worship of the "Great Moist Mother Earth" - Divanna.

In the 9th century, these tribal people stated there was no rule in their land and asked the Viking, Rurik to lead. He accepted. He is an ancestor of Vladimir, the famous ruler known for "Christianizing" Russia through forced baptism. The Vikings worshipped all of the gods in this land and brought their own. Vladimir worshipped these and participated in sacrificing humans.

In 988 A.D. he accepted baptism into the Orthodox Church for political gain. He married a Byzantine Princess under an agreement with the royal family that he would be baptized. After his marriage, Vladimir demanded all to be baptized. If anyone refused, he burned their homes and all their possessions. If this did not convince them to convert, he killed them. In Novgorod, the Volga River was full of dead bodies. While there, we prayed and poured anointing oil into the Volga asking God to purify the water of bloodshed, defilement, and death.

Vladimir replaced the pagan idols with names of biblical prophets and revered saints. For instance, Perun became Elijah. The Russians formed their own religion, resulting in the Russian Orthodox Church. It was evident that spirits of death, witchcraft, fear, and antichrist had gripped the lands and the inhabitants.

In Kiev, we met our contact, Glen, and mapped out locations to pray. I explained we had to find the area of the Trypillian culture, and also the Devich Mount because the Lord revealed this to be a key location. Glen said he would attempt to locate it.

The following day we prayed throughout Kiev. Later, Glen met Greg and I and excitedly asked, "What have you been doing?" We responded, "Praying." He explained he was having difficulty in discovering the location of the Devich Mount and so he asked God to help him. Vlad, a graduate student from the Bible College Glen had founded came to him. He shared he had read Peter Wagner's book on spiritual warfare prayer and needed someone to help him engage in this form of intercession. He said he lives and ministers in a spiritually difficult region called Trepolie. Glen stopped him, "Vlad, say the name of the region again." He answered, "Trepolie." This is the Russian word for Trypillian. Vlad explained he had written his research paper on the area's ancient culture and pagan practices. Glen said there was a group in Kiev from Global Harvest Ministries under Peter Wagner looking for this location. Vlad knew all of the locations in which we wanted to pray and would take us there.

I felt the Lord directing us to pray in all small villages of the Devich Mount region. At the end of the day, we would climb the mount to pray. We made our way to a town called Vytachiv; which the Ukrainian Spiritual Republic named "the road to enlightenment."

Driving to the edge of a village, we came upon a windmill, a small wooden temple, and three cornerstones. Many of us headed for the cornerstones placed there to dedicate this land to the Great Moist Mother Earth. Greg and two other team members went to the wooden temple. It was locked. Jonathan, another team member, investigated the windmill, which had the Queen of Heaven stationed at the entrance. This village and temple are situated on the Dnieper River, named and dedicated to the Queen of Heaven.

The mayor of the city drove up. He had the key to the temple and windmill and gladly let us in. He even gave us total privacy. Did we pray! Inside the temple were items dedicated to the worship of the Queen of Heaven and to Kupala. On the wall was a friendship/spiritual covenant between this occult group and the village. It was sealed with an image of the Queen of Heaven. The covenant was signed in 1992; the same year Glen began his work with St. James Bible College.

I felt the spirit of prophecy and shared with Glen: *"The date on this covenant was a prophetic statement about their call to Kiev. The enemy was establishing the counterfeit at the same time the Lord was establishing His work for future generations of Ukraine. God was revealing to Glen this day the schemes of the enemy so that he and his leaders could do effective targeted spiritual warfare prayer to prevent future generations from being gripped by darkness, but brought into Kingdom purposes for their lives and the nation."*

We engaged in spiritual warfare prayer and broke the power of the Queen of Heaven. Glen broke this covenant and pronounced the move of the Holy Spirit. We anointed the seal and all the icons with oil and broke their power. Proclamations were spoken so that the true and living God would be worshipped.

To our surprise, the windmill was the private temple of Berdnyk. God made a way through the mayor to pray inside this hidden sanctuary. In it he had pictures of three temples he planned to build. It had portraits of Buddha and the Queen of Heaven. There was a file cabinet containing all the books he had written about the Queen of Heaven and his new age occult beliefs. On one of the walls was his vision statement. It spoke of walking in peace as a child and walking as a warrior. I felt a very strong warning. If this group was not dealt with, it could become a very dangerous cult causing bloodshed. We broke its power and asked God to lead these people to salvation.

We made our way to the five villages and prayed at each town center. Vlad shared about an Orthodox Priest in this region who carried great power, but was addicted to drugs. Vlad gathered pastors to the region to fast, pray, and evangelize. People got saved. Before this, the priest often came and frighten the people. He convinced them they were in a cult and bound for hell. He took their money saying the more they paid the more weight his prayers would carry to "help secure their place in heaven again." He then purchased drugs. Because of fear, the people refused to attend evangelistic teachings. We prayed, broke his territorial control, and interceded for his salvation.

Our focus then shifted to the first woman saved and delivered. She and her husband lead prayer meetings in an attempt to reach villagers. Vlad and Glen took us to their home where we prayed and asked God to bless this couple and their work. We ended our time with them by sowing a financial blessing into the work God was birthing through this precious man and woman.

It was then time to climb old Devich Mount. It is a huge burial mound of all the ancient people involved with the worship to Great Mother earth, and of those sacrificed to her. Two Christian women from the village below came to speak with us and asked, *"Are you Christians?"* We said *"yes."* They showed us the location where the Republic recently buried a time capsule and where they had drawn a six pointed star like the Star of David on the ground to show the burial site. The double triangle means diverse things in different cultures; the most interesting is the attachment to Vladimir. Before the forced baptisms, Vladimir had a sanctuary to the gods Perun, Dazhbog, Chors, Simargl, Stribog, and the goddess Mokosha. On the outside, he positioned these gods and goddesses like the star; drawn here by this new age occult group as a sign representing the connection of the worship of the Queen of Heaven to past, present, and future generations.

We repented on behalf of the people and practices. We broke the power of the antichrist spirit, the spirit of death, fear, witchcraft, control, and perversion. We read Scripture and worshipped the Lord. Glen, Vlad, Yana, and Eugene sang the Ukrainian communion song about the blood of Jesus. We laid hands on all four of these Ukrainians and asked God to bless their work and to further the Gospel and His purposes in Kiev through them. The group broke out in praise and thanked the Lord for His goodness and decreed Kiev to awake and arise. Outward to the North, South, East, and West, we proclaimed a loud united prophetic declaration of freedom. Nine keys with oil were planted with mustard seeds right next to the time capsule. Glen and Vlad returned that weekend to bury two Bibles written in Russian and Ukrainian.

The ultimate praise report is in this Devich Mount region. There are now nine thriving churches. Villagers are being impacted by the gospel as they receive salvation. God is moving in powerful ways. Friends, spiritual warfare can and does bring tremendous spiritual breakthrough and transformation.

Illegal Possession of a Territory

God established the earth and set all the nations and the people in their proper and divine place. But from the beginning of time Satan has set himself against the Lord and His plans. Satan, through his evil power, will use deception, division, accusation, and lies to draw us into his evil web. He is intentionally aggressive in order to gain more authority. And far too many times, we, the human race, have fallen for and played into his schemes of deception; giving him even more authority to execute his diabolical strategies. Satan has power to wield his weapons of deception, but he carries no direct authority over the earth or people unless we give it to him. This leads us to the following question. What are the enemy's schemes in gaining authority over the land?

In his ambition to seize and place regions and territories in darkness, Satan often possesses a land illegally. I say illegally because God gave this planet to Adam and not to Satan. Satan usurped God's original intended plan when Adam fell. Satan then defiles the land by keeping all those within a certain territory under his deceptions and lies.

"So it will be that when the Lord has completed all His work on Mount Zion and on Jerusalem, He will say, 'I will punish the fruit of the arrogant heart of the king of Assyria and the pomp of his haughtiness.' [13] For he has said, 'By the power of my hand and by my wisdom I did this, For I have understanding; And I removed the boundaries of the peoples And plundered their treasures, And like a mighty man I brought down their inhabitants'" (Isaiah 10:12–13).

But how does the land become defiled? As we studied in Lesson Two, we understand God empowered the earth's new caretakers, Adam and Eve, with understanding, inventive abilities, and an inborn talent for leadership in order to rule and reign. Our Father is always about the business of His Kingdom, and created humankind with the same calling and purpose. It was a natural outcome, therefore, that man be afforded the duty to steward or manage Creation. This included the land and all living creatures upon it.

After sin entered in, man started to struggle with the land. The enemy eventually gained access and man began to conform to unholy desires and practices. This successively opened the door for the enemy. And with the assistance of man, Satan gained control over the Lord's resources.

Satan's Strategies of Defilement

The Bible assures us that we are not to remain ignorant of the wiles of Satan, *"...in order that Satan might not outwit us. For we are not unaware of his schemes"* (2 Corinthians 2:11). If he can hinder God's intentions for the land and its inhabitants, he can keep mankind in bondage to darkness and in broken relationships with the Father. It is vitally important to Satan's unrelenting campaigns and strategies to dominate the territories of the earth. I believe the following illustrations portray chief tactics utilized by Satan in defiling land.

Shedding of Blood

The Lord spoke these words to the prophet Jeremiah: *"Then go out to the valley of Ben-hinnom, which is by the entrance of the potsherd gate, and proclaim there the words that I tell you, and say, 'Hear the word of the LORD, O kings of Judah and inhabitants of Jerusalem: thus says the LORD of hosts, the God of Israel, "Behold I am about to bring a calamity upon this place, at which the ears of everyone that hears of it will tingle. Because they have forsaken Me and have made this an alien place and have burned sacrifices in it to other gods, that neither they nor their forefathers nor the kings of Judah had ever known, and because they have filled this place with the blood of the innocent and have built the high places of Baal to burn their sons in the fire as burnt offerings to Baal, a thing which I never commanded or spoke of, nor did it ever enter My mind"'"* (Jeremiah 19:2–5).

The shedding of blood contaminates the land, especially when the bloodshed involves the worship of demon gods and goddesses. When the blood of the guiltless is cast on the land for wicked purposes, Satan then takes the bloodstained land as his possession. In a region where this manifestation of demon worship is perpetuated, strong spirits of death, fear, antichrist, and many times witchcraft will have a firm hold.

In the Old Testament Molech was the pagan god worshiped by the Ammonites. The sacrifice of children was a requirement for his followers (see Leviticus 20:1–5). Lilith is another demonic entity we can identify in Scripture and who was also revered in Jewish mysticism (see Isaiah 34:11). *Lilit* is the Hebrew word for "screeching owl" or "night monster." This was a demonic spirit who was believed in Jewish tradition to harm or kill children in the night hours while they slept. Many of us involved in spiritual warfare prayer and spiritual mapping believe that these are the demonic principalities responsible for abortion. Through the bloodshed of innocent babies, Satan claims territories. We learn more about this deity in Lesson Six. Satan and his cohorts also claim land in which wars, traumas, shootings, and murders have occurred. By causing bloodshed through ungodly sinful practices, the blood spilled by man's hands defiles the land and many times will release a stronghold of death, fear, and manipulation in the exact regions where the violence and death occurred.

Applying it to Your City:

In Lesson Two we listed locations of abortion clinics. Are there historical sites where battles were fought in your region? If so, list them:

1. _____
_____
_____

2. _____
_____
_____

3. _____
_____
_____

Were there any Indian massacres in the history of your region?

1. _____
_____
_____

2. _____
_____
_____

3. _____
_____
_____

Was there a history of slavery and physical beatings and/or deaths of those slaves?

1. _____
_____
_____

2. _____
_____
_____

3. _____
_____
_____

Sexual Immorality

Leviticus 18:1–23 defines unlawful sexual relations. Verses 24–25 explain the results of sexual immorality:

"Do not defile yourselves by any of these things; for by all these the nations which I am casting out before you have become defiled. For the land has become defiled, therefore I have brought its punishment upon it, so the land has spewed out its inhabitants."

Remember the story of the Gentlemen's Clubs in Lesson One? Consistent, ungodly sexual practices in a region establish a stronghold of perversion and whoredom. In idolatrous worship the disciples are frequently required to commit adultery, fornication, and prostitution. And when adultery, fornication, and prostitution are propagated in an area, the enemy has gained control and the land is cursed. As shown in the following Scriptures in which God is speaking through the prophets, the result is the reduction of territory for those involved.

"'If a man divorces his wife and she leaves him and marries another man, should he return to her again? Would not the land be completely defiled? But you have lived as a prostitute

with many lovers—would you now return to me?' declares the LORD. Look up to the barren heights and see. Is there any place where you have not been ravished? By the roadside you sat waiting for lovers, sat like a nomad in the desert. You have defiled the land with your prostitution and wickedness. . . . Because Israel's immorality mattered so little to her, she defiled the land and committed adultery with stone and wood" (Jeremiah 3:1–2, 9 NIV)

"You built yourself a high place at the top of every street and made your beauty abominable, and you spread your legs to every passer-by to multiply your harlotry. You also played the harlot with the Egyptians, your lustful neighbors, and multiplied your harlotry to make Me angry. Behold now, I have stretched out My hand against you and diminished your rations. And I delivered you up to the desire of those who hate you, the daughters of the Philistines, who are ashamed of your lewd conduct" (Ezekiel 16: 24–27).

Broken Covenants

Covenant is defined as a binding and solemn agreement made by two or more individuals.[2] Throughout the Bible we see that the Lord established many covenants with His people. These comprised not only binding contracts to preserve the children of Israel for the purposes of the Lord, they were also a means of protection. Anytime a covenant is made with God, Satan will seek to destroy the pact. He does this primarily through deceit. Once deceived, man then opens the door to defilement by listening to lies and by rebelling against the Lord.

"The earth mourns and withers, the world fades and withers, the exalted of the people of the earth fade away. The earth is also polluted by its inhabitants, for they transgressed laws, violated statutes, broke the everlasting covenant.

Your Kingdom Come

Therefore, a curse devours the earth" (Isaiah 24:4-6).

Recognizing the History of Your Region

Were the broken covenants in your area between the white men and Native Americans? If so, how many and what years did they occur?

_____
_____
_____
_____
_____

Has there been repentance for these broken covenants? If not ask the Lord to begin to orchestrate divine connections and relationships in order for repentance to occur.

If the above question applies to your region begin to seek the Lord concerning restitution. The Lord might have you give a gift of restitution as a prophetic act of healing to those Host Nations people of our land.

Did broken covenants occur between some of the founding fathers of the region or even early governmental leaders? (Basically you want to discover if this is an issue because until it is dealt with it will continue to have a hold on the region and might be effecting and causing division and disunity, even among Christian churches and believers.)

_____
_____
_____
_____
_____

The Problem of Not Asking God for Wisdom

Throughout Scripture we are instructed to seek the Lord and abide by His ways so that the outcome will be blessing, supply, favor, protection, etc. Leaders and believers who choose not to follow God, His law's, statutes, and His wisdom are in reality rebelling against Him. This in turn leads the Lord to lift His hand of blessing and protection. These people have permitted their territory to be corrupted by Satan. Actually, every time we as believers come into a region and begin to build our own kingdom agenda without asking the Lord for His plan, we are in turn not blessing the land. We must know and hear His divine plan in all that He has called us to do.

"I brought you into the fruitful land to eat its fruit and its good things. But you came and defiled my land, and My inheritance you made an abomination. 'The priests did not say, "Where is the LORD?" And those who handle the law did not know Me; The rulers also transgressed against Me, and the prophets prophesied by Baal And walked after things that did not profit'" (Jeremiah 2: 7-8).

Idolatry

I purposefully saved this point for last. You have probably noticed that in many of the Scripture references included in this lesson that idolatry is mentioned numerous times. Idolatrous worship is the main focus behind the shedding of blood, sexual immorality, changing God's laws, and not asking God for wisdom. The Lord detests idol worship. This is clearly expressed in the First and Second commandments.

"You shall have no other gods before Me. You shall not make for yourself an idol, or any likeness of what is in heaven above or on the earth beneath or in the water under the earth.

You shall not worship them or serve them; for I, the LORD your God, am a jealous God, visiting the iniquity of the fathers on the children, on the third and the fourth generations of those who hate Me, but showing loving kindness to thousands, to those who love Me and keep My commandments" (Exodus 20: 3-6).

In the First commandment, the Lord is directing this primarily against the worship of spirits (demons) through spiritism, divination, and idolatry. The Second commandment forbids the worship of other gods and any image made of them. Now it is not wrong to wear a cross necklace or to have a picture of Jesus in your home. What is forbidden is bowing down to these objects or images and worshipping them. Worship to the Lord is based on God's Word and His personal revelation and relationship with Jesus. It is not founded on or in the bowing down to an image made by human hands.

The following Scriptures refer to idol worship and the clear anger the Lord holds toward this practice.

"Manasseh was twelve years old when he became king, and he reigned fifty-five years in Jerusalem; and his mother's name was Hephzibah. He did evil in the sight of the LORD, according to the abominations of the nations whom the LORD dispossessed before the sons of Israel. For he rebuilt the high places which Hezekiah his father had destroyed; and he erected altars for Baal and made an Asherah, as Ahab king of Israel had done, and worshiped all the host of heaven and served them. He built altars in the house of the LORD, of which the LORD had said, 'In Jerusalem I will put My name.' For he built altars for all the host of heaven in the two courts of the house of the LORD. He made his son pass through the fire, practiced witchcraft and used divination, and dealt with mediums and spiritists. He did much evil in the sight of the LORD provoking Him to anger" (2 Kings 21: 1-6).

Satan the Unlawful Tenant

"'The children gather wood, and the fathers kindle the fire, and the women knead dough to make cakes for the queen of heaven; and they pour out drink offerings to other gods in order to spite Me. Do they spite Me?' declares the LORD. 'Is it not themselves they spite, to their own shame?' Therefore thus says the Lord GOD, 'Behold, My anger and My wrath will be poured out on this place, on man and on beast and on the trees of the field and on the fruit of the ground; and it will burn and not be quenched'" (Jeremiah 7:18-20).

In strategic-level spiritual warfare, praying against demonic principalities, territorial spirits behind idol worship, and false/demonic religious beliefs, structures, and practices is the dominant focus. Idol worship is still rampant in the world today and comes in many forms. One thing I have learned in my 21 years of experience in spiritual warfare prayer is that the enemy is not very creative. These same deities of Baal and the Queen of Heaven that are referenced in the above Scriptures are still very alive and active today. These demonic principalities are usually the driving force behind all idolatrous worship we still witness today. Demonic entities are also the motivating power behind, Islam, Freemasonry, Wicca, Buddhism, Hinduism, abortion, the drug cartels, and all other forms of pagan practice and worship. The opening story of our experience in Russia is a strong example of how these entities work to gain power over entire regions.

In my personal experiences and many years of research, I am a firm believer that the Queen of Heaven is the most formidable demonic force we contend with on this level of intercession. Peter Wagner states in his book *Confronting the Queen of Heaven*, *"The Queen of Heaven is the demonic principality who is most responsible under Satan for keeping unbelievers in spiritual darkness."* [1] The more I travel and the further I delve into historical research of the nations of the world, the more I see the Queen of Heaven and her deception uncovered in some form. It typically involves the worship of the moon goddess in the form of Isis, Diana, Artemis, Ishtar, Cybele, Minerva, and Lilith just to name a few of her adaptations.

Alongside her you will find her partner and counterpart Baal. Where you see the Queen of Heaven, Baal will also be there in some form, such as Allah, Osiris, Apollo, Zeus, Buddha, Shiva, Horus, Attis, etc.

While you might think that these issues are not real, the evidence shows otherwise. The history of our nation did not begin with the discoverer Christopher Columbus. There were hundreds of years of demonic presence prior to the coming of the Spanish, French, and pilgrims.

Making Spiritual Warfare Relevant to Your Region.

List places of idol worship or temples of false religions in your city. Are these locations active in their worship?

1. _____
_____
_____

2. _____
_____
_____

3. _____
_____
_____

4. _____
_____
_____

5. _____
_____
_____

However, on the positive side, there were also many wonderful beliefs brought into our land as well. Some are read in the Mayflower Compact written and signed by the pilgrims in November 1620.

"In the name of God, Amen. We, whose names are underwritten, the Loyal Subjects of our dread Sovereign Lord, King James, by the Grace of God, of England, France and Ireland, King, Defender of the Faith, e&. Having undertaken for the Glory of God, and Advancement of the Christian Faith, and the Honour of our King and Country, a voyage to plant the first colony in the northern parts of Virginia; do by these presents, solemnly and mutually in the Presence of God and one of another, covenant and combine ourselves together into a civil Body Politick, for our better Ordering and Preservation, and Furtherance of the Ends aforesaid; And by Virtue hereof to enact, constitute, and frame, such just and equal Laws, Ordinances, Acts, Constitutions and Offices, from time to time, as shall be thought most meet and convenient for the General good of the Colony; unto which we promise all due submission and obedience. In Witness whereof we have hereunto subscribed our names at Cape Cod the eleventh of November, in the Reign of our Sovereign Lord, King James of England, France and Ireland, the eighteenth, and of Scotland the fifty-fourth. Anno Domini, 1620." [2]

When creating the Mayflower Compact, the signers believed that covenants were not only to be honored between God and man, but also between each other. They honored covenants as part of their righteous integrity and agreed to be bound by the same principles found in the Compact. John Adams and many historians have referred to the Mayflower Compact as the foundation of the U.S. Constitution which was written more than 150 years later. America, indeed, was begun by men who honored God and set forth founding principles by the words of the Bible. They lived their lives with honesty, reliability, and fairness toward establishing this country for the sake of survival. Many of America's founding fathers have been quoted in regards to living Biblical values.

Focuses for the Week.

Not only is it time to uncover and understand where Satan has defiled territory, but it is also important to recognize those spiritual activities that God wants to do in these areas.

Come prepared to share those things you have discovered in the next scheduled lesson. Be sure to complete the questions sometime later if you were not able to do so in the study time.

Now take time to list the things God is doing in your region. It is important to see His plans and activities increased in your region! Come prepared to share with the group:

1. _____
_____
_____

2. _____
_____
_____

3. _____
_____
_____

4. _____
_____
_____

5. _____
_____
_____

Spiritual Mapping

Lesson Four: Spiritual Mapping

As we researched the extensive and involved history of Egypt, we quickly realized that we would be dealing with its roots in the ancient religion of Freemasonry. One of the team members, whom I will call "Paul," had been a 33rd degree Mason, as had his father before him. When Paul learned the truth about Freemasonry, he denounced his association with it, broke all ties to the society, and threw out anything he possessed that was affiliated with it. The Lord had made it plain to us that Paul would be the point man for our prayer assignment. God was going to use him mightily.

We scheduled a day to visit the ruins of a temple. It was established by the pharaoh whom we had discovered to have been one of the initiators of Masonic practices. We had no doubt that all of the idol and icon worship perpetuated during his reign would be represented there. Paul was in intercession all night and all day prior to arriving at this location. Alice and I, as the leader and co-leader of the team, felt strongly that something strategic would take place on this site.

When we arrived we found that the site was closed because of excavations. Gigi, our guide, was a Christian on fire for God. She got out of the van to convince the workers to let us in.

I need to pause and reference a bit of background information here. Because I have the same skin and hair coloring of Egyptian women, many people believed I was Egyptian. (On this trip I actually received three marriage proposals; one man offered Alice a thousand camels for me!) Well, at this location my "new identity" came in handy. We could see that Gigi was having a challenging time. So Alice instructed me to sit in the front seat of the van, take off my sunglasses and smile at the men supervising the entry to the site. It worked! We hid our amusement as they ushered us in.

When we entered the ruins we were amazed. All around us stood large obelisks with hieroglyphics on them. Obelisks are mentioned in God's Word in Jeremiah 43:13, *"He will also shatter the obelisks of Heliopolis, which is in the land of Egypt; and the temples of the gods of Egypt he will burn with fire."* These contain pagan symbols and images symbolizing the worship of demonic gods and goddesses. I wish there was a more subtle way to state this, but this image in Freemasonry represents the male phallic symbol of Osiris. As we will discuss later in this lesson, Osiris is the ancient Egyptian sun god and is also many times referred to as the god of the underworld and Hades. It is also common to read in Egyptian mythology that the obelisk is a representation of Re, the father of Osiris.[1] The hieroglyphics at this location included the Masonic symbols that we see today. We made our way to the entrance gate of the temple and began to pray. Gigi told us to pray speedily because she was not going to be able to stall the workers much longer.

Paul spoke forth prayers of identificational repentance (a concept which we will discuss at length in Lesson Five) and denounced Freemasonry as a demonic secret society. Alice then instructed him to break the power of Freemasonry off the land and to cut its power to the other nations where it had spread. As soon as Paul broke the power of Freemasonry, it immediately began to rain. We were excited and several of us started to weep. Gigi then said we had to leave quickly because the workers were losing patience. We promptly obliged.

Once on the van she asked, *"Do you realize the miracle we are in?"*

We responded, *"Yes, the Lord told us He would come in the clouds, rain, and water, and He did."*

Gigi then explained, *"I am thirty-three years old; I was born and raised in Egypt. This is the month of October, which is known as the dry season. I have never in my lifetime seen it rain in Egypt in the dry season. This has never happened."* We were all stunned.

Not only did it rain, it rained a lot! It was a Houston, Texas, kind of rain. It lasted four hours with strong gusty winds. That night at dinner, the hotel and restaurant staff were standing at the windows watching it rain. Some decided to go outside and celebrate by dancing in the rain. They did not know what to think.

As we left the restaurant that evening, the manager was standing by the door watching it rain. We asked what he thought of it. His answer proved to us that God can use anyone to confirm His plans. This man did not know who we were and had not met us, but he looked right at us and responded, *"It is because you are here that it rained."* Speechless, all six of us turned the corner to leave the restaurant and began once again to weep.

The final amount of the rainfall was one and three-fourths inches. The normal *annual* rainfall in that part of the world is one inch. God can and will manifest in the natural realm breakthrough that has occurred in the spiritual realm. Isn't He an awesome and miraculous God?

Spiritual Warfare and Spiritual Mapping are a Powerful Team

As witnessed in the above testimony, spiritual warfare and spiritual mapping work together as a powerful weapon. They are a team. Actually, spiritual warfare is more likely to be less effective without the tool of spiritual mapping. When we combine the two it helps to avoid what I term the piñata method of intercession. This is where we pray and hope that one of the prayers will hit the mark. Usually the thought is, *"If we just keep praying and saying something, then eventually we will swing the final blow and defeat the darkness."* I believe that this type of praying has little effect and many times causes the enemy and his army of darkness to laugh instead of being alarmed and defeated by our prayers. Let me explain.

I sometimes hear intercessors comment that instead of researching an area prior to a spiritual warfare campaign, they travel to the location "to feel the land." Then they ask God to bring prophetic revelation of the enemy's schemes. God is able to reveal issues concerning the territory we are praying over. I personally have experienced this many times. However, I do question our ability to discern and prophetically hear the complete historical extent of Satan's defilement in a land. Why? First, I believe it is difficult to prophetically receive hundreds of years of historical information. And second, we see time after time, just as shared in Lesson Three about the breakthrough in Russia, miracles happen because the intercessory team is already knowledgeable about the strongholds they will face. When research and spiritual mapping are done correctly, prayer teams are able to hit the ground running.

Actually, all through the Israelites' journey to the Promised Land, the Lord instructed his leaders to send spies into the lands they were getting ready to overtake and possess (see Deut. 1:21–23, Numbers13:3, Joshua 2:1, and Joshua 18:8). These spies went into the land to see the layout of the terrain. They went to see what provisions were available. They also went in to observe the armies they would be going up against. They realized that it is always a good idea to know the strengths and weaknesses of your enemy ahead of time. The information obtained by the spies was used in making decisions for the next step in taking possession of the land.

I have witnessed many times those who do not want to make the investment of time in order to do due diligence to be a well informed soldier for the Lord. They want to intercede, make prophetic declarations, and then happily pronounce that the spirits over the region have been defeated. I have been in numerous services where I have witnessed this dominion rule declaration released as a regular confession of many believers. The voice of the Church has resounded with the desire to see the manifestation and revelation of our God-given right of ruling and reigning. This is a righteous goal, but in most cases it will not be accomplished because it has not been preceded by confession.

Authority is inextricably tied in with responsibility. It presumes not only knowledge but the rightful use of our position in Christ. It means understanding the original plan for man, walking in prayer and intimacy with the Father, understanding our role in restoring creation, walking in obedience to the Father's direction, knowing our sphere of influence, and engaging in our God ordained assignments in the territories He has given us. But all of that starts with a humble confession of our sins and weaknesses.

Yes, God can certainly order victories across regions when we pray, but it is informed intercession that we must have in order to be ultimately effective. Having the essential facts and revelations at the foundation of our prayers prepares the way for powerful transformations. Informed, trained, and appointed foot soldiers on the ground in covert assignments are required in order for there to be the measurable breakthroughs of change, awakening, and conversion.

Spiritual Mapping Defined

Spiritual mapping is defined as the practice of discovering the spiritual conditions operating in a specific community, city, or nation. By gathering objective information (historical facts) and combining it with spiritual impressions (prophecy, revelation, words of knowledge, Scripture, dreams, and visions) believers are given a map by which to discern open doors between the spirit world and the material world. Only then are we able to strategize and pray accordingly. In other words, spiritual mapping draws vital conclusions from the historical facts and Spirit-led insights that have been gathered. Spiritual warfare is the intercessory assignment based on these conclusions.

At this point, I want to strongly emphasize that spiritual warfare and spiritual mapping are not about presenting an opportunity for us to flex our spiritual muscles. The ultimate purpose is the reality that large numbers of conversions are unlikely to occur unless we discern the nature and origin of the obstacles. We must receive God's strategies for their removal and for the transformation of the people.

Satan has created these obstacles to the Gospel so that those who are lost will not come to salvation. The good news is that Satan's strategies will not succeed when we agree with God. The Bible says that *"the one who is in you is greater than the one who is in the world"* (1 John 4:4). God has granted believers power for evangelism through warfare prayer.

The desired outcome of spiritual warfare is the redeeming of the land and the salvation of those held in darkness by territorial spirits. We pray for the purpose of setting free those who are trapped by false religions, Satanism, mystic religions, Freemasonry, Eastern Star, Islam, witchcraft, Wicca, New Age, atheism, etc. We also want to see God's plans and blessings come to these areas. Spiritual mapping is necessary for believers who want to engage in strategic-level spiritual warfare prayer!

Effective, Fervent Prayers Hit the Mark

Numerous times I have witnessed in others and experienced myself the exhilaration, zeal, and fervency in prayer that occurs as an outcome of mapping. Granted, any and all anointed prayer gatherings where the Lord speaks and moves are an inspirational and faith building experience. But it is awe-inspiring to know that because of spiritual mapping our prayers are targeted accurately and do hit the mark! I believe that this is the deeper message of James 5:16: *"The effectual fervent prayer of a righteous man availeth much"* (KJV). In order to pray strategically, we must pray accurately.

I have three wonderful daughters, Kendall, Rebecca, and Katie. They are all familiar with the different mom voices I use. They distinctly know and recognize the difference between my calm voice, and the "you are in trouble voice." If one of them is in a dangerous situation and I need to gain their attention quickly, I am going to speak out her name with authority. If I call the wrong name, then she has every right not to respond, authority or not.

The same principle applies in strategic-level intercession. Identifying the names of the gods, goddesses, and territorial spirits influencing the region in which we are engaging in war adds authority, accuracy, strength, and effectiveness to our prayers. Satan is a legalist. If the spirit over the region is a spirit of death, but I address it as witchcraft, then I have missed the mark. Even though I have authority, the territorial spirit will not be defeated because it knows I have not prayed accurately and therefore will continue to grip the region. This is why I am so devoted to spiritual mapping. It empowers us to expose the evil strategies of the enemy in order to pray with wisdom and knowledge, and to stealthily conquer demonic strongholds over regions.

Reflect on your city or state. What areas could benefit from spiritual mapping and spiritual warfare prayer? Many of the lists formed from pervious chapters would apply to this list.

_____
_____
_____

Your Kingdom Come

_____
_____
_____
_____
_____
_____
_____

Gathering the Facts

We will discuss team dynamics in Lesson Five, but I want to emphasize right now the importance of each team member doing their share of the research and mapping. There will be those who are gifted at research and others who are not. But all team members who are part of a warfare campaign should do their share of researching the history. The team leader or intercessory group leader should ensure that research assignments are made for each member. This will make the project easier to accomplish.

During the research phase, many historical facts and hidden truths will be revealed. Numerous demonic schemes will be exposed. God is always faithful to lead the team to the right book, internet article, television documentary, history museum, etc. The following are suggestions of how to move forward in your research.

1. Foundational history: It is important to go back as far as you can in the history of the region. Here are good starting points.
- What is the earliest known information about the region you are studying?
- Was the foundational history peaceful or aggressive?
- Was there bloodshed?
- Were there Broken Covenants?

SPIRITUAL MAPPING

2. Original People Groups:
- What people groups fought over or settled in the area?
- What brought them to this specific area?
- What were their religious beliefs and practices?
- Were there battles between the white men and the First Nations people of the region?
- What did the First Nations people believe and worship?
- Does there need to be repentance and restitution made between people groups and races?
- Was there racism and slavery?

3. Key Historical Leaders:
- Who had the greatest influence in making key decisions?
- What were the political and religious beliefs of these leaders?
- Was a door opened over the area because of these beliefs?

4. Historical sites:
- Which sites have had significance on the people and the land over the years?
- What was the motivation for the construction of these major sites?

5. Spiritual history:
- Were the spiritual practices pagan and/or idolatrous?
- If so, what gods or goddesses were worshipped?
- Is there worship of these gods and goddesses still practiced today?
- Is the worship still active?

- How has past pagan worship been adapted into present day pagan worship?
- Active temples of pagan worship might include worship of the Queen of Heaven, Allah, Buddha, Hindu deities, Satan, Diana, Lilith, and the gods of Taoism and Shintoism.

6. Secret Societies:
- Were there any secret societies involved in the founding of the region?
- What were the hallmarks of those societies?
- What influence do these societies have today?

Freemasonry

No study on strategic-level intercession is complete without discussing the topic of Freemasonry. This is a significant concern in our nation along with many others because many of the tenets of this secret society were embraced and practiced by a large number of our founding fathers.

The roots of Freemasonry stem back to pagan practices and worship in ancient Egypt, which was steeped in the adoration and idolatry of demon deities; Ra, Osiris, Isis, Horus, and numerous other demonic gods and goddesses. In his book, *Free from Freemasonry,* Ron Campbell quotes from Moses Redding's *the Illustrated History of Freemasonry:* *"Egypt has always been the birthplace of the mysteries. It was there that the ceremonies of initiation were first established. It was there that the truth was first veiled in allegory, and the dogmas of religion were first imparted under symbolic forms."*[2]

While on the surface Freemasonry appears to be a good and charitable organization, we have to look at the foundational beliefs that formed this secret society. I am aware that many in Freemasonry are not aware of the origins of that which they are involved in. If they take the time and research the society they will discover pagan roots.

Many of the symbols and words spoken in initiation rituals are centered on Osiris, the ancient Egyptian Sun God, who is an adaptation of Baal. Isis, the ancient Egyptian moon goddess also known as the Queen of Heaven is likewise represented in symbols and words.

Horus, the son of Osiris and Isis, is depicted and revered as the Egyptian messiah and is represented by the all-seeing eye, meaning he knows and sees all. This symbol of Horus is plainly seen above the pyramid on our U.S. one dollar bill.

Freemasonry allows you to worship the god of your choice. So, if a Muslim is initiated he will pledge his allegiance to Allah, the god of the Qur'an. The Bible, then, will be moved off the altar or pushed to the side and the Qur'an will be given honor. Masons believe that they have a higher god above all other gods. His name is "The Great Architect of the Universe," who the 33rd and Supreme Degree Masons teach is Lucifer. They further perpetuate this Luciferian doctrine by claiming that Satan is the evil brother of Jesus and that he is equal in his evil power with Jesus. Freemasonry over the years has adopted and welcomed every satanic god and goddess in the world from every pagan belief and practice. Once you begin your research on this topic you will also quickly discover the things we have learned.

I once engaged in a conversation with a 32nd degree Mason in the Masonic Lodge of which he was a member. We were there requesting a historical tour and he gladly obliged, and also engaged in conversation with us about their beliefs. He assured me that he was a Christian. He explained that they have members from every religion and walk of faith, and that Freemasonry is not a complete Christian organization. I inquired if he felt comfortable having to give the Qur'an and Allah a seat of honor in initiation rituals. And if in his Christian faith this was bothersome to him. He responded: *"If you view God the way most Christians do, then yes this would be bothersome, but Masons do not view God this way. We believe that we, as Masons, have a God that is higher than, Allah, Jesus, Buddha, the cows worshipped in India, the Hindu dieties, etc. He is the God of Freemasonry and He unites all of our faiths on the same level and then we worship Him, our Masonic God, as the Supreme Being. Our God of Freemasonry is higher than all other Gods and beliefs including Jesus."* This statement was spoken to me two years ago by an active Mason. I knew that what he shared with us was true because of our extensive research into Freemasonry over the past twenty-one years. But it is still shocking when you actually hear these comments so blatantly expressed by a dedicated Mason. The following are other alarming quotes written by Masons.

"For every Masonic writer who says that Freemasonry is not a religion, there are five Masonic writers who claim that it is a pagan religion. While they may disagree as to which pagan religion, they are all agreed that Christianity is wrong and its teachings must not be allowed in the Lodge." [3]

"A considerable amount of excision was necessitated by the alteration of the clause in the (Masonic) Constitution which changed Masonry from a Christian to a non-Christian basis... Anything Christian was eliminated." [4]

"Masonry does not preach a new religion... Drop the theological barnacles from the religion of Jesus, as taught by Him, and by the Essenes and Gnostics of the first centuries, and it becomes Masonry. Masonry in its purity, derived from the old Hebrew Kabbalah as part of the Great Universal Wisdom Religion of remotest antiquity." [5]

There are many organizations that are a part of this Freemason structure. Eastern Star, De Molay, Jobs Daughter, Knights of Columbus, Odd Fellows, Shriners, Modern Woodmen of America, Rebekah Lodges, Daughters of the

Spiritual Mapping

Eastern Star, Elks Lodge, Moose Lodge, Eagles Lodge, Ku Klux Klan, the Grange, Ladies Oriental Shrine, Constellation of Junior Stars, and many more. Mormonism and Freemasonry are one in the same. Joseph Smith, the founder of Mormonism, was a Mason and many Mormon rituals are similar to Freemasonry.

The background of these demonic deities and the occult and pagan beliefs perpetuated through Freemasonry is too lengthy to discuss in this curriculum. It takes a good solid four hours to teach on this topic. I have included a list of great resources in the back of this book to aid you in further studies of this society. This will be instrumental in praying for your regions.

Mapping Your Region.

Who were the founding fathers of your region?
_____
_____
_____
_____
_____
_____

Were they masons? If so, who?
_____
_____
_____
_____
_____

How many Masonic Lodges are in your city?
_____
_____

How many churches and government buildings are dedicated by Masonic cornerstones?
_____
_____
_____

Determining Strategic Issues

One trap believers fall into in strategic-level spiritual warfare is what I call symptomatic praying. In others words they focus on the manifest problems in a particular region instead of dealing with the foundations of the struggle. To engage in successful and measurable intercessory outcomes, we must learn to distinguish between prevailing bondage and root bondage.

Prevailing bondage is the systematic recurrence over time of spiritual symptoms that indicate a much deeper bondage. *Root bondage* is the original sin committed against the land. Hear me on this statement, when researching, mapping and praying, the chief focus should be to uncover and expose the root bondage. The following is a list of root bondages that have controlling effects on land and its people:

- War.
- Trauma: the enemy will take advantage of the open door of trauma when great wounding or devastation has occurred. The result is an established stronghold. For example, a location where there have been repeated deaths such as tragic car accidents, suicides, and homicides. A "spirit of death" would be the spirit in operation in this area.
- Bloodshed: This might include abortion, deaths, murders, killing of the innocent, massacre sites, and areas with a lot of gang violence and shootings.
- Land violations: This is defined as evil or demonic abuse or infringement on the land by Satan for the purpose of

gaining more territory. This includes the wrong use of land for satanic worship, altars dedicated to demon gods and goddesses, bloodshed, greed, racism, bestiality, etc. The enemy will use these means to pilfer the land that is the Lord's in an attempt to claim it as his own. Many times New Age groups, Satan worshippers, and Masons (just to name a few) will place time capsules and worship stones on the land, claiming it for their own.
- Covenants made with darkness: This is a contract or vow made with a demonic being. This could have been established by a key historical leader, a people group, or a people engaged in demonic pagan worship. This contract serves as an open door of authority to this entity in order to perpetuate its influence on the land and its inhabitants.
- Demon worship.
- Broken Covenants.
- Deceptive/political leaders.
- Early pagan spiritual beliefs and practices, especially by the original people group on the land.
- Sexual immorality.
- Occult practices.
- Witchcraft.
- Freemasonry strongholds.
- Temples of active idolatrous worship such as Islamic, Hindu, and Buddhist temples.
- Queen of Heaven worship and its adaptations: Diana (Roman), Artemis (Greek), Cybele (Anatolian, that is Turkish and also later Roman), Lilith (Jewish Mysticism), Isis (Egyptian), Sophia (Greek and Russian), Santeria (Mexico and Latin America), Santa Muerte (Mexico), Xi

Wangmu (China, Japan, Korea), The Lady in Blue (Southern United States) and the list goes on and on.
- Baal worship and its adaptations: Osiris (Egyptian), Zeus (Greek), Apollo (Greek), Jupiter (Roman), Attis (Turkish), Allah (Middle East), Shiva (Hindu), Molech (ancient Semitic god still prevalent in Middle East, North Africa), Hercules (Roman and Greek) and this list could also continue on and on.

Identify issues of prevailing bondage in your city. List what you find:
_____
_____
_____
_____

Identify and discuss the root bondages in your city. (There will be more than one)
_____
_____
_____
_____

The Use of Geometry in Demonic Strategies

Some of you might be asking what geometry could possibly have to do with spiritual mapping and spiritual warfare strategies. The answer is quite a lot! The word *geometry* comes from the Greek word *geometria*. It means to measure the earth. Older dictionaries explain that the fundamental purpose of geometry was the art of measuring the earth or any distances and dimensions on it. These measurements are achieved through points, lines, planes, and spheres.

Spiritual Mapping

When mapping locations to find root bondages often geometric designs will be revealed. One key component is the concept of a *ley* line. The individual credited for the rediscovery and theory of ley lines is English photographer Alfred Watkins. "Watkins was riding his horse one day when the surrounding landscape suddenly came "alive" like a flood of ancestral memory." [6]

Mr. Watkins discovered that numerous prehistoric sites, such as standing stones, earthen burial mounds, and other similar locations, fell into straight lines for miles across the countryside. As a result he spent years investigating such alignments both on the ground and on maps. Actually, the use of ley lines in architectural design stems from ancient Egypt, and also can be seen among the Incas, the Aborigines of Australia, those who practice Feng Shui, and in locations in Spain, Mexico, New Mexico, Washington D.C., etc.

The Encarta World Dictionary defines ley lines as straight lines linking ancient landmarks and places of worship. They are believed to follow particular routes and are popularly associated with mystical phenomena. These landmarks are usually located in high points on the landscape.

Spiritually these high points are *power points* or places of energy that have been dedicated to cultic practices or idolatrous worship. Many times you will discover pagan temples, demonic altars, obelisks, and idols on these places of energy. I define a *ley* line as two or more power points that interact in order to hold an area in a certain kind of bondage. They depend on mismanagement of the land. The lines act as a feeding trough, giving the enemy access to the area. Thus, all the territory and people within the plane that is formed by these lines and power points are held in bondage.

In many ancient cultures these ley lines were often referred to as spirit ways, meaning the spirits could travel between power points which were also termed spiritual vortices. Those in New Age practices today and individuals involved in architectural designs for Masons understand and practice *geometria* and the use of ley lines in their construction. The following shares how even ancient cultures embraced this practice.

> Archaeological evidence of the ancient practice of building spirit ways has survived best in the Americas because it has experienced less cultural upheaval as in the Old World. A brief north-to-south survey shows this. In Ohio, between 150 BC and 500, the Hopewell Indians built geometrical earthworks covering many acres. They built them with straight linear features which seem to have been ceremonial roadways. In 1995, archaeologists announced the discovery of a 60-mile-long, straight Hopewell ritual road connecting earthworks at Newark with the Hopewell necropolis at Chillicothe.
>
> In the California Sierras, prehistoric Miwok Indians left behind the remains of very straight tracks. Archaeologists in the 1930s described them as "almost airline in their directness, running up hill and down dale without zigzags or detours." Mysterious prehistoric Indian roads have been found in Utah, Colorado, and Arizona. The most dramatic examples in the United States are those that converge on (or diverge from) Chaco Canyon, a cult centre of the lost Anasazi people, in the high, arid desert country in northwestern New Mexico. These Chacoan roads stretch for sixty miles beyond the canyon, and possibly much further, linking Anasazi ceremonial "Great Houses," of which there are many dozens scattered throughout the desert area surrounding Chaco Canyon. [7]

As the Body of Christ, we have been entrusted with the mission of breaking the power of these lines and reclaiming the land for God's glory! Let's no longer permit the enemy to gain further influence over our cities, regions, and nations. The "energies" operating between power points need to be broken and the land set free from spiritual darkness. What do we do when ley lines are uncovered in our research? Plan an effective strategy and pray!

When ley lines are discovered the goal is to break the spiritual power of the enemy that controls the region. Many times our teams will pray at each power point that has established the ley line, sever the demonic power from the site, and shut the open door that allowed Satan's control. There have also been times when we have stood directly on the ley line between the power points and have broken the demonic power. When in this situation listen to the direction from the Lord and He will guide you as to how to pray.

Consider your city or the region you are located in. Do you know of locations that might involve ley lines?
_____
_____
_____
_____

What are the power points associated with these ley lines?
_____
_____
_____
_____

Assembling the Information

1. To aid you in this process here are some good places for research:
    - Libraries.
    - Credible internet articles and websites.
    - E-library. It does have a monthly fee so I suggest using it only when you are in a research mode.
    - Local historical museums.
    - Many Masonic lodges will give history tours that are very informative. We state we are there to learn about the history of the region. Or, we will say we are history students. We do not share that we are spiritually mapping the region and want to gather information about how to pray against the demonic beliefs of Freemasonry. Many times the Lord will make a way at the end for us to pray for the person giving the tour, or simply share that we are Christians. Remember, the person is not the enemy. The beliefs that are the demonic roots of this society are what we are against.
    - Historians that live in your region.
    - In some cities you can request that the policeman who patrols your region come to your home or church. They can tell you the types of activities that are occurring as far as crime, gangs, and drugs are concerned. Sometimes they even know of witchcraft groups or satanic worship in a region.

2. Now is the time to begin to assemble all the Lord is revealing. You can do so by compiling a team notebook. The following are suggestions.

- Combine all the prophetic revelation including dreams, visions, Scriptures, and prophetic words the Lord has revealed into one section.
- As the facts are mapped, the issues that carry the most significant weight will become obvious. The Lord will give spiritual insight throughout the process. Don't forget to focus on the key root issues in order for you to discover in your region what was shared in this lesson.
- Divide the notebook into the sections for each of the sites that you will be researching and praying over.
- It will also be wise to map out all the Masonic lodges in your region or city.
- Find out how long they have been there and what political or historical leaders were instrumental in introducing the secret society to your area.
- Get a map of the city and begin to mark on it the points that the Lord highlights. Identify power points connected by ley lines.

3. As the research process unfolds, it is wise to have meetings once or twice a month to discuss what the team has discovered, and then to pray and to hear the Lord for further strategy.

Rules of Engagement

Lesson Five: Rules of Engagement

The phone call from my friend, Sarah, was an exciting opportunity to do warfare concerning the Francisco Vasquez de Coronado expedition of 1540 through 1542. Every time she reaches out for assistance there is something supernatural and awesome that transpires. She explained that a Christian state government leader whom she is in close fellowship with had contacted her that day. The Lord spoke to this leader about the need to pray concerning the Coronado expedition through his state and also our nation those many years ago. He felt strongly that some of the practices that took place during this expedition had opened doors for spirits of mammon and greed. This state leader knows the voice of the Lord, but also recognizes who to contact when it involves a strategic prayer assignment. And my friend, Sarah, and her team were the ones.

Sarah needed my assistance in uncovering the historical facts of why the Coronado expedition had opened doors to these spirits. To further add to this forming strategy, two other prophetic intercessors had received direction from the Lord that this would also involve an exposing of the human sex trafficking industry. With all of this prophetic revelation flowing, it was time to confirm and back up all of this through research. One of the spiritual mappers/researchers in our prayer network had the answers.

When Coronado came to Mexico and also to America, it was for the purpose of finding gold. There was a legend that had spread to Spain concerning the seven cities of Cibola in the New World. It was said that these cities contained great amounts of gold. Coronado greatly desired to explore these cities. Throughout his journey he traversed from Mexico, through New Mexico, Arizona, Texas, Oklahoma, and into Kansas. Along the way he kidnapped Native American women and girls to carry on his expedition. He used them for labor, but also to provide a sexual outlet for his men. Basically they were used as sex slaves. Research explained the greed and also the sex slavery. Prophetic revelations confirmed the findings.

Sarah and I prayed knowing it was time to deal with this matter. Amazingly, on the day that this Christian state government leader wanted to do this prayer assignment, my husband, Greg, and I were in Spain; the country of Coronado's birth. We mobilized intercessors and leaders to be positioned at the exact time and on the same day in each location were we planned to pray. Greg and I stood at the port in Spain, while other believers stood in Mexico, New Mexico, Arizona, Texas, Oklahoma, and Kansas. They were located in places where the original expedition had stopped on the journey. Everyone joined in on a prayer/warfare conference call. We also had Native Americans present for the purpose of identificational repentance. We wanted to repent for what the Spanish had done to the Native American women and young girls. All participants prayed in agreement. We then renounced and broke the power of the spirits of mammon and greed, and further broke all power points and ley lines from Spain all the way to Salina, Kansas where the expedition finally ended. It was a powerful time of intercession.

Within four days of this warfare prayer initiative, a sex ring operation spanning five continents, including Spain and the United States, was exposed and disbanded. Over six hundred people were arrested and many young girls were rescued from the horrible life of sexual slavery. All of this took place in July of 2011. Warfare prayer when coupled with government leaders and a prepared and trained army of believers can affect great change, and justice can and will be served.

Rules of Engagement

Are You Ready for Battle?

It is exciting to hear of the powerful testimonies of breakthrough. Now let's discover what is necessary to engage this level of governmental prayer.

Has God spoken? Is He calling you to a warfare prayer assignment? The question then is, are you ready for battle? This question is significant. Scripture says:

*"...for the weapons of our warfare are not of the flesh, but divinely powerful for the destruction of fortresses. We are destroying speculations and every lofty thing raised up against the knowledge of God, and we are taking every thought captive to the obedience of Christ, **and we are ready to punish all disobedience, whenever your obedience is complete.*** (2 Corinthians 10:4-6, Bold emphasis added).

Strategic-level spiritual warfare must not be entered into lightly. Make no mistake, this is war, and when engaging in praying at this level we are entering into a very powerful spiritual battle. Believers must walk in obedience and holiness in order to accomplish warfare goals. I have witnessed many zealous prayer warriors who had entered into spiritual warfare before they were emotionally, spiritually, and physically prepared. The consequences have been severe, and the backlash from the enemy devastating. For example, individuals who are plagued by fear, or who participate in sins such as pornography, adultery, addiction, lying, rebellion, or even unforgiveness have no business engaging in warfare prayer. A pure heart is required to pray at this level. You cannot come against the giants in the land until you have dealt with the giants in your own life. We cannot tear down or defeat what we are still building up. If we go into battle before overcoming our own giants, the enemy will diffuse our efforts and bring a strong counterattack. Only foolish, inexperienced, and unwise people move into spiritual warfare prayer without personal holiness.

Making it Personal

Now might be a good time to revisit the personal preparation steps we discussed in *Encouraged to Intercede Lesson Three* and in *Prophetic Intercession Lesson Three*. Make sure that there are no open doors in your life that can make a way for backlash from the enemy!

Not only is it necessary that we are prepared for combat, but likewise our families must also be ready. Family units need to be prepared in order to stand firm against repercussions of the warfare. A support and prayer agreement with your spouse is valuable. Prayer coverage over your children is essential. Before I proceed into a spiritual warfare prayer focus, my husband and I are in complete accord so that I can move forward in the assignment without personal interference.

In my earlier years of warfare intercession, there were instances when I began to move into warfare prayer and he promptly and wisely counseled me to stop. He recognized that in my zeal I was entering into a battle that was not mine. And yet there have been numerous times when he has encouraged me to accept an assignment even when I was hesitant or overwhelmed. The Lord designed marriages to move forward in united empowerment. I value and respect the wisdom, prayer support, and agreement that my husband provides for me. This allows us to better advance into all the Lord has called us to do.

When I first began to answer the call of deliverance, intercession, and strategic level spiritual warfare prayer, I had no training. I was attending a ladies Bible study which was taught by my dear friend, Alice Smith. As she taught, I knew the Lord was calling me to learn as much about prayer as I could. She challenged those of us present, "If you want to be involved on the front lines and know you are called, submit yourself to someone who is in leadership or a seasoned intercessor." The Lord's presence was intensely drawing me, and it felt as if that statement was directed right at me. After praying and hearing further from the Lord, two days later I approached Alice and submitted myself to her mentoring and leadership. I have never regretted that move.

Applying this Principle Personally

If you are new to this level of intercession and lack experience, I want to challenge you to ask God to place a mentor in your life. Let's stop and pray:

Lord right now I submit myself to You and I welcome the prompting and leading of the Holy Spirit in my life. Direct my steps in this process. I welcome the prayer leader and mentor you have for my life, and I submit myself to the process of spiritual growth. Lord, teach me in this season all that you have designed for me to learn. I am expectant of all that You will impart to me. Thank you, Lord, for Your direction and the divine connections You are presenting in my life. In Jesus' name, Amen.

Confirmation of Assignment

I have discovered that as the Lord begins to speak a new warfare agenda, He will bring confirmation of the mission. It is essential to ask the Lord to confirm the assignment prior to moving forward. Many times, as prayer warriors, we encounter revelation from the Lord and in our eagerness, venture into warfare prayer before we have fully received confirmation and the Lord's strategies. Confirmation can come through prophetic words, dreams, Scripture, or through the release and blessing of those we are aligned with. During this season begin to record, below, the different ways the Lord speaks and confirms the prayer assignment.

Record of Confirmations:

1. _____
   _____

2. _____
   _____

3. _____
   _____

4. _____
   _____

Spiritual Blessing from Those You are Aligned With

Spiritual Warfare is serious business. Compliance and a teachable spirit is a requirement before stepping into strategic-level spiritual warfare. I am in close relationship with Peter and Doris Wagner as well as many other leaders. Many times I will speak to those with whom I am closely associated. I want their input, blessing, and wisdom before moving into warfare. When I served as Prayer Coordinator of Houston House of Prayer, Eddie and Alice Smith were the pastors of the church. I always invited their blessing and insight before engaging in warfare. If those who have gone before me and love me do not feel that I am to move forward, I do not. If they are in agreement, then I gladly press on. I also surround myself with those who recognize the value of spiritual warfare prayer. Leaders who have no understanding of this form of intercession are not good counselors. It is good to ask wisdom and blessing from those who have the insight necessary for you to fulfill your calling.

Self-proclaimed prophets and spiritual warfare intercessors who are not walking under the direction of the Holy Spirit must be avoided. Stay away from people who have no spiritual covering. A familiar line that you hear from those with unhealthy authority issues is, "I am accountable to God. No man has room to speak into my life. My life is not anyone else's business." This is an unsafe and unscriptural response! Commonly, these are individuals who have deep wounds from the past. They are in need of releasing forgiveness to those who have wounded them, and then to go on and receive deliverance and healing from the Lord. These individuals do not make dependable team members, and typically question the authority of the team leader throughout the prayer assignment. This can make for an unpleasant experience for the leader and the team. This also opens doors for the enemy to unleash counter attacks.

If you are struggling with unhealthy authority issues, ask God to bring healing to you. He is the God of healing and deliverance. Submit yourself to your pastor or to a deliverance team for prayer. God loves you and desires to set you free from the hurts of the past!

Moving in God's Timing

God is a God of timing. Nehemiah can teach us wisdom about advancing in God's timing.

"By night I went out through the Valley Gate toward the Jackal Well and the Dung Gate, examining the walls of Jerusalem, which had been broken down, and its gates which had been destroyed by fire. Then I moved on toward the

Fountain Gate and the King's Pool, but there was not enough room for my mount to get through; so, I went up the valley by night, examining the wall. Finally, I turned back and reentered through the Valley Gate. The officials did not know where I had gone or what I was doing, because as of yet I had said nothing to the Jews or the priests or nobles or official or any others who would be doing the work" (Nehemiah 2:13-16, NIV).

Nehemiah saw, embraced, and accepted God's call to restore the walls of Jerusalem. He did not determine that one day he would ride into Jerusalem and herald the mission the Lord had presented to him. He secretly rode at night and studied the wall and its destruction. He acquired discernment of the condition of the wall before unveiling the restoration strategy. When he shared the vision of the rebuilding project to those who would be recruited, the word was alive and active. The people of Jerusalem accepted the task and all moved collectively in unity. When the enemy attempted to spoil the reconstruction of the wall, Nehemiah and the Jews were positioned and able to continue in unity. They were impenetrable.

As warfare intercessors, we are to react in the same manner. God will divulge an assignment, but it could be weeks, months, or even years before the timing is right. 1 Chronicles 12:32 states, *"And the sons of Issachar, men who understood the times, with knowledge of what Israel should do."* (NIV) Walking in an Issachar anointing, and then interpreting and knowing the seasons we are in, and also knowing how to pray accordingly, is important. As God begins to disclose a prayer assignment, ask him for accurate timing. Scripture refers to time in *chronos* time and *kairos* time. *Chronos* time is time in general. *Kairos* time is the exact point of time in which something should be executed. Entering into warfare before the correct time opens doors to the enemy. This is where we need one another. If you are uncertain, ask your spouse, pastor, spiritual mentors, or personal intercessors for their input.

The Value of Team Dynamics

In a physical battle against an enemy, one man would not be able to engage and survive, especially if he faced a large host. The same is true in spiritual warfare prayer. We need a team of soldiers to empower God given strategy in order to ensure victory. Praying spiritual warfare prayer requires a team. It is unwise and dangerous for one warrior to engage in territorial warfare without the backing and support of a skilled team. Those who are called have to be trained, submitted, and prepared as a battalion deployed and ready to face the enemy.

If you are moving forward with a prayer assignment, then you will also carry the responsibility of mobilizing a team. If you are a team member, the following criteria is important for effectively participating in and interacting with the team leader and other team members.

1. ***Prayer and seeking the Lord for confirmation of His team members for this assignment.*** He will be faithful to orchestrate the formation of the team.

2. ***Extend the invitation only to those with whom there is relationship.*** This is valuable as the team is formed. There is great wisdom in walking in relationship with those whom you will engage with in this type of a warfare assignment. I always tell people that there is a difference between those I enjoy a good lunch with, and those I go to war with. I was once a team member on a team in which the leader invited an individual to participate at the last minute. There was no history of relating. Just one lunch that lasted an hour. As a result, we spent more time dealing with the personal issues of this individual than with fulfilling the Lord's prayer agenda that we had spent

months preparing for. It was a distraction and very frustrating for the team members.

3. ***The team must consist only of those who are ready for battle.*** It is important to ensure that all team members are ready and prepared to engage in the warfare prayer assignment. Team leaders must know all of those on the team. This means knowing their spiritual condition as well.

4. ***Form a team with diverse spiritual gifts.*** A diversity of the gifts will strengthen the team. Just as discussed in Lesson Four of *Prophetic Intercession*, in corporate prayer gatherings it would be boring if all of us prayed in the same manner and giftedness. This same idea applies to prayer teams with a strategic warfare focus. Diversity makes for a beautiful flow of all of the gifts of the Holy Spirit.

5. ***Multiplication is always good. Include a rookie who is ready.*** One practice I always try to implement is to invite a newly recruited and trained intercessor to the warfare initiative. As leaders, it is imperative that we are always looking beyond ourselves in order to help to multiply God's army. Therefore, discipling and mentoring future leaders should be a focus in training teams.

6. ***Seek people who have legal authority over the target area because of their bloodline.*** What do I mean by legal authority? An individual with legal authority through his or her bloodline is one who is a descendant of a person responsible for the spiritual condition and atmosphere of the assigned territory. It is not required to have such an individual on the team, but if the Lord makes this connection during an assignment, he or she will carry a large amount of authority and may prove to be a powerful weapon when praying over the land and over issues concerning his or her forefathers.

There is another benefit to having the help of a person who has legal authority through the bloodline. Not only might you gain physical access to a certain place through this bloodline authority, as we did in the above example, but you might also achieve greater spiritual victory in a particular area that has been cursed. Nehemiah 1:6-7 states: *"Let your ear be attentive and you eyes open to hear the prayer your servant is praying before you day and night for your servants, the people of Israel.* ***I confess the sins we Israelites, including myself and my father's house have committed against you.*** *We have acted very wickedly toward you. We have not obeyed the commands, decrees and laws you gave your servant Moses."* (Bold emphasis added).

In this passage Nehemiah repents on behalf of the Israelites, himself, and his forefathers. He takes responsibility for the corrupt practices of past generations. This action is termed *identificational repentance*. An individual with legal authority through the bloodline carries the legitimate right to repent for the sinful actions of his or her forefathers, and to break any resulting defilement or curse over the land. This proves to be a potent weapon in strategic warfare prayer.

Let's make it personal: What issues in your family line might require identificational repentance? For example: Freemasonry involvement, ancestors who were involved in Native America massacres and, perhaps, ancestors who were involved in idol worship.

_____
_____
_____
_____

Are there areas in your region where these issues are a concern?

_____
_____
_____

Begin to seek the Lord to see if He desires a warfare strategy.

7. ***Be careful of controlling personalities.*** One thing I have learned as a prayer leader of warfare strategies is the need for team members to follow the team leader willingly and to work well within a team atmosphere. Those who want control make situations difficult for the team leader and the team members. Those who tend to be controlling can participate, but it is important that the leader speak with this individual to ensure that they will be teachable and willing to work with the dynamics of a team setting. On a warfare assignment, the team leader should not have to be concerned about engaging in argumentative discussions. This will distract from the assignment at hand.

8. ***Secure the team.*** Before moving forward with a strategic warfare initiative set a deadline date for team members who want to participate. It is imperative to know who will be involved. It is good to create an atmosphere in which there will not be a lot of changes once the research and team meetings are in full operation. However, it is still good to add team members as the Lord raises up new members that He wants involved.

9. ***Begin to hold prayer times.*** Now that the team is secure and in place, begin to hold regularly scheduled prayer times. If some of the team members are not local, include them in conference calls.

10. ***Mobilize intercessors for each team member.*** At this point, I implement the practice of asking each team member to line up personal intercessors to provide prayer coverage before, during, and after the warfare assignment. We make it a practice to require a minimum of five intercessors per team member. Explain the importance of inviting intercessors who understand what the warfare team is doing and engaging in. This level of warfare assignment should not be a training

ground for personal intercessors, but to enlist those who already have an understanding of spiritual warfare prayer.

Begin to make a list of those who you will personally invite to intercede for you and the team:

a._____
_____

b._____
_____

c._____
_____

d._____
_____

e._____
_____

11. *Agree to move together in unity.* "*Behold, how good and how pleasant it is for brothers to dwell together in unity!*" (Psalm 133:1) The enemy recognizes an intercessory warfare team that is not walking in unity. If he sees or witnesses actions or words of disunity he will take full advantage of the situation. Satan and his cohorts will use this open door to bring further discord, rebellion, accusation against the team leader and team members, jealousy, and contention. This in turn will bring backlash and counterattacks against the team. To put it bluntly, if a warfare prayer team is walking in disunity, they might as well pack their bags and go home. Their purpose and prayer focus will be diffused and thwarted.

To prevent this from occurring, it is imperative that the team leader explain to the team the uncompromising need for team unity. When a team is trained and the leader has expressed knowledge and wisdom in this area, it is possible for all involved to make correct responses in situations where disunity can arise.

12. ***Increase through worship.*** As the team begins to pray and to worship together something wonderful begins to happen. While worshiping as one, hearts draw close to the Lord and to each other because it is in His presence where an impenetrable unity is formed. The following verse explains this beautifully.

"Now may the God who gives perseverance and encouragement grant you to be of the same mind with one another according to Christ Jesus, so that with one accord you may with one voice glorify the God and Father of our Lord Jesus Christ" (Romans 15:5-6).

Through worship, two complimentary actions take place that are vital for successful teamwork. The team is built up in faith and the Lord pours out revelation knowledge. The more the team ascends into the heavenly places in worship and prayer, the more faith and divine revelation flows. As the team worships, God will reveal strategies for the upcoming warfare initiative. Each revelation will prove to confirm the facts revealed through research. Now that we understand the principles of team dynamics, let's move forward into the final lesson of this curriculum in order to learn how to pray for insight and breakthrough.

Tasks to Complete Before Advancing.

1. Hold a team meeting and discuss the importance of unity.
2. As a team, commit to one another and to the Lord in order to move together in unity.
3. As a team, seek the Lord for the timing of the assignment that He has been outlining for the team.
4. As discussed above, share with one another the areas where you could step into identificational repentance as a team member.

Rules of Engagement

5. Begin to invite and mobilize personal intercessors. Each team member should be responsible to invite their own personal intercessors.
6. Continue to record all of the Lord's confirmations concerning this assignment.
7. Together with your team leader/prayer leader, move forward with the blessings of those you are spiritually aligned with.

Engaging in Battle

Lesson Six: Engaging in Battle

The closing testimony of breakthrough included in this prayer curriculum shares a warfare prayer focus concerning abortion. Regrettably, the primary incident that the media focused on lent itself to a wide array of interpretations, and consequently invited a good deal of controversy.

First, the moral issue involved, namely abortion, is one of the more contentious of public concerns in America today. Second, the tragic murder of Dr. George Tiller of Wichita, Kansas, an outspoken abortionist, on May 31, 2009, greatly complicates the matter. Tiller's untimely death shocked and dismayed all of us who were praying about and dealing with the sanctity of life in Kansas. For us, believing in the sacredness of life would most assuredly have included the sanctity of Dr. Tiller's life. It is a sorrowful reality that he died after our spiritual warfare initiative. But, this was not my desire, nor the desire of anyone else on our team. Our prayers were centered on a much more harmless closure to the high-profile support of abortion in Kansas. Preferably, the answer should have come through the justice system.

A Word about Abortion

My belief system affirms that human life begins at conception. Consequently, I disagree with those whose beliefs tell them that an unborn child is simply organic tissue without life, which may be removed without guilt, similar to the removing of an appendix. I believe that ending an unborn life is as morally wrong as terminating life after birth. To put it more bluntly, I think abortion is a form of murder. As I shared in Lesson Three, the killing of the innocent is among the primary weapons the enemy employs in his bid to corrupt peoples and lands. This reminder will serve as a moral and spiritual principle for the field application of spiritual warfare in Kansas.

My first trip to Kansas was in 2005. I was invited by recognized pastors, Sandy Newman and DeeAnn Ward. They asked me to teach a group of hungry and attentive intercessors; pastors and leaders who were fully ready to study the importance of spiritual mapping and spiritual warfare. To my delight, during the first teaching session, it was evident that the Lord had placed me with a passionate army of believers who were prepared to begin the journey of spiritual mapping, welcoming prophetic revelation from the throne room, and who were enthusiastic about putting into action warfare strategies in order to see transformation.

Wichita, Kansas housed an abortion clinic run by a doctor who was recognized as one of America's most prolific abortionist, Dr. George Tiller. In his lifetime career, he aborted no less than 60,000 unborn babies. Abortions, including late term abortions, were the only medical procedures he performed in his practice. Sandy, DeeAnn, and others whom I was training felt strongly that the Lord was directing them to contend with this death structure in their state.

Since the initial training, I have returned to Kansas numerous times. The trip in the fall of 2007 proved to be a divinely-appointed and directed strategic-level spiritual warfare assignment. For months, believers in the state had been aggressively researching and praying that the spiritual root, or demonic principality behind the infamous abortion clinic, would be revealed, so that strategic prayer could defeat it. Another organization, Operation Rescue, held three prayer initiatives in front of Tiller's Clinic throughout the year of 2007. There was much focused prayer, but we recognized that the "principality" (literally a demon) itself needed to be exposed and defeated in order to issue the final spiritual blow that would guarantee the closure of the clinic.

Engaging in Battle

In preparation for our upcoming prophetic action, Sandy, DeeAnn, and I met with Stephanie Norton, their lead intercessor and researcher. We prayed asking the Lord to disclose the stronghold. At that moment, the Lord unmistakably brought back to my memory a dream I had in 1994 in which He revealed to me the demonic spiritual entity called Lilith. She is mentioned in Isaiah 34:14. The Hebrew word *lilim or Lilith*, means night monster, night hag, or screeching owl. In the dream the Lord expressly showed me this territorial false deity was one of the principal forces behind death and abortion. After further research, I understood why.

Lilith is an ancient false deity, depicted as a nocturnal great-winged goddess with bird-claw feet. She carries a ring or rod of power signifying that she is among the first ranks of the gods. She is a seductress known as the Goddess of Death or Hades. "The Talmud says that Lilith was formed by the Lord in response to Adam's request for a mate. According to the patriarchs, God used filth and sediment to create her, rather than the pure dust he had used for Adam. The children of Lilith were demons."[1]

Lilith, according to legend, was Adam's first wife. Eventually, she objected and refused to lie submissively beneath Adam as he wanted. She left and fled to the Red Sea where daily she gave birth to more than one hundred demons. Angels were sent to assure her she would die if she did not return to Adam. Lilith reasoned that it was not possible for her to die since she had charge of all newborn infants. So God penalized her by killing one hundred of her babies each day. Remember this is legend.

Even in the description given of this demonic deity, we recognize the lies of the enemy. Lilith was not formed by God in the Garden of Eden before Eve. It is easy to see how the enemy in his evil schemes attempts to bring confusion and deception. Many in Jewish mysticism still believe in this demonic entity and engage in superstitious practices to protect their newborn children from an untimely death at the hands of Lilith.

As I shared this revelation we all felt strongly that this was the principality responsible for death through this abortion clinic. The next day they drove me to the airport for my return flight home. We decided to stop in front of the clinic to pray. A few minutes into the prayer, I heard the voice of the Lord, *"Becca, bind the territorial spirit operating behind the killings of this clinic."* The amazing thing is at the same exact time Sandy and DeeAnn heard the Lord speaking this as well. With all three of us in agreement, I spoke out, *"In the name of Jesus I bind the territorial spirit of death, I bind you Lilith and say that you no longer will be able to execute the bloodshed of the innocent and unborn from this location. You will no longer advance in your demonic strategies and agendas. You are bound!"*

After my flight departed and as Sandy and DeeAnn made their journey home, a fierce windstorm blew across the state of Kansas. Two days later Sandy and her staff returned to the church offices only to discover an amazing surprise. In the only tree on the church property an owl was bound with fishing line used to hang decorations. They called a wildlife ranger to the church to free the bird. Remember that Lilith is characterized as a screeching owl!

Upon freeing the owl and examining it, the ranger told Sandy: *"Based on the level of dehydration and the amount of bird waste below the tree, I can determine a fair estimate of the length of time the owl has been here. Do you recall the windstorm that blew across the state two days ago? I believe the wind made it impossible for the owl to fly and forcefully blew it into the tree where the fishing line bound it."* Sandy immediately called and exclaimed, *"Becca, one hour after you prayed and bound Lilith who is the screeching owl demonic entity of death, the Lord sent a sign. Through a fierce windstorm, an owl was blown into our tree and bound by fishing line!"* We both rejoiced and then prayed to receive the next part of the prayer strategy.

For the next twenty-one days, believers across the state of Kansas and the nation began a period of fasting and prayer in the night hours due to the fact that Lilith is a nocturnal spirit. The idea was to pray and war during the hours when her demonic activities were the strongest. It was an amazing twenty-one day focus. During this time, new legal cases were instituted against Dr. Tiller and his practice, on top of the already existing ones. They focused on his repeated pattern of illegal late term abortions. *"Tiller now faces two Board of Healing Arts investigations that could cost him his license. He faces 19 criminal counts of illegal late-term abortions that could cost him huge fines, and he faces a grand jury investigation that could net literally hundreds of additional counts of illegal abortions from the past five years that could cost him his freedom,"* said Operation Rescue President Troy Newman.[2] Even patients began to come forward and give shocking revelations of all the illegal reasons and actions surrounding their abortions in Tiller's clinic—Women's Health Care Services.

From 2007 on, things continually intensified for Dr. Tiller. He was continually involved in court hearings. Repeated accounts of his illegal activities were exposed. Statistics show that the abortion rate of post viability abortions performed at Tiller's clinic dropped 23% in 2007 and in subsequent years. The following is a report from 2009 by Troy Newman, President of Operation Rescue. His ministry was housed next door to the Tiller clinic. *"During the first part of this year, our focus was on efforts to try late-term abortionist George Tiller for criminal charges that we discovered and exposed. Unfortunately, Tiller was acquitted of performing illegal late-term abortions in March. But minutes after the verdict was read, the Kansas*

State Board of Healing Arts released a statement indicating that they had filed an 11-count petition against Tiller on those same charges, and that the burden of proof was different than in a criminal case. They assured us that the case was progressing. Those counts were based on a complaint filed by Operation Rescue staff. We expected to see discipline, perhaps even the revocation of Tiller's license, within six months."[3]

This, obviously, is what we had prayed for, and we felt that God's hand was working to put a stop to Dr. Tiller's activities. At the risk of being repetitious, let me say very emphatically that in the midst of our praying, not one time did we pray or even consider praying for Tiller's demise. Our hearts' cry was for his spirit to soften and turn from this practice of aborting babies. We prayed for his salvation and God's subsequent blessing on him. The news that he had been gunned down in his church was appalling, sad, and repulsive to those of us who had been praying. The abortion clinic was closed and now the largest city in Kansas remains abortion free.

How to Advance in Onsite Prayer

Now it is time to pray onsite with insight and with the faith that you and your team will begin to see miraculous outcomes and testimonies. These types of breakthroughs are not just reserved for people like myself and our teams. As I have traveled and trained throughout the world, many who have heard and responded to this training are also seeing supernatural breakthroughs and transformations within their regions.

In this lesson I am not attempting to put God in a box and insist that you follow all of these steps. The need is to follow the direction of the Holy Spirit. First and foremost, pray and do as the Lord directs. He will be faithful in telling you what to pray about and what not to pray about.

Engaging in Battle

Some of the locations that you think will carry the most significant spiritual weight will not, and those you thought would not be significant will prove to be otherwise. Or, you might end up spying out the land, and later take what the Lord reveals and apply it to a future prayer assignment. Perhaps, an intercessory team has already prayed over this location and you sense this when you arrive. Possibly, you and your team might be the first to pray on this location and you start to feel as if you are chiseling away at a demonic foundation that will take more than one prayer time to destroy. Do not become discouraged if this is the case. Be obedient to your prayer directive by allowing the Lord to orchestrate the strategies and breakthroughs. However, after stating all of the above advice, I do want to give tips and suggestions that will aid you in how to engage in battle once you are on location.

1. ***Be expectant!*** First and foremost, be expectant, enthusiastic and fervent! He who has called you will be faithful to give you the direction, insight, and prophetic revelation you need in order to complete your assignment. In your obedience, God will take you on an awesome spiritual adventure.
2. ***Discern Spiritual and Physical Conditions.*** When onsite, be sure to discern what is spiritually and physically occurring. Listen for further revelation from the Lord. If you have a guide, ask him or her to share spiritual and historical information they are aware of. This is especially helpful in museums, in international warfare prayer initiatives, and around historical buildings and monuments. More times than not, a casual statement can prove to be a vital piece of information.
3. ***Pray in obedience.*** After using your discernment and observing the area, the team should pull together and begin to pray. Discuss all relevant research information discovered in the spiritual mapping process and in prophetic revelation.

When the team reaches agreement on the direction to pray, follow that direction.

4. ***Pray with your eyes open.*** Why?
   - First, closing our eyes and bowing our heads in prayer shows respect to God. However, I refuse to show respect to the enemy and his army of darkness.
   - Second, praying with our eyes open and in confidence represents a position of authority. Can you imagine a trained soldier going into a physical battle with his eyes closed? Absolutely not! He would most assuredly be shot and killed. The same is true with spiritual warfare prayer. We want to engage in the battle with our eyes open and in a position of authority.
   - Third, you might miss a miraculous event that is unfolding as a result of intercession.

5. ***Pray together as a group.*** When praying onsite gather together and pray in close contact with all of the team members. It is key that you agree with each other's prayers. As revelation comes, the strategy will build and breakthrough will come. Now is not the time for each team member to be praying separately. There is power and unity as you agree in intercession.

6. ***Read aloud the Scriptures that the Lord reveals.*** Be sure to read out loud and in agreement those Scriptures the Lord highlights while onsite, as well as those which were revealed beforehand—those that apply to this specific assignment. God's power will become evident as the Word is declared.

7. ***Repent for the sin and corruption on the land.*** Now is the time to engage in identificational repentance. Even if there is not a team member with authority through the bloodline, the sins of the people in that particular region will still need to be repented of and washed clean by the blood of the lamb. As a team, pray in unity and confess and repent because of the defilement on the land.

8. ***Break the power of defilement and the effects of territorial spirits off the region.*** For example, if Freemasonry is the issue, here is a sample prayer:

In the name of Jesus, we command all spirits attached to Freemasonry that you are plundered today. Together in agreement, we say to the spirits of death, witchcraft, antichrist, lying spirits, spirits of infirmity, and all spirits of mammon, your assignments are broken off of this region. Every place where you have gripped this place with your lies of deception, they are cancelled now in Jesus name. We break your power generated through the foundational leaders of this region. All dedications, in the land, which were made to the gods and goddesses of Freemasonry we cancel your power now.

Lord, cause these lodges to shut down. Lord, we welcome your light to shine forth on this land and its inhabitants. For those who are gripped in darkness, we thank you for a harvest of souls. For those who are actively involved in the Masonic lodge, Lord touch their hearts and minds, and may they respond to the truth of Your Word and to the revelation of Jesus Christ. Cause them to leave the lodges. And Lord, we rejoice that life and submission to Your Spirit and Word will come forth. Let there be a hunger for righteousness and Your presence. Lord, where this land has been gripped by darkness, we now set that darkness aside and dedicate this place to You and to Your purposes.

9. ***Never pray against a person; our focus is to break off the defilement and demonic schemes from the land and the region.*** When engaging in spiritual warfare prayer we have to fully understand this kingdom principle, *"For our struggle is not against flesh and blood, but against the rulers, against the powers, against the world forces of this darkness, against the spiritual forces of wickedness in (the heavenly places"* (Ephesians 6:12). Therefore, we should never pray harm

against an individual, or for curses to be heaped on people, or that judgment will come to a person. Jesus died on the cross for all humankind, including those who have allowed and welcomed sin into their land. Pray and deal with the spiritual influences at hand and ask God to touch the hearts of those trapped in darkness and evil practices.

10. **Perform prophetic acts.** Remember all of the testimonies shared throughout this curriculum and the discussion we had concerning prophetic acts and declarations in *Prophetic Intercession Lesson Four*. Remain sensitive and flexible as the Lord directs you in these acts. It is not wise to bring harm or destruction to idols, relics, or icons in a temple. Do not destroy property while performing prophetic acts.

11. **Speak forth prophetic declarations.** Be bold as the Lord leads you as a team. Agree out loud with the proclamations God reveals and encourages. And pray in faith. Remember you and your team are partnering with the Lord and becoming His ministers of reconciliation—His voice for breakthrough.

12. **Pray until breakthrough happens or you sense the assignment is completed.** As a warfare team you will need to discern when breakthrough has occurred. The following are examples to help you to know when this takes place:

- You might go from weeping or travail to peace and no tears.
- Where everyone is fully engaged in warfare intercession, suddenly there is a sense of knowing that the warfare burden has lifted. There is a calm and confidence among the team members.
- God will speak that breakthrough has occurred.
- There will be a sudden breakthrough or manifestation in the weather when the breakthrough has occurred.
- You will have completed praying through all the Lord has revealed for that particular location and onsite assignment.

13. ***Release God's purposes on the land.*** Where darkness has gripped the region, begin to speak forth and release the Lord's purposes for the region. The sample prayer given above in Number 8 shows how to pray in this manner.

14. ***What about the redemptive gift?*** The redemptive gift is God's original purpose for the land before poor management and the enemy's schemes of defilement stole it away. Pray for the gift to return.

15. ***Ask for the salvation of lost souls.*** In faith, pray in agreement for souls that have been trapped in darkness that they will come to salvation.

16. ***Ask that, where there have been injustices, righteousness will prevail.*** Pray in agreement that the injustices and the ungodly laws of the land will be overturned and that righteous, wise laws will be passed.

17. ***Worship the Lord and rejoice in the breakthrough He has brought.*** I cannot over emphasize the importance of worship throughout the entire process of a spiritual warfare assignment. Worship is one of the most powerful weapons of warfare. Worship and exalt the Lord as the breakthrough comes. Numerous times the Lord has directed our teams to worship and magnify His name even in public places. Be willing to do so when he directs you to!

Accepting the Call

What an awesome journey we have been on over the past 18 weeks of this study. We have gone from the basic foundations of prayer and intercession, to praying onsite with the kind strategic warfare intercession that ushers in transformation. Throughout the world, we see men, women, and children destroyed through sin and the schemes of the enemy. Friends, God is calling forth a warrior Bride, one dressed in a wedding gown, yet at the moment outfitted in army boots and positioned for war.

    I teach the following truth throughout the world. How humiliating that Satan should be impacted by an imperfect Bride who has partnered with our Lord in defeating the schemes of darkness. Psalm 44:5 decrees, *"Through thee we will push down our enemies: through thy name we will tread them under that rise up against us"* (KJV). Now is the time for you, as a team, to put into practice all that you have learned, to stand in your regions and territories as wise warriors, and be the ones to see kingdom transformation. Trust Him in the journey, and above all expect and believe that as you intercede you will see and experience great breakthroughs, a harvest of souls, and an ignited passion and move of spiritual awakening. *And Lord, in the midst of the transformation, we give You all the glory, all the honor, and all the praise. In Jesus' name, Amen.*

NOTES

NOTES

Lesson Two

1. *A Documentary: Transformations I*, directed by George Otis, Jr. (Lynwood, WA: The Sentinel Group, 2002), DVD.
2. Sarah Pollak, "Guatemala: The Miracle of Almolonga," CWNews, June 10, 2005, CBN.com.
3. Ibid.
4. Ibid.
5. Ibid.
6. Ibid.

Lesson Three

1. C. Peter Wagner, *Confronting the Queen of Heaven* (Colorado Springs, CO: Wagner Publications, 1998), 24.
2. *The Mayflower Compact,* Pilgrim Hall Museum. http://www.pilgrimhall.org/compact.htm (accessed, January 12, 2012).

Lesson Four

1. **obelisk:** a four-sided free-standing pillar, normally monolithic, tapering inward as it rises, terminating in a small pyramid. Obelisks were produced in Egypt from at least the latter part of the Old Kingdom (fifth dynasty, late third millennium BC) until the Ptolemaic period (late fourth century BC). Associated especially with the cult of the sun god Re, whose primary worship center was On (Heliopolis), obelisks were apparently seen as resembling the rays of the sun, the podium being the primeval hill over which the sun rose, and became symbolic of royal rejuvenation. Jeremiah 43:13 refers to the obelisks of Heliopolis, literally 'the pillars of the sun temple which is in Egypt.' As a pair flanking a temple entrance, two obelisks represented the rising and setting sun; as models in tombs they related to

resurrection. On, Thebes (center of the cult of Amun-Re), and Pi-Ramesse (a capital of Ramesses II) had major obelisks, products of the eighteenth-twentieth dynasties (ca. 1546-1085 BC), the tallest of which exceeds 105 feet. The obelisks elsewhere were generally shorter. Some obelisks were themselves, as divine symbols, objects of a cult. Obelisk-type pillars, inspired by Egyptian models, were erected at Byblos (Phoenicia) and at other Syro-Palestinian sites. There are now more major Egyptian obelisks in Rome than in Egypt; one was even moved to New York's Central Park.

See Achtemeier, P. J., Harper & Row, P., & Society of Biblical Literature. 1985. *Harper's Bible dictionary*. Includes index. (1st edition). Harper & Row: San Francisco.

2. Moses W. Redding, *The Illustrated History of Freemasonry* (New York: Redding & Co., 1901), 56-57.
3. Dr. Robert Morey, *The Origins and Teachings of Freemasonry* (Southbridge, MA: Crowne Publications, Inc., 1990), 115.
4. J.S.M. Ward, 33° Masonic Historian *The Higher Degree Handbook*, 25.
5. J.D. Buck, M.D., F.T.S., S.R., 32°, *Symbolism of Freemasonry* (Cincinnati, OH: The Robert Clarke Company, 1897) 66-67.
   NOTE: The Kabbalah is widely recognized as one of the best known books of Occultism.
6. David Taylor, *"Putting Things Straight (Introducing Earth Mysteries)"*, www.whitedragon.org.uk (1994).
7. Paul Devereux, *"Ley/Ley Lines,"* Abridged summary of paper given at the "WEGE DES GEISTES - WEGE DER KRAFT (Ways of Spirit - Ways of Power)" conference in October, 1996, in Germany, accessed December, 28, 2001.
   http://www.pauldevereux.co.uk/new/html/body_leylines.html

NOTES

Lesson Six

1. Buffie Johnson, *Lady of the Beasts: The Goddess and Her Sacred Animals* (Rochester, VT.: Inner Traditions International, 1994), 83.
2. Written by Operation Rescue, Tillers License at Stake as KSBHA Launches New Abortion Investigation, October 4, 2007.
http://www.operationrescue.org/archives/tiller (accessed July 15, 2010).
3. Written by Operation Rescue, Operation Rescue's Top Ten Stories of 2009, December 3, 2009.
http://www.operationrescue.org/page/7/?s=Tiller+Archives (accessed July 15, 2010).

Leader's Guide

Introduction

It is with much prayer and great excitement that this prayer curriculum has been prepared. It is our prayer that this much needed training will empower and bless many throughout the Body of Christ. As we begin this journey I want to commend all of the Pastors, Leaders, and Intercessory Prayer Leaders who are leading your prayer group through this training. I assure you it will empower, not only individuals, but also the church or ministry that the Lord has called you to. Prayer provides the basis of blessings for believers personally, corporately, and also in our cities and the regions around us.

This guide is a tool to provide guidance for those who lead during this 18 week study. I want to say upfront that the most important instruction I can give is to follow the leading of the Holy Spirit. However, this material will aid you in what we have seen to be effective tools in training and equipping others in prayer and intercession.

It is up to you if you choose to read each week's lesson out loud together, or you assign the lessons to read beforehand and then discuss what the Lord is revealing to each person during the group time. It will take some time to read each lesson out loud as a group; therefore I would recommend assigning the reading before each group gathering. This will lead to times of open discussion and stronger group bonding and experiences.

The first two segments of the curriculum, *Encouraged to Intercede* and *Prophetic Intercession* will apply to all in your training. When beginning the third segment, *Spiritual Warfare*

Prayer, you might discover that there are those who do not want to pray at this level. This is fine. If all involved in the first two segments do want to continue to the third part of this curriculum, this is also good. I do want to advise you that those who pray at the spiritual warfare level need to be ready and prepared to do so. This level of intercession is not to be entered into lightly. As the leader you want to make sure that those you take onsite to pray with spiritual warfare prayer over cities and regions are absolutely ready to do so. There might be those who go through this part of the training, but who do not want to engage in praying over the spiritual issues of a city. This is also acceptable. There is usually a smaller group who prefer to engage in this type of prayer.

Now, to encourage each of you leading, I want to express that God has anointed you for this leadership role and I am certain He will give you all you need as you guide those participating. It is going to be a wonderful 18 week process. It is such a beautiful experience to see the Body of Christ equipped and walking in a dynamic personal relationship and prayer life with Jesus. If for some reason you need further advice and counsel during this process, you can contact our ministry at chi@christianharvestintl.org or call 719-243-3302. Our team can answer questions and give extra support.

Let's pray as we launch into this new spiritual journey and season.

Lord, thank you for this opportunity to lead and empower those within this prayer group. May Your anointing, presence, wisdom, love, and peace be with me. I ask You that during this time all You want shared, imparted, and accomplished will come to fruition. Lord, thank you for anointing me for this leadership assignment and cause those I am training and myself to grow into and become the prayer warriors and army You have designed for us to be. It is a privilege to partner with You and Your kingdom in intercession.

Leader's Guide

May You be lifted high and exalted in this time. Lord, we give You all the glory, honor, and praise. Amen.

Encouraged to Intercede
Lesson One
Inheriting the Promises of Prayer

- ✓ Begin the lesson time by welcoming everyone to this 18 week spiritual journey.
- ✓ Be sure to share with them your heart as the leader and all you feel the Lord wants to accomplish through this study.
- ✓ As the leader of this group it is good to be transparent with the group throughout this journey and to also share with the group how your personal relationship with the Lord is growing.
- ✓ Open in prayer, inviting the presence of the Holy Spirit to envelop all you are doing.
- ✓ If you are reading each lesson out loud as a group, assign different people to read throughout the lesson.
- ✓ Give time for people to write their responses to the questions during the lesson time. If people feel free to share, have discussion time out loud about the different areas where growth needs to occur. Actually, you want to encourage transparency and sharing times throughout the entire 18 week journey. I am sure you will find that the group is excited to share as the study progresses.
- ✓ After reading through the lesson or discussion time, take about 15 minutes as a group and welcome the Lord to guide you individually and as a group in sincere, relevant, persistent, purpose focused, and faith filled prayers.
- ✓ Make sure that if at any time you feel or sense the Lord moving in the lesson time and you need to stop and pray

with the class, by all means follow this leading and do as the Lord is directing.
- ✓ In closing, go through the points of what each person needs to do before the next lesson.
- ✓ If choosing to read the lessons before each session, assign the group to read Lesson Two.
- ✓ Strongly encourage those participating to begin journaling during this time.
- ✓ Close in prayer and also make sure to provide any personal ministry time needed to encourage all of those in the training.

Encouraged to Intercede
Lesson Two
From Prayer to Intercession

- ✓ Welcome everyone to the class and open in prayer.
- ✓ Have a brief discussion time of all that has transpired since the last class in everyone's prayer life.
- ✓ Give place for testimonies and answered prayers.
- ✓ If reading the lesson out loud as a group, assign those who will read in this lesson time.
- ✓ Pray together, out loud, the prayer about believing God for the miraculous. The prayer in the lesson provides a guide. If the Lord begins to move, then follow His leading and pray as long as He directs. You may even want to break the prayer group into groups of 4 to 5 and have them pray together in agreement for those prayer requests where they are believing for the miraculous.
- ✓ Have a class discussion time over the questions asked in the *Let's Reflect* portion of this lesson. Give them time to record their answers, but allow some to share with the

class. To break the ice in these situations, it would be good for you as the leader to share some of your personal experiences in response to these questions.
- ✓ Pray the closing prayer together as a group. Welcome the presence of the Holy Spirit and invite the Lord to speak to the group. Encourage sitting and waiting on the Lord. He might direct some to a Scripture. Some might have a closed vision, and some an impression. Encourage the group to share what the Lord is revealing. Worship music playing in the background is always helpful in this atmosphere. It is not necessary, but it is helpful. In the second segment of the curriculum, I will have you take the class through some fun activities that will activate and encourage the group to hear the Lord's voice. But for now, teaching the class to learn to sit and receive from Him is the most productive focus.
- ✓ In closing, go over the steps for the next lesson.
- ✓ Assign the reading of Lesson Three, if the group is reading the lessons between weekly scheduled sessions.
- ✓ Dismiss in prayer.

Encouraged to Intercede
Lesson Three
Who is to Intercede?

- ✓ Welcome everyone to the meeting.
- ✓ Open in prayer.
- ✓ Make time for personal testimonies of miracles and breakthroughs that group members have witnessed since the previous meeting. Be sure to remind them to record the breakthroughs in their prayer journal, including the date of the answered prayer.

- ✓ This week's focus is personal in that it is helping individuals to identify personal weaknesses that might be hindering their prayer/spiritual lives. Therefore, as the leader of the group share the areas that you feel are appropriate where the Lord has touched things in your life. This will encourage transparency and trust within the group.
- ✓ Make time for the group to do the exercise at the end of the lesson if they have not already done so. I have included the steps below:
  - ➤ This is the cleansing time in our personal lives in order to be obedient to rid ourselves of all that might be hindering our intimate prayer and intercession time with the Lord. Have a piece of paper and pen handy. As the Lord shows you each issue write it down and repent for each thing He reveals.
  - ➤ Maybe you struggle with a competitive and performance driven attitude like I did. Invite the Lord to help you prefer others better than yourself. Trust me. He will be faithful to give you opportunity for this to happen!
  - ➤ Continue to seek the Lord concerning areas in your life that you need to bring before Him and make right.
  - ➤ Also, ask the Lord to show you any items or forms of entertainment you need to rid your home of.
  - ➤ Are there things that are hindering your relationship with the Lord that you need to pull away from?
  - ➤ Is there someone you need to forgive? Does the wrong need to be made right?
  - ➤ After you have completed this process, mark a big X through the paper and write on top of it, confessed, repented and forgiven on _____.
  - ➤ (Include the date and time). Then take the paper, tear it up and throw it away. This is a prophetic action done to show these sin patterns and issues have been forgiven

and are now officially no longer a part of the new season the Lord is taking you into.
> Invite the Lord to cause you to walk in higher realms of holiness.
✓ In this lesson time, make sure to have personal prayer time for the prayer group. If it is helpful, break the class into small groups and have them pray for each other in areas that are hindering their personal walks.
✓ Assign the reading of Lesson Four and dismiss in prayer.

Encouraged to Intercede
Lesson Four
Who or What Do I Pray For?

✓ Welcome the group to this week's session.
✓ Open in prayer, welcoming the presence of the Lord.
✓ Allow about 15 minutes for personal testimony.
✓ If you are reading through the curriculum together as a group begin the reading time.
✓ If the lesson was read before the group session, take the time to discuss different aspects of intercession members of the group have experienced.
✓ Discuss "travailing" in intercession and "wrestling" in intercession. Have different group members share their thoughts and experiences in these areas.
✓ In this lesson, I encourage a time of worship leading into the group prayer time. Songs focusing on worshipping the Lord that glorify Him will welcome His presence.
✓ Invite the Holy Spirit to direct the group's intercession time. Pray as He leads the group, and continue the intercession time until you as the leader feel the burden has lifted.

- ✓ In closing, assign the reading of Lesson Five. If this is being done between sessions encourage the group to personally follow the steps at the end of Lesson Four before the next meeting.
- ✓ Dismiss the group.

Encouraged to Intercede
Lesson Five
The Father's Heart of Mercy

- ✓ Open in prayer.
- ✓ Give time for testimonies. Encourage them to share the new ways they are experiencing God in their prayer lives, and also the answers to prayer they are witnessing. There is power in testimony and through testimony faith is built.
- ✓ If reading Lesson five together begin the reading time. If assigned before the weekly meeting move into the time of sharing and discussion.
- ✓ Ensure that each person has listed those people, businesses, etc. for which they are praying for God's mercy to be made known.
- ✓ Have a focused discussion time concerning fasting. Encourage the group to share their honest feelings about fasting.
- ✓ Whether or not this is a new experience for the group, I suggest a fasting/prayer chain for the week. On this fasting/prayer chain assign each person a day that they are to participate. Some may choose to fast all day and some one meal. Encourage everyone who is medically able to fast to participate in this exercise.
- ✓ You may choose to have a concentrated prayer focus for the week. It could be the church or your city. Maybe there are those within the church who are ill. They can become

the focus for the week. Another idea is praying for those who are lost. Also, the focus can be on those people who simply need God's mercy to be shown to them.
- ✓ Have a time of prayer, asking the Lord for His grace and strength for the upcoming fasting week.
- ✓ Assign the reading of Lesson Six.
- ✓ Dismiss the group.

Encouraged to Intercede
Lesson Six
The Joy of Intercession

- ✓ Welcome the group and open in prayer.
- ✓ Allow time for everyone to share concerning their fasting experiences.
  - ➢ Was it easy?
  - ➢ Was it difficult?
  - ➢ Were there answers to prayer?
  - ➢ How did God meet them during this time? Were there new spiritual experiences?
- ✓ Once everyone has shared move into focusing on Lesson Six.
- ✓ Explain to the group that corporately you will move into a time of entering God's presence.
- ✓ If it is possible to have intimate worship songs intermingled with the prayer time, I would highly encourage you to incorporate this during this intercessory time. Live worship would be good. I suggest starting off with two to three songs.
- ✓ Before the worship time, assign Scriptures provided in Lesson Six to be read out loud by individual group members. Other Scriptures can be included as well. It is

important that they focus on the greatness, goodness, and magnificence of the Lord.
- ✓ As the presence of the Lord increases in the room, move into focusing prayers on the Father, then on Jesus, and finally on the Holy Spirit.
- ✓ Then follow the leading of the Lord through the prayer time. You as the leader be strengthened to gently speak what you feel the prayer direction should be.
    - ➢ It might be sitting in His awesome presence as a group and exalting Him in worship.
    - ➢ He might lead you to pray through specific assignments.
    - ➢ He might have the group sit silently as He individually touches each person.
    - ➢ Trust His leading and encourage the prayer group to take that direction.
    - ➢ If a member of the group begins to take the prayer time off course, gently say, *"Thank you for praying. How about right now let's stay on the focus the Lord has given. We want to partner with His agenda right now. We will be glad to agree with you at the end of our prayer time concerning your prayer concern."*
    - ➢ When you speak in this manner it will gently keep things on track.
- ✓ Encourage each intercessor to journal what the Lord is speaking during this time.
- ✓ Most importantly, do not rush this time.
- ✓ Once the prayer time is complete. Allow time for sharing all the Lord did and how awesome His presence was in your midst.
- ✓ Pass out the second part of the curriculum, *Prophetic Intercession* and assign the reading of Lesson One.
- ✓ Dismiss the group.

Leader's Guide

Prophetic Intercession
Lesson One
We "Can" Hear God's Voice

- ✓ Welcome the group and open in prayer.
- ✓ As we have done in *Encouraged to Intercede*, allow time for personal testimonies.
- ✓ Move the focus to Lesson One of *Prophetic Intercession*.
- ✓ Ask the group to share their thoughts about hearing God's voice and prophetic intercession.
- ✓ As the leader, share times when the Lord has spoken prophetically in your life and the impact that it had.
- ✓ Allow others to share.
- ✓ Move into a prayer time in which you welcome God to begin to speak prophetically to the group.
- ✓ Encourage the group to share what He is revealing. It will be faith building for the group to see how God is speaking to each person. And it will also help to confirm each other.
- ✓ In closing, assign the reading of Lesson Two.
- ✓ Dismiss the group.

Prophetic Intercession
Lesson Two
Learning His Voice

- ✓ Welcome the group and open in prayer.
- ✓ In this session, we are going to practice hearing God's voice for each other. Many times these activities are termed prophetic activations. This means we are making room for cultivating hearing the encouraging, edifying, and comforting voice of God on behalf of others.
- ✓ In the first exercise break into groups of three to four.

- ➢ Explain that the group will take turns praying and speaking encouraging words to each other.
- ➢ They are to pick the first person to receive. You as the leader pray and ask the Lord to speak to the group members. Give them about one minute and then have them begin to speak what the Lord showed them concerning the prayer recipient. Each member needs to share what they are hearing.
- ➢ Then rotate to the next person in the group. Continue this exercise until each person has received words.
- ➢ Have several people share testimonies of the confirming words they have received.
- ✓ Now have a time of discussion with the group concerning the different ways God speaks that are explained in Lesson Two. As the leader ask for those who have dreams to raise their hands and have a couple of them share. Find out those who are gifted in receiving visions—those who experience impressions from the Lord. Have a personal testimony time from a couple of individuals when a prophetic word has greatly impacted them. Having this discussion out loud will begin to help the group understand and realize the gifting of those among them.
- ✓ Now have a time of prayer. I would suggest in this prayer time focusing on the church or ministry that is hosting this course. Ask the Lord to begin to speak words of encouragement concerning the ministry. Maybe you will feel led to focus on your city or region. But welcome the Lord to release His prophetic revelation and pray in agreement with Him.
- ✓ Encourage group members to journal and date their dreams, visions, promises from Scripture, impressions, etc…
- ✓ Assign the reading of Lesson Three and dismiss!

Leader's Guide

Prophetic Intercession
Lesson Three
Prophetic Protocol

- ✓ Welcome the group and open in prayer.
- ✓ As we continue to practice throughout these lessons, it is personal testimony time! Allow 15 minutes for those who have experienced breakthrough to share.
- ✓ Open Lesson three and go through all the hindrances to prophetic intercession. Allow time, I would suggest 5 minutes, for self-reflection and examination after the discussion time.
- ✓ If some people feel the freedom, break into groups of three to four and allow time for personal ministry in areas focusing on places or hindrances where members need breakthrough.
- ✓ Talk through the green and red lights of prophetic revelation. Some people may be skeptical because of seeing or hearing of abuses from the past. Take time to engage in a good discussion by walking through these topics encouraging the group that prophetic intercession will be handled with integrity and scriptural values.
- ✓ If there are some who have been hurt or wounded by abuses in prophetic intercession allow time to minister to those who need healing in these areas.
- ✓ Assign the reading of Lesson Four.
- ✓ Dismiss in prayer.

Prophetic Intercession
Lesson Four
Breakthrough!

✓ In this group session, as the leader you will want to schedule a prayerwalk. You will put into practice all the steps I have given following Lesson Four. I have included these steps below.
  - ➢ Schedule a time for a prayerwalk.
  - ➢ Ask the Lord to show the assigned area for this prayer venture.
  - ➢ Be sure to have at least one prayer partner.
  - ➢ If the prayer group is larger than six, be sure to divide into teams and assign each team a location to pray. I prefer teams no larger than 6 people in this type of assignment.
  - ➢ Assign a team leader to each team.
  - ➢ Discern what God is saying concerning the land and the people.
  - ➢ Make a journal of all that He is revealing.
  - ➢ Pray, welcoming His presence.
  - ➢ Speak that His light will dispel the darkness.
  - ➢ Believe that God will move and touch lost souls.
  - ➢ Do prophetic acts as led by God.
  - ➢ Speak forth prophetic proclamations as He leads.
  - ➢ Speak to those who are out and about.
  - ➢ If He directs you, share the Gospel message with those you come in contact.
  - ➢ Be expectant.
  - ➢ Have fun.
  - ➢ If divided in teams, after prayerwalking gather together and share all that transpired and the revelation the Lord revealed.

Leader's Guide

- ➢ Schedule another time to prayerwalk and be sure to pray through all the prophetic revelation the Lord has released.
- ✓ Assign the reading of Lesson Five and dismiss in prayer.

Prophetic Intercession
Lesson Five
Corporate Intercession

- ✓ Welcome the group and open in prayer.
- ✓ It is testimony time!
- ✓ Lead the group through a discussion of the different intercessory gifting and anointings.
- ✓ Have group members share what they feel their primary focuses are in intercession.
  - ➢ Did they discover new things about themselves as a result of this lesson?
  - ➢ Do they now feel they have a clearer understanding of their individual gifts?
  - ➢ For how many in the group did this teaching bring a freedom and clarity to accept who they are gifted to be?
- ✓ Now it is time to lead the group into a corporate prayer time as discussed at the end of the lesson. As the leader encourage individuals to be free in their gifting while learning to stay on the targeted prayer focus.
  - ➢ Encourage the group to resolve in their hearts not to judge others in their anointing and gifting, but to embrace the diversity that God has given each individual.
  - ➢ Tell them to be expectant that God will meet you as a group and supernaturally move.

- ➤ Remind everyone to not cross over into judging other's giftings, but rather receive and welcome the diversity of gifts.
- ➤ Pray toward one focus, not several random directions which will prove to be ineffective.
- ➤ Keep your attention on God, the unity of Spirit, and the divinely birthed assignment for the hour.
- ✓ Assign the reading of Lesson Six and dismiss.

Prophetic Intercession
Lesson Six
The Power of Prophetic Intercession

- ✓ Welcome the group and open in prayer.
- ✓ Make time for personal testimony!!
- ✓ In this session, you as the leader are going to put into practice the steps outlined at the end of Lesson Six.
- ✓ Now is the time for your intercessory group to seek God to discover how He would have you make an impact. It is time to discover and engage.
  6. What is our corporate prayer assignment that will effect change?
  7. Pray as a group and invite Him to reveal new prayer assignments and strategies.
     a. It might be prayerwalking.
        1. Maybe it will be a certain region in your city.
        2. Maybe it will be praying for the neighborhoods that surround the church.
        3. It might be an area downtown where there are the homeless, poor, drug addicted, runaways and prostitutes.
     b. It might be forming different intercessory groups within the church with prayer focuses such as:

Leader's Guide

   1. The Church
   2. The Pastor
   3. Families
   4. Government
   5. Nations
8. How might your church intercessory group affect society through your prayers? Ask Him. He will show you.
9. Maybe He will direct your church to coordinate and pray corporately with other churches in your region for your city.
10. Be obedient to the direction He speaks and be expectant that it will succeed and grow. Do not be discouraged if growth takes time. Once a church or prayer group engages in corporate prayer, the enemy will try to oppose it. Be committed and persistent in what the Lord is birthing. In time the growth and multiplication will come. When I began my most recent prayer group five years ago, one person initially participated. Now, we have grown to a regional prophetic prayer gathering involving pastors, ministry leaders, and intercessors from across our city and beyond. Our prayer time averages 50 to 100 prayer warriors.

✓ Once as a group you have discussed this and also sought the Lord over your assignment, say yes to His direction and welcome the Lord to guide you as a group as you begin this journey for bringing change.
✓ Pass out the third segment of the curriculum *Spiritual Warfare Prayer.*
✓ Assign the reading of Lesson One and dismiss in prayer.

Spiritual Warfare Prayer
Lesson One
Explanation of Spiritual Warfare Prayer

- ✓ Welcome the group and open in prayer.
- ✓ Allow time for personal testimonies of breakthrough.
- ✓ In this portion of the prayer curriculum and in this particular lesson, you are entering into the reality of being a well oiled strategic prayer group.
- ✓ You want to allow discussion time for all the questions presented in this lesson. For many this will be a whole new way of looking at and perceiving their regions and cities.
- ✓ Begin with ground-level spiritual warfare. As the leader share your answers to the questions and then have group members share. Pray in agreement for those who have been listed as needing breakthrough that the Lord will bring them into a place of freedom and victory.
- ✓ Move into a discussion about occult-level spiritual warfare. Be prepared as the leader to present areas in your city that you know to be gripped or trapped in this form of darkness. Have the group share as well. As instructed in the lesson, ask God to loose those trapped in darkness and also seek Him for a prayer strategy to see this area of your city transformed.
- ✓ Move into a discussion time about strategic level spiritual warfare prayer. As the leader and as a group, share the revealed spiritual warfare prayer assignments for the region. The Lord will be faithful to speak and bring confirmation among the team. It will be inspiring and exciting to watch as this unfolds within the group!
- ✓ Assign the reading of Lesson Two and dismiss in prayer.

Leader's Guide

Spiritual Warfare Prayer
Lesson Two
Creation is Waiting

- ✓ For this lesson, bring a map of the city or region and also stick-pins or a pencil to mark on the map all the locations God is highlighting for your group.
- ✓ Welcome the group and open in prayer.
- ✓ Allow time for personal testimony.
- ✓ I want to share with you as the leader, that Lesson Two's reading will have been very different for many people. The reason I have included this chapter is to share stories of where and how God has brought freedom and blessing to people and also to their region and land. God not only wants to bless us as people, but also the land and cities in which we live! Encourage them that this is an exciting and wonderful part of our inheritance in God's Kingdom. God created us as His sons and daughters. He also created the earth and the land. He loves all of His creations and wants and desires to bless all of it.
- ✓ Spend time in prayer before the discussion time.
  - ➤ Thank the Lord that He has called and positioned each of you in your city and region.
  - ➤ Ask Him to continue to give you His heart and plans for the area.
  - ➤ Invite Him to guide the discussion time and to reveal every place He desires for there to be focused intercession in your city/region.
- ✓ Be prepared to share with the group the areas of the city where there are those who are suffering because of sin.
- ✓ There might be more places that you and the group members have uncovered beyond the five guiding questions represented at the end of this lesson. This is fine.

The questions at the end serve as a guide to jumpstart the discussion.
- ✓ Assign the reading of Lesson Three and dismiss the group!

Spiritual Warfare Prayer
Lesson Three
Satan the Unlawful Tenant

- ✓ Welcome the group and open in prayer.
- ✓ Take some time for personal testimony.
- ✓ Bring the map of the city/region to this group time and plan to bring it to all the city strategy meetings. It is important to mark on the map all the areas the Lord shows the group.
- ✓ Have a discussion time from the questions asked in Lesson Three.
- ✓ Make time to discover the history of your city where God was not asked for wisdom or His laws have not been followed. Begin to record these.
- ✓ Remember that the points in these lessons serve as a guide. If God shows you or the group other issues to focus on include these in your discovery/mapping process.
- ✓ Make a list of at least five good things that you see God doing in your city/region. Take some time to thank Him for all the good He is doing.
- ✓ We do not want our complete focus to be on darkness, but also on the good and blessed kingdom activities that God has already begun!
- ✓ Assign the reading of Lesson Four and dismiss the group!

Leader's Guide

Spiritual Warfare Prayer
Lesson Four
Spiritual Mapping

- ✓ Welcome the group and open in prayer.
- ✓ Allow time for personal testimony.
- ✓ This will likely be the first time some of the people in your class will have heard teaching of this nature on Freemasonry. Some might not like what they hear, and some of may have had personal past involvement or ancestors who have been active in this secret society. The good news is they can receive prayer and freedom from the open doors to generational curses that this secret society brings over lives. There is a prayer titled, *the Prayer of Release from Freemasonry*. I would suggest going to the following www.jubilee.org.nz/prayers/freemasonry/ and printing out the prayer. If there have been several in the group who have participated or have had past generations involved, I would suggest scheduling a night where, as a group, you can read through this prayer together in order to break the demonic influences. It takes about 1 ½ hours to do this, so I would schedule it separate from the regularly scheduled group meeting time. I require this for all team members who intercede at a strategic spiritual warfare level over regions. We cannot deal with the giants in the land until we have dealt with the giants in our own lives. We also have available on our website a four-hour teaching on Freemasonry in a class setting. It can be ordered in our web store at www.christianharvestintl.org.
- ✓ In this lesson you and the group have now entered into deeper into the spiritual mapping phase.
- ✓ Take time to discuss and answer the questions asked in the lesson.

- ✓ As the leader of the group, you will oversee this mapping process. I have included the steps listed below at the end of the lesson to guide you in this discussion time.
- ✓ Now is the time to begin to assemble all the Lord is revealing. You can do so by compiling a team notebook. The following are suggestions.
  - ➢ Combine all the prophetic revelation including dreams, visions, Scriptures, and prophetic words the Lord has been revealing into one section.
  - ➢ As the facts are mapped, the issues that carry the most significant weight will become obvious. The Lord will give spiritual insight throughout the process. Don't forget to focus in on the key root issues discovered in your region that were shared in this lesson.
  - ➢ Divide the notebook into those sections per each site that you will be researching and praying for.
  - ➢ It will also be wise to map out all the Masonic lodges in the region or city in which you will be praying.
  - ➢ Find out how long they have been there and what political or historical leaders were instrumental in introducing the society to your area.
  - ➢ Get a map of the city and begin to mark on it the points that the Lord is highlighting. Identify if they are power points connected by ley lines?
- ✓ As the research process unfolds it is wise to have meetings once or twice a month. You can also use the group lesson times to discuss what team members have discovered and then to pray to the Lord for further strategy.
- ✓ Assign the reading of Lesson Five and dismiss the group.

Leader's Guide

Spiritual Warfare Prayer
Lesson Five
Rules of Engagement

- ✓ Welcome the group and open in prayer.
- ✓ Allow time for personal testimony
- ✓ In this group gathering, hold a team meeting and discuss the importance of unity.
- ✓ As discussed in the lesson, have the team commit to one another and to the Lord in order to move together in unity.
- ✓ As a team, seek the Lord over the timing of the assignment He has been outlining to the team.
- ✓ List the different areas where team members can step into identificational repentance?
- ✓ Now is the time for each team member to invite and mobilize personal intercessors. Each team member is responsible do this.
- ✓ Continue to record all of the confirmations the Lord gives concerning this assignment and add it to the team notebook.
  - ➤ _____
  - ➤ _____
  - ➤ _____
  - ➤ _____
  - ➤ _____

  - ➤ Ensure that the team moves forward with the blessings of those you are spiritually aligned with.
- ✓ Have a time of intercession to continue to seek the Lord over the assignment He is birthing.

- ✓ Assign the reading of Lesson Six and dismiss in prayer.

Spiritual Warfare Prayer
Lesson Six
Engaging in Battle

- ✓ First of all I want to say, congratulations! You have taken this group through an intensive and in-depth 18 week intercessory training course. Good job!
- ✓ Welcome the group and open in prayer.
- ✓ Allow time for personal testimony.
- ✓ As the leader, congratulate the group on the completion of the prayer curriculum.
- ✓ Take the time to discuss the points made throughout Lesson Six.
- ✓ Now is the time to set a date for the prayer assignment. Schedule the date and move forward with praying onsite with insight.
- ✓ Now is just the beginning. It is my prayer that you now have an informed and trained group of intercessors that will benefit the church and your region.
- ✓ I would suggest that the group continues to meet and carry through on all the prayer assignments that God continues to reveal. You as the leader and as a group will need to decide if you want to come together weekly or monthly, or for what fits your schedule. Allow the Lord to continue to guide and speak you.
- ✓ Once you begin to pray for your region, the Lord will continue to speak concerning further assignments. There might be prayer assignments which occur back to back or several months apart. The key point to remember is to be

Leader's Guide

open for the Lord to continue to reveal different assignments for your region.
- ✓ Be sure to write reports after each assignment and add them to the team notebook. Just as it is awe inspiring to read reports and dates of personal breakthrough, it is also faith building to write brief reports concerning breakthroughs in your church and region.
- ✓ Schedule the next prayer meeting.
- ✓ Close in prayer thanking the Lord for this incredible 18 week journey and dismiss the group.

CPSIA information can be obtained at www.ICGtesting.com
Printed in the USA
BVOW03s1324120813

328451BV00003B/6/P